D0458565

Praise for *Meganets*

"*Meganets* will forever change the way you think about the digital world. It is an eye-opening account of the relationships we create—and which are often created for us—online. It is the foundational book explaining the sweeping social changes that created our present and will transform tomorrow. David Auerbach has written both a warning and a blueprint for a better future."

—Amy Webb, CEO, the Future Today Institute,
and author of *The Big Nine* and *The Genesis Machine*

"Auerbach has written a fascinating, mind-expanding book that is not about the future of technology but about the future of society. We are still early in our journey toward understanding how the interaction of data and computing are fundamentally changing our lives. *Meganets* gets us further down that road. Two important takeaways for me: First, the metaverse is not some future state—it is here now, expanding and evolving daily. And second, algorithms don't run the world—they create a rich, sometimes productive, and sometimes toxic new ecosystem that is an organic interaction of humans and machines already well beyond any person, company, government, or algorithm's control."

—Alan Murray, CEO, Fortune Media,
and author of *Tomorrow's Capitalist*

"Auerbach's *Meganets* warns the networked systems that channel our words, images, and ideas are already too complex for humans to govern, however we might try. A necessary book, bracing in places, but not without hope."

—Jordan Ellenberg, author of *How Not to be Wrong*

"Auerbach is the opposite of a conspiracy theorist: he explains how there's often ultimately no person, institution, or discernable group behind big systems and the events they shape. He's interested in how to deal with that fact—building up responsive structures instead of tearing anything down."

—Jonathan Zittrain, George Bemis Professor of International Law and professor of computer science, Harvard University

"Auerbach knows better than anyone that the very act of writing about technology is an assertion of the preeminence of the human. His signature command of conscience and fact make his work that rarest thing: indispensable."

—Joshua Cohen, Pulitzer Prize–winning author of *The Natanyahus*

"How often do we hear people vainly protest—'But I'm not on social media!'—as if the problems we confront in our new technological reality could be solved by individual lifestyle choices alone? In fact, the forces that shape our online experience jumped the fence long ago, and there is now no protective barrier between the digital and the 'real,' between our online experience and our experience of the entirety of social reality. Algorithms and gamification shape our newsfeeds, but they also shape our transportation routes, our credit ratings, our labor, and even our health. This new reality requires a big-picture thinker ready to take on the problem in all its complexity, and Auerbach proves himself more than up to the task. In stunning, lucid prose and with unsparing analytical acumen, *Meganets* reveals just how profoundly our world has been transformed over the past generation of technological innovation. Auerbach offers no easy answers, yet the depth of his expertise and the far-reaching scope of his vision already provide a model for the sort of thinking we will need if the beast we have summoned is ever to be tamed."

—Justin E. H. Smith, Université Paris Cité, author of *The Internet Is Not What You Think It Is*

MEGANETS

HOW DIGITAL FORCES BEYOND OUR CONTROL COMMANDEER OUR DAILY LIVES AND INNER REALITIES

David B. Auerbach

PublicAffairs
New York

PublicAffairs
Hachette Book Group
1290 Avenue of the Americas, New York, NY 10104
www.publicaffairsbooks.com
@Public_Affairs

Printed in the United States of America
First Edition: March 2023

Published by PublicAffairs, an imprint of Perseus Books, LLC, a subsidiary of Hachette Book Group, Inc. The PublicAffairs name and logo is a trademark of the Hachette Book Group.

Print book interior design by Linda Mark

Library of Congress Cataloging-in-Publication Data
Names: Auerbach, David (David B.), author.
Title: Meganets : how digital forces beyond our control are commandeering our daily lives and inner realities / David B. Auerbach.
Description: First edition. | New York, NY : PublicAffairs/Hachette Book Group, 2023. | Includes bibliographical references and index.
Identifiers: LCCN 2022029526 | ISBN 9781541774445 (hardcover) | ISBN 9781541774438 (ebook)
Subjects: LCSH: Internet governance. | Internet—Social aspects. | Metaverse.
Classification: LCC TK5105.8854 .A94 2023 | DDC 004.67/8—dc23/eng/20221017 LC record available at https://lccn.loc.gov/2022029526

ISBNs: 9781541774445 (hardcover), 9781541774438 (ebook)

LSC-C

Printing 1, 2022

For Eleanor and Iris

Also by David Auerbach

Bitwise: A Life in Code

Contents

吾生也有涯，而知也无涯。

Your life has a limit, but knowledge has none.

Zhuangzi

Galloping in unceasing flow ever ahead, denied any further control over their fate, the disconsolate company were borne terribly over the edge of the visible world.

Thomas Pynchon, *Against the Day*

INTRODUCTION

The New Minds of the World

> Woes by wrong imaginations lose the knowledge of themselves.
>
> Shakespeare, *King Lear*

FOR ALL THE MASTERY AND KNOWLEDGE THAT HUMANS HAVE obtained over nature, from charting the movements of the planets to machine-assisted flight to the mapping of genomes, there remain areas in which our chief accomplishment has been to realize the limits of our understanding and control. Take the chaotic system known as the weather. Despite all the technology deployed to monitor the skies, the tides, and everything in between, our predictions can still be so inaccurate as to be unable to predict whether a hurricane will hit a city tomorrow or whether it will rain in a particular space an hour later. The weather system is too complex, too chaotic, too nonlinear to allow for perfect fine-grained predictions. Much the same holds for the tectonic plates beneath the earth's surface: we monitor them incessantly but still cannot anticipate when the next big earthquake will hit. And there is the brain itself, where the deeper we delve, the more we find difficulties in determining how our minds arise from this mass of tissue and neurons.

In human society, economics has steadfastly proven resistant to any sort of high-confidence modeling, leading to its moniker "the dismal science." We may approximate the purchases and sales of herds of people and corporations at a macrolevel, but the flows of commerce remain frustratingly susceptible to sudden and unpredictable shocks, whether in the economic crisis of 2008 or in the wild fluctuations and multiple crashes of the trillion-dollar Bitcoin cryptocurrency.

In the last decade, that sense of bafflement at the complex workings of the human and social sciences has spread to our increasingly vexed everyday interactions, online and offline. The weight of the larger world weighs more heavily on our work, our lives, and our families. The digital world connects us to the bigger picture nonstop. The large and the small no longer seem so distinct. The flood of information and the possibilities for expression given to us by the internet feel more like traps than opportunities, offering us the illusion of control only to bury it under sheer incomprehensible chaos.

Our image of computers remains one of clear, discrete control, a salvation from the messy and opaque systems of the natural and human worlds. Today, however, this could not be further from the truth. While the mainframes of the 1960s and the PCs of the 1980s were localized and simple enough to permit us a near-perfect understanding of the work they did, the rise of large-scale internet-based networks, Facebook and Google chief among them, has obliterated most of that certainty. Our computer networks today are just as immune to fine-grained control and perfect prediction as the weather, tectonic plates, or the prices of cryptocurrency.

The history of the technological baton passing from Microsoft to Google to Facebook has become a familiar tale of innovative disruptions. We ask ourselves questions about whatever bits of these disruptions happen to come to the forefront of public consciousness: Will AI be a tool for good or evil? Can we make algorithms fair and bias-free? How do we get disinformation off the internet? These big questions of today are fundamentally misformulated because they don't take into account the new world in which we already live. Without realizing it, we are already immersed in a world administered by enormous computer networks fundamentally out of our control. If we insist on seeing our online lives as resulting primarily from human intentions or algorithmic logic, we have missed the forest for the trees. We fool ourselves into thinking we can make quick fixes or prevail upon corporations and governments to protect us from the harmful byproducts of technology. We search for where the power really lies, when it does not lie anywhere—or else it lies everywhere at once, which is no more helpful.

The real story centers around increases in size and speed—computer systems that grew from modest, containable size into leviathans too great and too fast to be seen in their entirety. It is the story of how the engineers who built these systems were as carried away by them as the people who used them. Like Moore's law, the enduring maxim that computational processing power will double every two years thanks to advances in semiconductors, it is the story of exponential growth, not only in computing power but also in the amount of computable data and the size of the networks that compute it. But the story is more than that. It is also the story of exponential growth in the amount of human behavior computers capture, the tightening feedback loops that alter human behavior, and our increasing inability to control those changes.

For all the talk of the metaverse—much of it merely a debate over what the metaverse even *is*—the fundamental difference between the metaverse (whatever it will be) and the internet today is not quality but quantity.[1] The metaverse threatens to add virtual reality (fake physical space), "augmented" reality (digitally enhanced real physical space), and cryptocurrency-driven NFTs (non-fungible tokens, which are artificially scarce digital assets to buy) to the existing potent online world, but all of the metaverse's changes will amount to the same thing: *more* data, *more* connectivity, *more* transactions, *more* complexity. The movement from Web 1.0 to Web 2.0 to the metaverse and onward has not stemmed from radical new technologies. Rather, the change in online life is like the evolution of the brain, growing ever more complex until surprising new phenomena emerge purely through that complexity—along with that much less ability to understand what is going on. The metaverse, for all practical purposes, is already here, growing incessantly. We lose more control to it by the day.

The consequences of wrapping our world in networked computation have not merely been lifestyle changes but also the increasing and steady growth of autonomous networks—*meganets*—not under the control of their corporate or governmental administrators. To understand today's world, we have to think not like a sapiens, nor like a state, but like a server. A server—or more accurately, a collective army of servers—sees the world as computable data, floods of numbers representing every facet of life in more and less accurate ways, in quantities so great that much of the *meaning* of this data is lost, even as we feed ever more data into the system. In turn, our servers feed that data back to us, and we come to see the world the same way. Without realizing it, machines and humans are building a new world together, a world we cannot control in the way we controlled the old world.

FACEBOOK'S UNPLANDEMIC

The biggest face of this chaos and transformation has been and remains Facebook. Facebook has become a magnet for all complaints about the internet more generally—and not without reason. Nobody likes Facebook, but everyone uses it. It is a fount of misinformation, a petri dish in which false facts and crazy theories grow, mutate, and metastasize. It sucks up our time, bastardizes our emotions into a handful of emoticons, and bludgeons us with inflammatory content. Worst of all, it harms our civic life by creating insular virtual subcultures that shut out anything that contradicts their worldviews, allowing extremism to grow in all directions.

That, at least, is the conventional wisdom. While some of these charges may be exaggerated, none are fundamentally untrue. The phenomena they describe exist on Facebook, and they do cause harm, as even Facebook's own employees admit. Despite studies showing that quitting Facebook improved people's mental health, there are just as many articles explaining why people can't quit Facebook as there are preaching why they should.[2] Helplessness breeds anger. At the center of it all, Facebook CEO Mark Zuckerberg shrugs off boycotts from users and advertisers alike, blithely observing, "My guess is that all these advertisers will be back on the platform soon enough," the effects of the boycotts too small to make a difference on Facebook's bottom line.[3]

What is less understood, however, is *why* Facebook allows all this chaos to fester and boil over. Behind Facebook's seeming strength and Zuckerberg's intransigence is a near-adolescent helplessness not so different from that felt by Facebook's frustrated users. After the Cambridge Analytica scandal of 2016, in which Facebook gave information to a third-party application provider that was used to target potential Trump voters, one would have expected Facebook to wield an iron hand over abuse on its system. Instead, COVID-19 brought with it myriad conspiracy theories spreading through the veins of Facebook's network sometimes even accompanied by cryptic (and not-so-cryptic) incitements to violence. However much Zuckerberg rejects criticism, the platform cannot possibly be what he (or anyone) actually wants.

Facebook's critics appeal to the simplest explanation—greed—as the reason for why Facebook has refused to clamp down, but simple capitalistic greed doesn't even begin to explain the problem. Nowhere is it clear that the spread of bad information and leakage of information benefits Facebook compared to the chronic public relations nightmare now plaguing them, one which CEO Mark Zuckerberg had more or less given up on fixing. Just before the COVID-19 pandemic, Facebook publicly pledged to crack down on antivaccine misinformation that vaccines can cause autism in a news post entitled "Combatting Vaccine Misinformation."[4] By May 2019, the *Wall Street Journal* observed "not much happened," noting that Facebook still ran ads for antivaccine groups and that the top three vaccine-related Instagram accounts were the conspiracy-minded "vaccinetruth," "vaccinesuncovered," and "vaccines_revealed."[5]

Things only got worse when the pandemic hit. In early 2020, despite Zuckerberg himself working with the World Health Organization (WHO) and publicly (and seemingly sincerely) pledging that Facebook was "removing false claims and conspiracy theories that have been flagged by leading global health organizations," he could not make good on his own commitments.[6] By May, the infamous *Plandemic* video was flying across the platform unimpeded, while conspiratorial posts about the disease, masks, and vaccines increasingly populated people's walls.[7] The thirty-minute *Plandemic* video claimed to expose corruption among the medical and global elites, including the WHO and the US Centers for Disease Control, accusing them of profiting from COVID-19, even suggesting that the coronavirus was implanted in people through flu vaccination and activated by wearing face masks.[8] Exploiting existing paranoia, the video was talked up by sympathizers, but as a Harvard study showed, its appeal was mostly to the already converted, and the suppression of a second video by social media giants didn't prevent the impact of theories that were already running wild before the first video had even been released.[9] The video was only the visible tip of a much larger, unmovable iceberg.

Despite critics claiming that Facebook cares only about money, that explanation is almost too cozily reassuring. It would be simpler to believe that Facebook could fix the problem if only it cared more about doing the right thing instead of promoting lucrative clickbait. Internal documents, though, revealed that Facebook was trying, at least partly, to do what its critics desired. The company just couldn't. "Our ability to detect (vaccine hesitancy) in comments is bad in English—and basically non-existent elsewhere," read one memo.[10] The documents showed Facebook hapless, conflicted, and impotent, slowly recognizing the scope of the problem its own CEO had pledged to fix, yet literally unable to take sufficient action to address it.[11]

By the end of 2020, Facebook was limiting how much *any* content could be forwarded, regardless of what it said. New political advertising was entirely banned in the run-up to the November election.[12] One former content moderator complained that Facebook

> is not committed to content moderation, does not have a clear strategy or even a good handle on how to do it, and the people trying to do the actual work are under immense pressure to shovel shit uphill without proper tools or direction.[13]

He was not necessarily wrong. But hidden in his statement was the assumption that some other alternative, whether improved tools, better leadership, or external government regulation, could successfully address the problems he was pointing out.

Yet the blunt fact of one of the world's biggest companies failing to address ongoing, stinging criticism from all sides on an issue that doesn't greatly profit them in any way does not speak to malice and not even to incompetence. It speaks to an actual inability to solve the problems. And Zuckerberg's own frustration was that of an unfathomably rich and powerful man who could not control what he had created any more than its users could stop logging on to it. Zuckerberg's creation had become as autonomous as nature—as the weather, as the tides, as plate tectonics. This loss of control, more than privacy violations and the spread of disinformation, was a fact Facebook (the company) wished to obscure. In one internal Facebook memo the company's communications department worried, above all, about people thinking that Facebook employees *couldn't control their own networks*

> Limit the meme that we're slow to spot misuse—and can't control Facebook
> Limit the meme that we cannot control our systems—or are too slow to spot these different types of abuses.[14]

Facebook wants to quash such ideas partly because they *are* true—as much as Facebook takes pains to disguise it. Such a lack of control hardly suits one of the most valuable companies in the economy, one of the richest men in the world, and one of the largest and most powerful platforms in existence. And yet the evidence of the last decade makes Facebook's impotence hard to deny. The battle is not the elites versus the masses but the elites versus the networks they have themselves birthed, and the networks are winning.

THE MEGANET

The Googles, Facebooks, cryptocurrencies, and government systems of our world accumulate influence at a mystifying rate. The constant critiques and attempted regulation directed at these systems never seem to yield real reform. Such efforts run into a brick wall for one ultimate reason: no one is really in control. Even the companies and executives who run them are trapped by the persistent, evolving, and opaque systems they have created. What is it that has so destabilized our elites so that they have lost control of the very systems they built and run? With every passing day we intuitively sense a loss of control over our daily lives, society, culture, and politics, even as it becomes more difficult to extricate ourselves from our hypernetworked fabric. No explanation ever seems sufficient.

I saw this new world being created when I worked in the engine rooms of Microsoft and Google for more than a decade. I can say, for certain, that we did not know the impact of what we were creating. We were wildly overoptimistic about it, to be sure: Google's slogan "Don't be evil" made that clear. But moreover, we did not fully grasp the uncontrolled power of the systems growing around us. Very few among us not only understood that these new, huge networks could behave unpredictably and uncontrollably but that they were also becoming intrinsically *more* unpredictable and uncontrollable. And we did not know how to prevent this because the systems extended beyond our direct control. Yes, we controlled the code, but we did not control the people using it, nor did we choose the data that was being put into it. And the ever-growing networks moved faster than we could keep up with. Coarse-gained, approximate influence increasingly replaced total, microscopic control. We did not predict the consequences of that loss of control either.

When I transitioned to being a technologist, policy analyst, and writer, I moved to a world that was alternately dazzled by and resentful toward the new technological leaders. Yet nearly without exception, my colleagues assigned unwarranted agency to the creators of the technologies and tech companies that they criticized. They would tell me: "If only tech companies would change this, life online would be so much better!" Either regulation or user pressure could make Facebook, Google, Amazon, Apple, Microsoft, Twitter, and whoever else see the light and remove the ugliness. I would respond: "What you're asking for, the companies just can't do. It's too difficult. There's too much data and not enough ability to process it." Without exception, they would disagree. How could such big companies not be responsible for the world they foist on us? Whatever problem was wrought on society through social media or the internet more generally, whether it was fake news or online abuse or cryptocurrencies, the assumption was that the Mark Zuckerbergs and Steve Jobses of the world could fix these growing problems if only they had a stronger ethical core and less attention to profits—if only they would put people before profits and ethics before growth.

I overestimated tech companies myself. Though I had left Google by 2011, when it rolled out its social network Google+, I expected that on the strength of its successes, Google would be able to assemble a social network to rival and even surpass Facebook's. What I didn't expect was the aimless, confused product that followed, one that poked its nose into Google's more successful properties (Gmail, YouTube) without ever gaining traction. By 2015, Google+ was thoroughly irrelevant, and Google finally shuttered it completely in 2019. Just because Google had organized the web for utility and profit did not mean that it could organize people for the same ends. If one of the largest and most successful companies in history could not gain any ground in creating a social network out of its hundreds of millions of existing users, was there any more reason to think Facebook had any greater degree of control over *its* users?

□ □ □

This book is addressed to those who feel lost—or at least perplexed. If you feel at home in the world today, comfortable with the size and scope of daily and global events, what I say will likely seem superfluous or irrelevant. Yet it is rare that I meet people, however happy they may be, that do feel at home in such a way. Even the most successful and contented bemoan a world that, in its complexity and its inseparability, leaves them only with the options of being trapped in engagement or else opting out completely and escaping. Indeed, the happiest seem to have chosen the latter. Money has become less a tool for changing the world than for merely regaining one's autonomy. Fame and prestige have far more negative associations than when they were the preserve of a remote, elite class. Whether one is an internet celebrity, an influencer, or a movie star, fame today is more like having a target on one's back. Visible impact in the world has come to feel less important than privacy, autonomy, and independence—the freedom *from* the automated and semiautomated processes that sweep up most of us into routines from a very young age.

We repeatedly point to one or another phenomenon that seems to have created this new world: computers, smartphones, social media, data more generally. No doubt, the injection of exponentially growing computing power set the stage for the loss of control we currently experience. This unprecedented growth has created an unprecedented situation, but that nonlinear sheer size does not point to a way out of this mess we are in, nor does it fully explain what has happened. The fundamental explanation lies in how humans and technology have *combined* to form unfamiliar, disruptive phenomena.

The Industrial Revolution brought about great shifts in human existence as cities became centers of industry and modes of work drastically shifted, for better and for worse. Industrial technology and the science behind it were necessary precursors to the societal changes of the nineteenth century, but by themselves, they hardly explain the new economic and social organization that resulted. From looking at the steam engine, one would not immediately make the jump to filthy factories, child labor, and the migration from traditional rural life to the explosive growth of cities. Yet the Industrial Revolution lies in those social changes just as much as it does in the technology that spurred them. Similarly, today's enormous online networks have produced new forms of social, economic, and political organization, but we have been slow to perceive them because they are so unfamiliar to us. Growth and connectivity have fueled the invisible human-machine behemoths that I call meganets, radically restructuring our lives as drastically as the Industrial Revolution did—a fact that we are just beginning to comprehend. These meganets are fundamentally new combinations of huge numbers of people and enormous amounts of computational processing power. They evolve faster than we can track them. Their workings are opaque even to their administrators. And they irreversibly occupy our lives with an ongoing persistence that makes them inextricable from the fabric of society.

The driver behind our loss of control is neither "populist" masses of people nor technology per se but this new kind of force, something that did not exist even twenty years ago. It emerged sometime in the first decade of this century and exploded in the second, triggered by the massive deployment of mobile computing devices that connected huge numbers of people to the internet without interruption. The tight tethering of humans to global communications networks created this new sort of beast operating beyond the control of the individuals, companies, and governments that created them, commandeering our inner lives and daily reality.

Conspiracy theories are fundamentally comforting. When confronted with uncertainty and chaos, it is a reassuring backstop to imagine that in some secret location, behind closed doors, *someone* is still in control, orchestrating the mystifying events around us. Whether it's foreign governments, our own government, industry CEOs, or the 1 percent, hypothesizing conspiracies lets us believe that if only we could seize control from the secret actors, we could set things right. If no one is in control, then the worst may likely be true: no one *can* be in control. Unfortunately, it is this latter situation that is far more frequently the truth, and it is why, in the words of philosopher Kenneth Burke, we build our cultures by "huddling together, nervously loquacious, at the edge of an abyss."[15] It may not be a conspiracy theory to believe that Mark Zuckerberg is choosing to sow social unrest for profit, or that Silicon Valley elites are undermining democracy, but it is conspiratorial thinking. And it is incorrect.

Meganets, in truth, strongly resist attempts to control them as they accumulate data about all our daily activities, our demographics, and our very inner selves. They construct social groupings that could not have even existed twenty years ago. And, as the new minds of the world, they constantly modify themselves in response to user behavior, resulting in collectively authored algorithms none of us intend—not even the corporations and governments operating them. And in keeping with the exponential explosion in computation, they too will continue to grow at nonlinear rates, faster than we can keep up with.

From the internet came subrevolutions like Web 2.0 and social media, followed by an ongoing series of buzzwords that capture whatever new forms of growth we have discerned in meganets. Whether it's big data, the cloud, the internet of things, blockchain, augmented reality, or the much-ballyhooed metaverse, these labels all present partial time-sliced views of the larger, sweeping trend of the meganet sweeping up our lives into a part-machine, part-human leviathan.

THE CRYPTOMETASOMETHINGVERSE

The metaverse is here, and we don't know what it is. Not only has Facebook changed its name to Meta to signal its full-throated backing of this brave new world, but the *metaverse* became the business buzzword of 2022, with JPMorgan declaring it a $1 trillion business opportunity, while Morgan Stanley and Goldman Sachs raised the bet to $8 trillion.[16] Those are enormous numbers for one of the most nebulous concepts to have come down the pike since "the cloud." Yet even if the term itself fades as just another buzzword like the internet of things or big data, the technologies and networks being developed under the name of the metaverse will remain with us for a very long time and deeply alter our lives at a personal and global scale. Many of these technologies are already with us.

While popular discussion of the metaverse has focused on the long-latent promise of virtual reality (VR), that by itself isn't enough to explain the trillion-dollar expectations placed on it. Rather, much of the metaverse's promise relies on the hopes for an entire new universe of online goods to buy: not just accessories for virtual avatars but also tickets to virtual concerts and online "land" in the form of digital properties. In the blockchain-based online world of Decentraland, a cross between a role-playing game and a real estate development, people as different as Ariana Grande and JPMorgan CEO Jamie Dimon have purchased parcels of physically nonexistent land for upward of $12,000 and built virtual mansions on them.[17] Far beyond online gaming, this is the creation of a major new marketplace in which companies like Meta and Microsoft will act as sellers and brokers in much the way that Amazon today acts as broker and guarantor for its market of physical goods and third-party sellers.

The technology underpinning the marketplace is not VR, though VR will make digital goods more appealing and glitzier. Rather, the technology is cryptocurrency, or more precisely the blockchain algorithms that enable cryptocurrency to exist. So-called non-fungible tokens, or NFTs, act as decentralized proofs of ownership for virtual goods. Formerly, "ownership" of digital goods was something asserted by the company providing the particular world in which those goods existed. If I owned some sort of virtual object in some online virtual world or game, whether it was a really awesome axe in World of Warcraft or a cute skirt in Roblox, that object and ownership of that object were only valid in the world in which I had purchased it because there was no robust, universally agreed-upon mechanism for proclaiming my axe or skirt ownership somewhere else (Facebook, Instagram, wherever). NFTs (or equivalent technologies) obliterate those barriers, allowing for collective, universal, and indisputable agreement on who owns what. In effect, NFTs, blockchain, and cryptocurrency allow for a new international economy in which the virtual goods of all online worlds can be merged into one enormous market. The massive NFT crash of mid-2022 only hastens this consolidation by eliminating small players and speculators, allowing for domination of NFT transactions by established tech titans. Metaverse barons like Facebook and Microsoft will provide the biggest marketplaces, as well as manage many of the blockchain transactions. That is where that $8 trillion is to come from.

Yet there is a price to be paid for this lucre, and the price is paid in a loss of control. The metaverse is only the most visible evidence of the shocking hold that cryptocurrency, as well as the blockchain-based NFTs that are its offspring, has gained over the world. Cryptocurrency, once considered an eccentric and cultish enthusiasm of laissez-faire techies, has become a trillion-dollar phenomenon, a permanent part of the economic landscape attracting large-scale institutional investment. The peculiarities of its mechanisms, which are subject to the intrinsic workings and limitations of the meganet, threaten to have a far greater impact on the world than social media. The greater financial system has already absorbed cryptocurrencies into its workings, so that cryptocurrency's swings are no longer isolated. In early 2022, International Monetary Fund financial counselor Tobias Adrian observed increasing correlation between cryptocurrency and equity markets, declaring: "Crypto is now very closely tied to what is happening in equities. We can't just dismiss it."[18] The proof came only months later, with May's immense crash in cryptocurrencies and November's collapse of the much-vaunted yet fatally sketchy FTX exchange devastating but hardly destroying the market, simultaneously proving cryptocurrency's hold on us as well as our inability to control it.

The underlying nature of cryptocurrencies and NFTs, true to their origins, holds great risks. True to their designers' intentions, the benefits of cryptocurrencies are inseparable from their anarchic, consensus-requiring design. The history of Bitcoin and Ethereum is a chronicle of philosophical schisms, money heists, disreputable exchanges and outright scams, and disastrous bugs—none enough to undo the fundamental success of the technology but enough to raise great concerns over such technology underpinning $8 trillion of the world and enough to destabilize the rest of the economy should something go wrong.

When Bitcoin exchange Mt. Gox went bankrupt in 2014 after hackers stole $460 million in Bitcoin, the massive losses were ultimately only a minor setback to cryptocurrencies.[19] Yet such incidents underscore that when something goes wrong on the blockchain, *no one* can fix it because no one has control over it. *Everyone collectively* can fix it if everyone can agree on how to fix it. An economy built on blockchain, cryptocurrency, and NFTs is built on the faith that humans can reach consensus in dealing with any problem. Unfortunately, "everyone" can rarely agree on anything. If a crisis should arrive, there will be no Federal Reserve to step in because the nature of cryptocurrency doesn't allow for one, and another financial crisis like that of 2008 will loom. The massive crash of cryptocurrencies in May 2022 and FTX's subsequent implosion months later will seem mild in comparison to what is to come. The price of cryptocurrency is the risk of chaos.

No doubt the enormous corporations and world governments will attempt to rein in the wild west excesses of cryptocurrency. In some regards, they will succeed by providing greater guarantees and stamping out some bad actors. The metaverse promises to centralize many cryptocurrency transactions within massive corporate entities. But the fundamental design of cryptocurrencies prevents easy regulation and containment of any problems that arise within them, and over the course of this book, we will see how cryptocurrency and NFT algorithms are inextricably linked to the strengths and failings of human nature, as amplified by the meganet.

LOSS OF AGENCY

Today there is a pervasive fallacy of assigning greater agency to others than to ourselves. I was fortunate enough to step into a great many waters over the course of my careers as software engineer, journalist, part-time academic, and DC think tank fellow, gaining more perspective than any single position could provide. In each of them, there was a dominant strain of thought that assigned power to one or more of the other factions. Journalists saw Silicon Valley threatening their jobs and centralizing power. Tech workers saw journalists and politicians impinging on their lives. DC policy wonks saw a failed regulatory state that couldn't control corporate businesses. And academics felt at the mercy, more or less, of all of them. Each faction was convinced that someone else had the power. People are searching for where the power really lies, when it does not lie anywhere. Even Mark Zuckerberg, the target for so many grievances, is said by his own colleagues to be without a clear plan on crucial issues facing his company and his creation: "The whole point is, he changes his mind all the time."[20]

Such confusion originates from the simultaneous power and inadequacy of meganets. Even as we feel humbled by technology and tech companies, we wonder why they are so inept. *Financial Times* editor Elaine Moore summed it up when she asked in 2021: "If Big Tech has our data, why are targeted ads so terrible?" She was offended not just by the invasive tracking but also by the shoddiness of the results:

> I have been using Facebook platforms for more than a decade. The company has had the opportunity to track my movements and scrape information for years. Yet the end result is a random, largely inaccurate overview. If I were an advertiser I would want my money back.[21]

Yet there is a greater implication of this ineptitude. If companies cannot even target advertising well after collecting so much data, how on earth could they address the more profound problems of social disorganization and disinformation? If the best and the brightest cannot marshal their algorithms to a level of self-interested competence, what reason do we have to believe that governmental oversight would compel them to do better?

It is easy enough to think that our problems arise from tech companies' pursuit of profit. Yet despite their immense profitability, the meganets created by Facebook, Google, and others are hugely imprecise and, moreover, impossible to "fix," if fixing means removing all possibility of error, bias, and unintended consequences. The only full fix would be to shut the meganets down, which will not happen. But as long as they continue to grow in size and complexity, we must accept that these systems are too large for us to supervise and control in any traditional manner. Meganets cannot be controlled in the way we control an airplane or a factory. They can, however, be shaped and ushered in more benevolent directions. If not fixable, they can, with the right approach, be tamed.

SOLUTIONS, NOT FIXES

There have been two primary responses to the loss of control caused by our meganets. On the one hand, many simply shrug and accept it as the cost of the brave new virtual world gifted to us. The Amazons, Apples, Facebooks, and Googles of the world are too big, too central, and too profitable to ignore or boycott. The public-private data and surveillance infrastructure is too necessary, too ubiquitous, and too powerful to shut down. Cryptocurrencies are too anarchic, decentralized, and (sometimes) lucrative to shut down. Just as the recording and movie industries spent years fruitlessly fighting illegal file sharing before embracing the new technology of streaming, many people, whether CEOs, politicians, or ordinary workers, accept the consequences of the new technological world because they see no alternative. Elsewhere, in China, Russia, and even India, the greater population lacks even the agency to object to any particular impact of meganets on their lives. In the case of India's government-mandated identity system Aadhaar, there has been a societal shrug about it going "rogue" from its original intent. For cryptocurrency ecosystems, chaos, anarchy, and conflict are simply the norm.

On the other hand, there is a constant stream of selective, directed outrage whenever unacceptable consequences of the technology present themselves too visibly. Whether it's hate groups gathering on the internet, Facebook's Cambridge Analytica voter-profiling scandal, or Google's YouTube recommendation algorithms pointing to fringe content, media feeding frenzies now pop up regularly, calling either for greater self-policing or for government regulation. These crises usually fade away rather than being resolved, and the next one inevitably arises within weeks if not days.

As we have seen and will explore in more detail, the Facebooks and Googles of the world are not indifferent to such bad publicity, but they now view it as unavoidable—not because they choose to ignore the scandals but because their own creations are not sufficiently under their control. Calls for reform and regulation cascade, yet there is failure to achieve any real such reform: the best we seem to manage are pop-up notifications telling us that we can't use a website unless we accept their cookies, a useless and superficial mandate from the EU.[22] Can we really expect the nascent attempts at regulating AI, a far more complicated issue, to be any more adequate?

To fix something, we must know how it is broken. We will first get a grip on the nature of the problem facing us by exploring both the structure of the meganet and the effects that structure has on human interaction. Bearing in mind that the meganet is not wholly technological, nor wholly human, but an unprecedented combination of both, we will see how the traditional scale and organization of the world has been upended by virtual networks extending their tendrils through every populated inch of the planet, whether by smartphones, laptops, digital cameras, or one of thousands of other networked devices deployed throughout the world. By themselves, these devices are not so remarkable, but their integration and unification into huge nation- and globe-spanning networks is.

That unification creates the new phenomena that so vex us. Anyone can now broadcast information to hundreds of millions of others, and computers instantaneously react to that information and modify and amplify it further. All of this happens so fast, and so incessantly, and so broadly that no single entity, whether a person or a corporation or a government, can keep up with it. The consequences are the out-of-control incidents that flare up constantly online and offline, whether it's something as harmless as a flash mob or something as damaging as the spread of paranoid conspiracy theories.

We will then take a brief trip to the past to see how these changes snuck up on us. I was fortunate enough to be present at the birth of several of the most successful meganets in my time as a software engineer at Google and at Microsoft. I witnessed firsthand the nascent loss of control, which took even the most veteran engineers by surprise. While we knew what we were building technologically, none of us were wholly aware of how people would use our systems and what would be born once hundreds of millions of people were inextricably and ubiquitously tied to our systems.

Social networks are only the most visible manifestation of meganets—and not even their most supercharged manifestation. Social networks show how information and influence can spiral out of our control once meganets manage and conduct them, but even more severe possibilities exist when money is thrown into the mix. Here, the world of online role-playing games has something to teach us, as their "imaginary" economies have proven to be more real than even their creators imagined, with floating exchange rates and illegal transactions. The toy currencies of World of Warcraft, EverQuest, Pokémon, and many other games have yielded economies beyond their creators' control. It is no wonder that Microsoft and others see gaming as the new paradigm for online life in the metaverse era, replacing the social media of today.

Games also set the scene for cryptocurrency, the far more consequential economic manifestation of meganets. While cryptocurrency and blockchain technology are set to structure the metaverse, their history already contains plenty of predictions and warnings about how such a decentralized and chaotic technology may impact the global economy. We will see how cryptocurrency's remarkable explosion is based in a surrender of any kind of centralized control, as well as how that lack of control has already produced ongoing chaos within the crypto community. We will see how both cryptocurrency players as well as external entities have attempted to exert some kind of control, with mixed success, resulting in a paradoxically centralized decentralization riven with scams and schisms. And we will see how so-called crypto stablecoins like Tether and TerraUSD, proposed as a moderating influence on the fundamental anarchy of Bitcoin and Ethereum, are in fact not so stable after all on account of their meganet-like properties and how they threaten the world economy.

Beyond economics, politics has also fallen under the sway of meganets administered by governments themselves. In this, the West is behind other parts of the world. The government-run Aadhaar meganet provides an "identity service" for all India's citizens that, while officially optional, has become all but mandatory to utilize any number of crucial governmental services as well as to register for bank accounts and cell phones. As by now will seem inevitable, Aadhaar has slipped out of the control of the Indian government, its benefits bringing with it unavoidable flaws that the government had pledged to prevent. A comparison with China, a far less liberal society, is illustrative. While China subjects its citizens to far more monitoring and governmental oppression than India, this increase in control has ironically caused China to realize more quickly the limits of what such meganet-driven control can gain for them.

For all of the flood of information that drives the meganet, one major cure-all has been proposed: artificial intelligence and deep learning in particular. Deep-learning AI, some of its proponents argue, is a technique for taming the mountains of data and activity that are too great for humans, collectively or individually, to manage. And if an AI could monitor and prevent the negatives of the meganet, it would be nothing short of a godsend. Unfortunately, the reality is very nearly the opposite. While deep learning is uncannily skilled at analyzing analog data, the sheer opacity of deep learning (and of AI more generally) ends up amplifying the existing problems of meganets tenfold. Unable to grasp the nuances of human behavior and interaction, AI will end up dragging vastly more data into the meganet while obscuring what that data actually *means* to the meganet. As meganets continue to balloon in size and complexity, AI will make them *more* difficult to manage, not less, even though its technical achievements will still appear amazing.

If AI is not the solution, then what is? Many technological ethicists and policy specialists suggest a far greater degree of governmental regulation or at least self-regulation of how data can be managed. Such approaches, unfortunately, are pure placebos. Neither corporations nor governments can change the nature of meganets any more than they can control the weather or prevent natural disasters. By framing meganets' problems as a lack of will or ethics on the part of meganet-operating corporations like Google and Facebook, we search for solutions where none exist. Only by accepting that the problem is systemic and insoluble, centered around processes that we can neither fully understand nor control, can we hope to *cope* with meganets' negatives. There is a middle path between unrealistic idealism and defeatism. We can abandon the dream of *fixing* meganets while retaining some ability to *shape* their functions. When a hurricane hits, one does not blame the government for the hurricane itself—yet we expect the government to mitigate and address the damage done by the hurricane. The meganet, and its hurricane of dynamic data, cannot be brought to heel—but it can be mitigated.

To take one high-profile hotspot: How could one fix the degradation, balkanization, and radicalization of discourse on Facebook, Twitter, and YouTube? It can't be fixed by trying to stamp out unwanted discourse, nor by expecting the companies to police their platforms thoroughly, nor by creating regulatory agencies to demand such of companies. Rather, the problem is one of social engineering, albeit at a far greater scale than has ever before been seen. Instead of fruitlessly policing civility, social networks need to create mechanisms for dissipating and dehomogenizing discourse, mechanisms that aren't surgically targeted but instead will have subtle yet wide-ranging effects. I will discuss some of these potential mechanisms in detail later in this book, but such strategies include:

1. Injecting unfamiliar participants and elements into virtual communities
2. Randomizing and decentralizing meganet control mechanisms such as recommendation engines, ranking algorithms, and advertisement targeting

3. Intentionally "tainting" or "polluting" large meganet data stores and AIs with random garbage data
4. Breaking up and/or dispersing long-standing virtual communities
5. Creating and encouraging participation in new, heterogeneous virtual communities
6. Involving end users in correcting and dehomogenizing data and analytics

All of these mechanisms center on diminishing, disrupting, and breaking up the self-reinforcing feedback loops that meganets inevitably create.

These mechanisms will work most effectively if they are *not* surgically targeted because the size of meganets makes surgical targeting infeasible to begin with. We read about some problematic community only after it has metastasized into a malignancy that is too big and too toxic to treat. Only by applying soft social engineering universally can we improve the overall health of the online world. As much as we may wish for cancer drugs and chemotherapy to only target the bad cells of a human body, they do not work at so fine-grained a level. The same applies to these meganet control mechanisms.

The term *social engineering* is discomfiting. Despite widespread acknowledgment of the social problems created by meganets and the communities they foster, there is still a justifiable and sacrosanct ideal that association and discourse should remain more or less free from authoritative social control mechanisms. Realistically, however, meganets make a liberal, laissez-faire approach to social engineering unfeasible. Yet the social engineering I recommend will not have the effect of cracking down on free speech but of *preventing* the selective, ham-fisted censorship performed by corporations and governments in response to the complaints of politicians and media. There will always be some degree of social control on networks that are not complete anarchy. Even within intentionally decentralized networks such as Bitcoin or Twitter-competitor Mastodon, social control occurs through collective enforcement of norms; there is just no clear ownership of that social control. By implementing soft, nontargeted social engineering, we will ironically ensure a greater degree of freedom for meganet participants than we would by surgically attacking problem spots with hard social controls like censorship and ostracism.

Meganets disconnect our traditional sense of cause and effect. As with the environment, humanity collectively has difficulty addressing problems in which the causal links between behaviors and their larger effects scatter and grow unclear, problems where it's difficult to gauge whether a chosen course of action is actually improving things. Even in the face of overwhelming evidence that burning fossil fuels is contributing to economically and socially devastating climate effects, the lead time on climate change is so long that even if we were to stop all fuel-based carbon production tomorrow, we would not see the climate stabilize for years at best—and possibly a lot longer.[23] Likewise, containing meganets requires subtle, far-reaching interventions, and it will be far from obvious how they are helping. That is why it is first necessary to understand them, since over the next few decades, meganets will increasingly force our political institutions and social norms to evolve. Large corporations, polities, and hedge funds will still exert great force in the economic realm, but they will now compete with decentralized and near-anonymous aggregates of self-organizing traders, both in equities and in cryptocurrencies. Politics will be guided less by political parties and more by seemingly spontaneous groupings of like-minded—and angry—individuals. This seeming populist empowerment simultaneously creates blinkered microenvironments that corral and balkanize human thought and behavior. Self-determination will be a distant myth, as our personalities, characteristics, and habits will be gleaned from birth onward and used to sort us; humans will be subjected constantly to the decisions of algorithms and AIs that, when questioned, cannot be explained or reversed. This is our future with meganets. The loss of our old ways will be mourned, but it does not have to be all dark.

ONE

A WORLD TOO BIG TO KNOW

Automata [machines] can help us to skip levels of consciousness, and we often must respond to the strains of practical demands by automatizing ourselves.

HANS BLUMENBERG, "World Pictures and World Models"

We no longer understand the structure of human existence. Perhaps we never did; perhaps we only construct rationalized stories in retrospect that explain the immense changes spurred by the scientific and industrial revolutions. Yet until recently, the amount of knowledge was manageable. Today, the world itself has grown beyond collective human comprehension, thanks to the digital revolution and the titanic information networks it has created.

One example: In 2019, a group of Iranian architects entered plans for a dual-purpose skyscraper, Crypto-Park, into the *eVolo* magazine Skyscraper Competition. Designers Ramtin Taherian, Illia Attarpour, and Dadbeh Mohebbi Gilani proposed a two-thousand-foot vertical waterpark built around an enormous cryptocurrency mining operation, to be built in the hills of Tehran. The water would cool the energy-hungry cryptocurrency rigs, even as the rigs heated the water.

The architects intended Crypto-Park as a means of autonomous financial support and a way to do an end run around economic sanctions imposed on Iran.[1]

Crypto-Park was a conceptual proposal. Even the cryptocurrency obsessives at the Bitcoinist news site deemed it a mad idea.[2] But all the designers did was to place in one physical location activities that are already occurring around the world at similarly massive scale. Enormous Bitcoin mining rigs run deep around the world, consuming more electricity than the entirety of Sweden.[3] Invented currencies, from Bitcoin to Ethereum to Tether to the in-game currencies of World of Warcraft, remove governments as intermediaries and guarantors of value and replace them with corporations, individuals, or pure algorithms themselves. Around it all is the virtual life that technology has created for us, a world to which our "real" lives increasingly migrate day by day. And increasingly, the walls between online networks break down as data spreads out of control.

In 2020, Singapore's citizens were outraged by a leaking of data from a COVID tracing app to law enforcement. Singapore had mandated that its citizens install a COVID-19 contact tracing app, TraceTogether, before they could enter indoor public spaces again.[4] The always-on app, which could be installed on either a mobile or a dedicated wearable tracking device, used Bluetooth to keep a record of which other citizens a user had been in proximity with. Despite promises that the information gathered would be used exclusively for contact tracing, police easily obtained access to TraceTogether data in a murder investigation in May of that year, sparking outrage even in a country not known for its civil liberties.[5] As so often is the case, the sensitivity of the data posed little obstacle to its promiscuous spread, and even the legislative response was half-hearted. The bill passed in February 2021 still allows for use of TraceTogether data for investigations across seven types of "serious crimes" including murder, sanctioning the very violation of data privacy that had triggered the debate in the first place.[6]

We hear incessantly about such broken promises of privacy and security to the point where we are numb to them. Most such breaches happen in the private sector, but as governments move online and our official lives are increasingly encoded in data, the uncontrolled spread of data accelerates in spite of our best intentions and promises to contain it.

Take the Baltic country of Estonia, one of the first Soviet republics to break away as its parent nation fell apart. Estonia has aggressively pursued the digitalization of its citizenry and country, moving government services almost entirely online. It is commonly termed the most wired country in the world. In 2019, President Kersti Kaljulaid touted blockchain as the crucial technology securing wholly digital government services: "a majority of government services are offered 24/7 online, and data integrity is ensured by blockchain technology."[7] Yet Estonia's president had it wrong. There is no blockchain in Estonia's databases. The X-Road system that synchronizes them does use one algorithm—hash-based time-stamping, which is used to validate the exact time a particular transaction took place—which is also central to blockchain. But such time-stamping is no more blockchain than a wheel is a car.[8]

Princeton researcher Arvind Narayanan observed that the word *blockchain* itself was so hyped up that banks were eagerly trying to adopt the technology even when it was completely unnecessary.

> "Private blockchain" is just a confusing name for a shared database. . . . It's a bit like hammering in a thumb tack, but if a hammer is readily available and no one's told you that thumb tacks can be pushed in by hand, there's nothing particularly wrong with it.[9]

The reality of the blockchain, in fact, makes that hammer ill-suited for many purposes. The benefits of blockchain that Narayanan lists—"the level of security, irreversibility, and censorship-resistance"—are things that governments and banks *don't want* because they would entail a genuine and irreversible loss of centralized control.[10] True blockchain would remove power from the government while *dispersing* it across individuals, none of whom could control the entire system. It would be inimical to government's underlying goal of perpetuating itself. This is, in fact, the goal of the Bitcoin architects' anarchist vision: to take centralized power away from hierarchical human organizations and lock it up with impermeable algorithms.

The question is, What world results when we lose centralized power over our technologies? Whatever it might be is enough to baffle Estonia, and yet the financial potential of these technologies drives their continued integration into the fabric of the world. Rather than supplementing our lives with technological accessories, we are tightly wrapping our lives around technology and putting online networks at the core—like a waterpark wrapped around an enormous Bitcoin mining rig.

Whether a Bitcoin skyscraper or a contact tracing app, no such technologies would be deployed if they did not promise significant benefit to their users. And their benefits—and not merely financial ones—cannot be denied. The efficiency, convenience, accountability, and communication provided by computer and communication technologies has brought significant human value into the world. Yet what's unnerving about their downsides is not that they are necessarily catastrophic—the drawbacks of these new technologies are frequently more subtle than horrific—but that their downsides are so often unpredictable and difficult to mitigate. We do not feel plagued by these technologies for the most part, but we do feel increasingly unable to control them. And by "we," I do not mean only the users but also the corporations, governments, and even engineers who deploy these technologies. This uncertainty poses a threat not just to individuals' rights and privacy but also to businesses who have an increasingly difficult time estimating risks posed by new technologies—or even understanding them.

Even though smartphones, social networks, and the internet itself would appear hopelessly alien to someone who had been asleep for the last forty years, these changes have come gradually and slowly enough that the surrealness and novelty of decentralized finance or digitalized governance rarely strikes us as deeply as it should. Consider some of the bizarre questions confronting us day by day on social networks. Are you reading the words of a person or a bot? What content are algorithms hiding from you—or promoting to you? Do you belong to an organic group or an astroturfed operation? Are you seeing a picture or a deepfake? The controversy and uproar following the last two US presidential elections centered around debates that could not have taken place twenty years ago. The threat of viral misinformation dominated discussion of the 2016 election, with Facebook accused of letting third parties, both domestic and foreign, improperly access its data for purposes of electoral targeting. It was not only Republican-funded firms like Cambridge Analytica but also Russian trolls who cast a pall over the result. Similar viral misinformation spread like wildfire after the 2020 election, as dubious authorities popped up on Facebook, Twitter, and YouTube to spread conspiracy theories about manipulated voting machines and corrupt election officials, fomenting every bit of doubt they could. As a result, many finally realized that it is trivial to spread dubious information on the internet and that the sheer volume of that information means that some of it will inevitably go viral. It is only the first of many uncomfortable wake-up calls to come.

Westerners may feel coerced and even oppressed by Facebook and Google, but the governments of India and China have already created similarly ubiquitous systems. India's Aadhaar and China's nascent Social Credit System both display the same pitfalls as their established Western brethren: they are invasive, prone to mistakes, and susceptible to data leakage. Rather than taming the Facebooks and Googles of the world, governments are far more likely to mimic them in their own highly interconnected networks. As governments roll out mechanisms to prove COVID-19 vaccination, such as New York's Excelsior Pass or Canada's vaccine passport, these systems are built on top of a growing digital infrastructure that can instantaneously validate such passes and passports. It's anachronistic to see such passports as an omen of Big Brother–like monitoring because such infrastructure has long been in place far deeper in society (albeit less visibly). Already, government intelligence blithely tracks and amasses voluminous data files on all citizens in what its own technicians term "vacuum-cleaner surveillance."[11] In the West, such surveillance and tracking is mostly invisible, and most of the data goes unused and even unseen, but vaccine passports are one augur of an era in which governments will increasingly employ Facebook-like and Google-like networks for both the benefit and the tracking of citizens. China's Alipay Health Code, built by a public-private partnership including Ant Financial, automatically quarantines citizens by assigning them one of three colors—green, yellow, and red—assigned by centralized servers. A *New York Times* report could not determine what the specific triggers were: someone could go from green to red and back with no explanation. The mechanism is opaque, yet one Chinese woman was resigned to it: "Alipay already has all our data. So what are we afraid of? Seriously."[12] In mid-2022, Zhengzhou citizens found out one answer to that question when a number of them protested local banks freezing their deposits, and the local officials secretly flipped over a thousand protesters' codes to red to limit their movements.[13] As data, tracking, and connectivity grow, that opacity becomes the norm.

All of these networks have peculiar, unprecedented properties. They grow organically, they evolve rapidly and unpredictably, and they are decidedly imperfect. Above all, they are *not ultimately under our control.* No one has been especially keen to acknowledge this truth. Corporations prefer to say they are the masters of their creations, government agencies and watchdogs wish regulation of these networks to be possible, and no user would ask to be subject to the whims of some out-of-control proto-Skynet. Unfortunately, the exponential growth of computing technology and data collection has yielded a world that, upon examination, is too big for us to know.

What happens when our technological systems of control themselves prove uncontrollable, when they become semiautonomous—not as unitary minds but as large, complex systems like the weather or traffic patterns? They yield meganets.

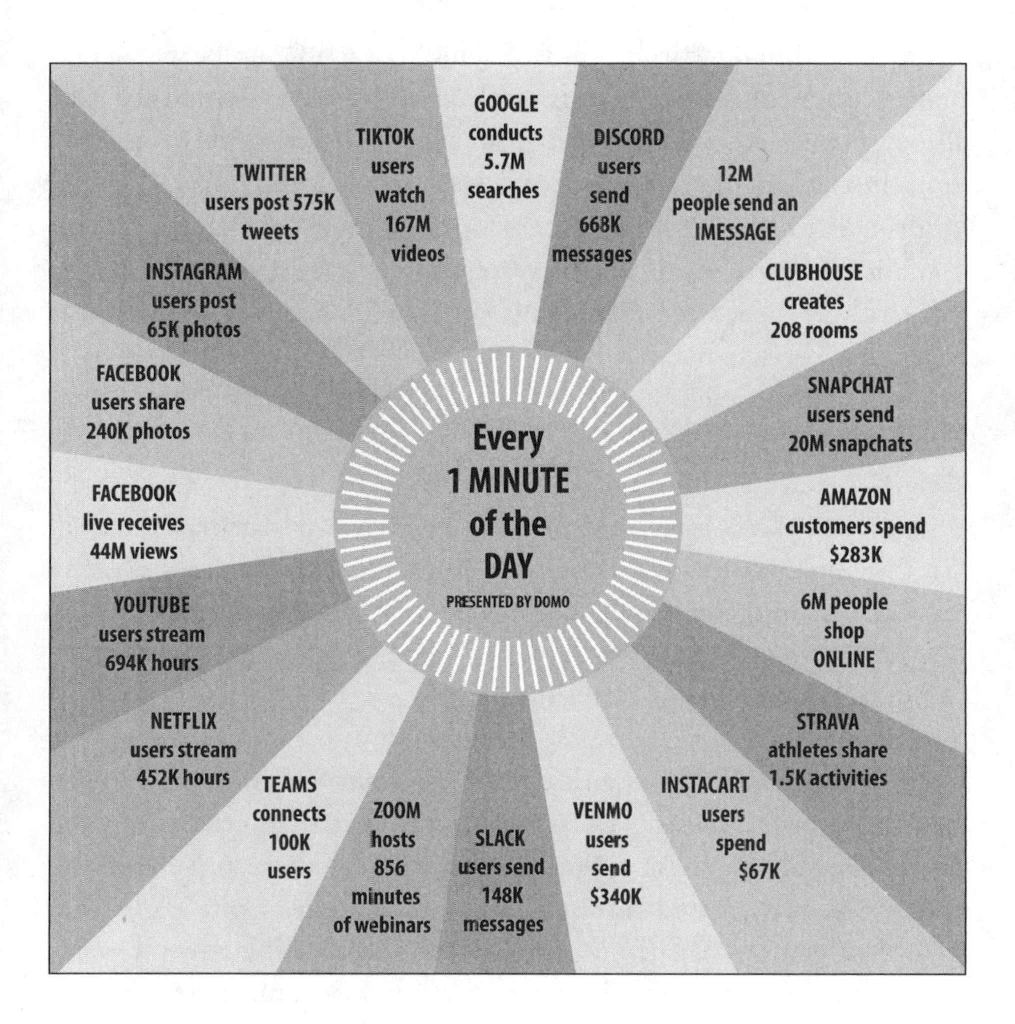

DATA ABUNDANCE

As recently as fifty years ago, the overwhelming majority of people's lives went undocumented and unrecorded. It wasn't data but simply life. We possessed neither the means to codify most of our lives as data, nor the resources with which to analyze and store it.

Things have changed. Our world has acquired a new substrate of *data*. Every single day, we now produce more computational data than was produced in the entire history of humanity up until the year 2000.[14] Nearly everything we do now carries with it a trace of computable data that can be recorded, preserved, analyzed, and synthesized. The change was not instantaneous. For much of the twentieth century, computers dealt almost exclusively with numbers: balance sheets, physical measurements, and other purely quantitative data. Today, however, computers can glean data from a picture, a conversation, and any bit of daily activity, usual or unusual, and the monitoring infrastructure exists for computers to access much of that activity automatically. In the last twenty years, computers have gone from seeing very little of the world to seeing nearly all of it—and with it, the whole world has become data.

In a 1984 article titled "Is It O.K. to Be a Luddite?" Thomas Pynchon observed:

> Since 1959, we have come to live among flows of data more vast than anything the world has seen. Demystification is the order of our day, all the cats are jumping out of all the bags and even beginning to mingle. . . . What is important here is the amplifying of scale, the multiplication of effect.[15]

Yet in the ensuing decades, the continuing inflation of data has had the opposite effect. The world is more mystifying than ever, and the unbagged cats are now buried amid a gale of noise and chaff. The power we have gained through the amplification of our efforts has grown so great as to become tangled in itself, creating new phenomena more confusing than those we attempted to control. The unveiling of reality has given way to a growing and chaotic series of onion layers, the fundament increasingly obscured.

When I joined Microsoft at the turn of the century as a software engineer, the company was at its peak of dominance with Windows and Office. I ended up by chance on Messenger, which became one of its few successful internet offerings at the time. Google was nothing but a start-up with a search engine and nothing else, while Facebook and YouTube did not exist. The social aspect of online life was little more than blogs and chat rooms.

By the time I departed Microsoft five years later to join Google and work on its search engine, the dotcom boom had crashed and Microsoft had lost a good deal of its prestige in the wake of the antitrust trial brought against it by the Department of Justice and ongoing delays to its Windows Vista operating system. Bigger changes were on the horizon. The momentum all pointed online: the web was exploding in size, and more than information moving online, *people* were beginning to move online. Friendster, MySpace, and Facebook heralded a new era of online presence, while YouTube and iTunes started the shift of content to digital distribution. The release of the first iPhone in 2007 augured the era of being always online, always reachable; the internet began to supplant the phone system.

These shifts have only accelerated. An entire generation has grown up unable to imagine a life without smartphones and streaming. Electronic payments have superseded physical currency in many parts of Africa. The idea of being offline has gone from the norm to a rare luxury.

In the first decade of this century, ensconced in the internet's crow's nest at Google, I realized that something new was being born, not in culture or in technology alone but through an unprecedented combination of them. Exactly why it was unprecedented—how it was different from the PC revolution or the commercialization of the internet—took me years to understand because there was no new technology driving this shift, only *so much more* of the same technology. During my time at Google, the company released Gmail and bought YouTube. MySpace and Friendster had exploded and stagnated, while Facebook was quickly rising. The internet was becoming something different, yet unlike the first online boom, this one didn't seem driven by any particular advances in technology. Instead, the change revolved around a critical mass of people, computers, and data coming together and interacting in fundamentally new ways. The world was reordering itself, sorting itself into massive networks to which people were always connected. Some were operated by corporations in plain daylight; others (like surveillance networks) were operated by governments in low profile. Still others, like Bitcoin, evolved under the radar before bursting anarchically into prominence.

The social history of computing is the story of how we have turned ourselves—our lives, our actions, our purchases, our words—into data, online and offline. We have become increasingly data driven, which means more than merely making decisions based on data. The data now determines what decisions we make in the first place. Take the endemic shift in the last twenty years from *searching* to *recommending*. At the dawn of the web, we typed in what we wanted to look for, whether into AltaVista, Lycos, or Google. Now, these networks increasingly tell us what we are interested in, recommending a never-ending stream of content. We off-load our choices to these networks, but it was only *after* millions upon millions adopted and engaged with these networks that they could make such recommendations. A new creature was born that could manage the data boom and absorb, filter, and recommend it: the meganet.

There was no one single innovation that created this creature. The general-purpose computer, the internet, the smartphone—each provided a great advance in the ability for the average human being not just to access data but also to *generate* it. The *cumulative* impact of this online networked growth, breaking through to a critical mass of connected people and data generation, triggered our new age of high-velocity, densely interconnected networks of people and computers. We have moved from information scarcity to informational abundance.

A curious fact emerges when it comes to the effects of these technologies on society: size really counts. Anyone who witnessed the first light bulb or automobile was immediately stunned. But only an expert or a visionary might have been dazzled by computational prototypes like Charles Babbage's analytical engine or the World War II military computer ENIAC (Electronic Numerical Integrator and Computer), which held eye-opening potential but were too primitive (or, in Babbage's case, unbuilt) to change the world by themselves. The revolutionary effects of the computer played out more slowly. They were driven just as much by what happened *after* the introduction of the new technology into businesses and homes. It was a slow-motion revolution, built by humans working in tandem with computers.

The result of this revolution is something beyond computers in themselves. It is a hybrid of countless computers perpetually attached to countless humans. It is the product of humans using computers to input, analyze, and output data, which then causes more data to be created, repeating the cycle at ever-increasing size.

Our existing vocabulary doesn't suffice to describe these data-generating networks. "Social networks," "the web," "the internet," "big data," and "digital life" all reflect some aspects of them, but none capture how sheerly organic and out of control these networks are. Artificial intelligence, particularly the deep-learning AIs that process and analyze petabytes of data in the bowels of Google and Facebook, has absorbed a lot of the praise and blame for qualities that would exist even in the total absence of AI technologies. Because there was no single technology that heralded these new larger networks of humans and computers, society searched for a culprit for why the world had turned so chaotic and hostile, and AI was in the right place at the right time.

Deep learning and AI play an important but ultimately secondary role in these new networks. They greatly amplify the unpredictability and power of meganets but only by virtue of the already existing large-scale assemblages of people, computers, and data.

TRANSISTORIZED

If there is a seed from which this entire revolution grew, it lies deep within computers, in the transistors that form the integrated circuits of most every electronic device. Specifically, it lies in the unprecedented scalability of the semiconductor technology underlying them and how engineers shrunk down the functionality of a three-inch vacuum tube to a transistor the size of a single virus particle.

The crux of the transistor revolution is the speed at which scientists have exponentially miniaturized semiconductors. That mind-boggling trend is the essence of Gordon Moore's observation in the 1960s, which came to be known as Moore's law, that transistors were being miniaturized at such a rate that the number of transistors capable of fitting into an integrated circuit was doubling roughly every eighteen to twenty-four months. And that in turn meant that devices whose capabilities were gated on transistor capacity—namely, key components of the computer such as the processor, memory, and disk space—were also experiencing exponential growth at roughly the same rate.

Against most predictions, Moore's law held up for sixty years. In recent years it has shown indications of slowing down, but the benefits (or damage) have already accrued.[16] The processing power and speed of a smartphone today is millions of times more powerful than mainframes that filled entire office rooms fifty years ago. The results of this bizarre, almost unprecedented change in scale are simultaneously obvious and elusive. Computational technology is now everywhere; data collection and analysis are now everywhere. Yet the simple existence of the smartphone doesn't begin to touch on what it means to have scaled-up computer technology to such absurdly high levels.

My first computer, an Apple IIe in 1984, had 128 kilobytes of memory (131,072 bytes). It used floppy disks that could store about 140 kilobytes (143,360 bytes). It had a CPU speed of a little more than 1,000 kilohertz, meaning that it went through over 1,000,000 clock "cycles" per second, during which all its hardware transistors opened or shut in accordance with processing the next primitive instruction. It was not cutting edge for its time but thoroughly acceptable for a home computer. Today, the computer on which I'm typing this has 16 gigabytes of memory (about 16 billion bytes). It has a 256 gigabyte hard disk (about 256 billion bytes). And its CPU has six cores, each running at 2.38 gigahertz (6 * 2,380,000,000 clock cycles per second), though clock speed numbers don't wholly reflect the increase in processor efficiency that has taken place since the 1980s. In every regard, today's computers are tens of thousand times bigger than computers of the 1980s, and their memory and disk storage are hundreds of thousands of times faster. When you use today's $1,000 iPhone, it is not obvious that it is as powerful as the $30 million, six-thousand-pound Cray-2 supercomputer of 1985, but you are indeed carrying around a tiny device that, with the use of a small rechargeable battery, can do as much as a refrigerator-sized mammoth from thirty-five years ago that required 200 kilowatts of energy to run.[17] Moreover, it's not even clear where all that computing capacity is even going. The Cray-2 was an elite machine, the fastest of its time, used for military and scientific research. We now have that much computing power in our pockets. The supercomputer of today (which would take the form of a server farm or data center, not a single machine) could do the work of ten thousand of those $30 million machines of 1985.

Think about what this would mean for technologies that have not scaled exponentially—which is to say, most of them. If batteries were ten thousand times more efficient than in 1980, one charge would power my phone for years. If fuel efficiency were ten thousand times more efficient than in 1980, cars and planes could travel for years on a single tank of gas. And if medicine could expand the human life span by ten thousand, human society would change so drastically as to be unrecognizable. Exponential growth in any of these fields would utterly transform the use of the underlying technology. We take it for granted that innovation in most technologies will proceed incrementally, if at all. At the same time, we forget exactly how anomalous the exponential miniaturization of transistors and integrated circuits has been. Any such exponential growth *should* yield results that are mind blowing and bizarre, but we fail to ask ourselves, "What are we doing with all this power?" because we forget that until recently, we did not have it.

Consequently it is a tricky matter to think of "the computer revolution" because it did not simply occur with the invention of the computer but evolved over a decades-long time span as computer technology vaulted itself into vastly more powerful domains. Yet unlike with automobiles or electricity, which were fully formed before they took over the world, the very nature of computer technology changed as it accumulated enough power and speed to generate and process more data than the world had ever known.

A QUESTION OF SIZE

Many articles and books try to explain what the internet is doing to us. This is not my goal, or at least not my starting point. Rather, I wish to look at certain structural commonalities among these new human-machine meganets and from there examine what limits we've put on ourselves by entrusting our lives to them. Meganets present a problem of size and scale whose implications are bizarre and even contradictory. Moore's law gives some indication of the nonlinear increase in technology, but it doesn't give any clue as to the underlying structural changes resulting from that increase. Things would be simpler if the practical upshot of that explosion in processing power and data still produced comparatively simple human phenomena. Cars and televisions are complex machines, but the average person can utilize them because expert knowledge and infrastructure create simple, manageable interfaces for them. But while computers present us with comprehensible (if sometimes creaky) interfaces to the web and internet, the very nature of meganets makes them nigh-impossible to understand and control. We will see many examples as to why, but the simplest explanation is that these networks are fundamentally too fast, too big, and, more than anything else, too *interconnected*.

Like the efficiency of transistors, interconnectivity grows exponentially. The simplest kind of network is *one to one*, or point to point. Physical mail, telephones, and text messaging all deliver communications from one entity to a single other entity. Adding a person to this network increases its size but not its complexity. Then there are *one-to-many* networks like radio and television and online mass media, where a small elite group broadcast their communications en masse to receivers, who all see and hear the same thing. Again, adding new broadcasters and receivers to one-to-many networks increases the size of these networks incrementally but not their overall complexity.

The internet gave us the first large-scale *many-to-many* networks, in which every participant theoretically possessed the ability to broadcast to every other participant. While the network's density was fairly sparse, in the early years of the internet and the web the explosion of social media in the last fifteen years realized the interconnected potential of the internet, giving us meganets. Each new participant connects to an arbitrary number of other members, so that everyone is simultaneously broadcasting on multiple channels and receiving the broadcasts of countless others across those same channels and others. Here is the combinatorial explosion: the links between participants no longer increase linearly but exponentially. Each person may now broadcast to millions of others as easily as she may privately message a single friend. No wonder we are overwhelmed, and no wonder we now need computational help to filter and organize this growing influx of data. This is the everyday manifestation of the underlying data boom.

These networks are simultaneously vast and claustrophobic, huge yet stifling. The sheer amount of data reminds us how much we are missing, even while we have the sense that the entire world is constantly looking over our shoulder online. The whole system can see us, even though we cannot possibly see it. The combination of unending access and unending surveillance leads to what Harvard professor Shoshana Zuboff, author of *The Age of Surveillance Capitalism*, termed a "perverse amalgam of empowerment inextricably layered with diminishment."[18] Our potential reach into the world has deepened immensely, and we have great choice over how we present ourselves and engage in the connected digital world. Yet our gain in control doesn't match the far greater gain in things we don't control: the online world grows faster than our agency does. Our supposed power becomes a placebo, providing an illusion of control over the things we do see, while what we don't see increasingly encroaches on us.

We find it increasingly difficult to distinguish between little and big. Distance—and physical space itself—has ceased to be a primary measure of size. When an exabyte (a million terabytes or trillion megabytes) of data can be stored in a single room, even as the books required to print that data at humanly readable size would be on the scale of the Great Wall of China, we lose a concrete sense of what *big* and *small* even are. The world of meganets breaks the human sense of space and size; the world is paradoxically bigger and smaller. It is more robust and more fragile.

The content delivery network (CDN) Fastly is one of a number of key players providing underlying server infrastructure to guarantee fast and reliable access to web content and streaming video. Such plumbing usually ensures that any particular technical glitch won't be noticed by end users, but when a misconfiguration in Fastly's platform took Reddit, CNN, Hulu, and thousands of other sites offline on June 8, 2021, tech analyst Ben Wood remarked:

> It's astonishing that one small piece of the immense jigsaw that powers the internet is able to cause such a massive outage. On the one hand, it's an unbelievably robust platform. On the flip side, these occasional blips underline the fragility of its fabric.[19]

By sheer dint of its importance, it hardly seems accurate to call Fastly "small," yet in purely numerical terms, it is only a minuscule portion of the overall internet. Is Fastly a big piece, a small piece, or both?

That paradox even extends to the very name I have given to these huge networks. The *mega* prefix comes from Greek, where it denoted something freakishly large, even godlike.[20] In 1873 it was cemented as a metric prefix designating a million.[21] It maintained its status as the largest prefix until the computer age, when far bigger numbers were becoming a practical reality. In 1960, the International System of Units added prefixes for a billion (*giga*) and a trillion (*tera*), both from Greek words applied to titans, giants, and leviathans—not just freakishly huge but monstrously so.[22] They, too, are no longer remarkable. Today, my personal hard disks hold several terabytes, and Google and Facebook deal in exabytes of data. Today, a megabyte is simultaneously huge—a million is no small amount—and tiny, dwarfed by the overwhelming mass of data we have created. This disturbing and permanent distortion of perspective flows out of meganets' exponential growth.

ENTER THE METAVERSE

From the miniaturization of the transistor to the explosion of data, the distortion of our very idea of physical space continues. The recent talking up of the metaverse (sometimes known as Web 3.0) promises to push these distortions further. Despite Facebook's rebranding to Meta and a boom in companies claiming to fuel metaverse technology, many are hard-pressed to say exactly what the metaverse is. This, I argue, is a consequence of the nature of the meganet.

Dictionary definitions of the metaverse are less than helpful:

Oxford English Dictionary:

"a virtual-reality space in which users can interact with a computer-generated environment and other users"[23]

Merriam-Webster:

"a highly immersive virtual world where people gather to socialize, play, and work"[24]

The curious thing about these two definitions is that they more or less describe the internet as it already exists. Don't we already socialize, play, and work in an all-too-immersive online world? That world may not be *The Matrix*, but all the connecting tissue is already there. "Virtual reality" colloquially describes physically simulated worlds that appear as tangible as the real world, but when we go online (and we are almost always online), we inhabit a world as virtual and absorbing as any—just less flashy and less sensorial.

Some other sources point a little closer to what the metaverse might be.

Victoria Petrock (eMarketer):

"the next evolution of connectivity where all of those things [like shopping and social media] start to come together in a seamless, doppelganger universe, so you're living your virtual life the same way you're living your physical life."[25]

Matthew Ball (metaverse venture capitalist):

"a successor state to the mobile internet, as well as a platform for human leisure, labor, and existence at large."[26]

Sara Fischer (Axios):

"bringing people together in a virtual interactive world."[27]

Meta Horizon:

> "a social experience where you can explore, play and create in extraordinary ways."[28]

Wikipedia:

> "a buzzword for public relations purposes to exaggerate development progress for various related technologies and projects."[29]

In all these definitions, save the last, the metaverse is a combination of the internet, social media, e-commerce, and online games: Facebook plus Snapchat plus YouTube plus Roblox plus Fortnite plus Bitcoin. It is the internet, except more so, online life blown up to the point where it can replicate and surpass offline life. As to *how* this enlargement will happen, details are scarce, but they revolve around new forms of interactivity like headsets and feedback gloves, which will shut out the physical world and replace it with a convincing fiction all the better to substitute for offline life.

There is still something terribly vague about all of this. In answer to the question of what one would actually *do* in the metaverse, the Associated Press offered this answer: "Things like go to a virtual concert, take a trip online, and buy and try on digital clothing"—and work from home.[30] This is all notable but hardly revolutionary. Crypto and gaming entrepreneur Shreyash Singh described the metaverse in similarly incrementalist terms:

> Web 3.0 offers even more functionality and interoperability than any of the preexisting services, so the possibilities for remote work, teleconferencing, telemedicine, remote socializing and so much more become profoundly enhanced. I would say it is reasonable that the metaverse will become a significant part of the regular individual's life in the coming decade and beyond.[31]

Indeed, it is entirely reasonable to say that remote work, teleconferencing, telemedicine, and remote socializing will become significant in years to come because *they already are.* Simply spreading *existing* online technologies and connectivity around the world will make a more profound difference to the world and online life than introducing new technologies. Later on, we will see that the true nature of the metaverse lies less in anything flashy than in the goal of monetizing existing online interactions, which is why the metaverse is so hard to pin down—it is a new way of making money off what's already out there. True, technologies falling under the metaverse rubric will likely improve many areas of online life, as well as make them more profitable, but on close examination, the metaverse seems to be less a life-changing phenomenon and more a bundle of emerging technologies to be grafted on to the existing internet, in much the way deep learning and big data were (and continue to be).

Deep learning and big data are significant aspects of the internet, as we will see in the coming chapters, but they too are secondary to the fundamental and deceptively simple concept of the meganet: the perpetual connection of billions of people through computer technology. Ironically, while deep learning and big data describe reasonably discrete and well-defined paradigms of processing data, the metaverse is a far bigger umbrella. Once VR headsets and cryptocurrency have been put under a single rubric, there is room for just about anything. So if we think of the metaverse as "the coming changes to the internet in the next decade," it will likely be far more accurate than focusing on anything in particular that Facebook or Microsoft are doing right now. Even if the name fades out as a momentary buzzword, its changes will remain.

Ultimately, the metaverse promises a continuation of meganet-driven trends that are already firmly in place: a loss of our sense of scale, a loss of local and globalized control, and even a loss of specific meaning. As a vague term for which no one seems to have an authoritative definition, the metaverse is the *reductio ad absurdum* of the meganet era. Not only can we not control the technological systems we have built, we also can no longer even pin down the words by which we call them. We are simply building out and building bigger, though not necessarily better.

THE DEFINITION OF A MEGANET

The internet opened up broadcasting channels to everyone, replacing transient, point-to-point communications by phone with enduring, one-to-many communications. Meganets coalesced these new broadcasting channels—hundreds of millions of them—into a new kind of evolving entity, where these assemblages of individual channels feed back upon one another with increasing speed. This transition has had greater consequences than even the most techno-optimistic and techno-pessimistic among us have grasped. Microsoft, Google, and other companies and governments have supplied the technology, infrastructure, and platforms for the networks in which virtual interaction, data collection and creation, and analysis take place, but that is not the whole story. The high-speed, feedback-driven evolution of these networks is not under the control of those who create and administer those networks. As we will repeatedly see, it is not wholly under anyone's control.

The general purpose computer has been around for seventy-five years, and the internet for over fifty, yet only in recent years have those technologies and their user bases grown to the point where we need to examine them from a new and greater distance. Over the last twenty years, both data processing and artificial intelligence made their stunning leaps only after centralized control was abandoned in favor of a looser, less controllable model. There has been a price to this success. Today, it is no longer we who are controlling how our servers see the world. It is they who are controlling how we see the world. Whether at Facebook, YouTube, or the National Security Agency, aggregations of machines running opaque algorithms—meganets—now present constantly evolving visions of the world for us faster than we can test and correct these visions.

A fundamental reframing is necessary to understand the radically destabilizing effects these networks have had on human society and to understand their unprecedented nature. Shoshana Zuboff has described the creation of a "behavioral surplus" in how these networks capture, quantify, and capitalize on human interaction and activity, but equally important is the structure of the network itself.[32] A meganet is *a persistent, evolving, and opaque data network* that controls how we see the world. Whether it uses AI or heuristics, whether it describes people, money, or products—these questions are less important than those three qualities.

A meganet is *persistent* because its value comes from it never being offline and never being reset. If you were to restart Facebook, clearing its data stores but maintaining all its code, its value would evaporate. Yet even if you kept the data and only disconnected Facebook from the world for a month, its value would plummet sheerly from its information being out of date and users leaving the platform. The value is not in its algorithms, nor in the sum total of its data, but in a meganet's ability to respond to changes and update itself, keeping in sync with the world. There is no way to restart or even pause a meganet without destroying it.

A meganet is *evolving* because thousands if not millions of entities, whether users or programmers or AIs, are constantly modifying it. Google's search results are not the product of fixed algorithms or even of trained machine-learning models but of a constantly shifting library of disorganized ranking criteria and an incessantly changing index of web pages. Take a snapshot of Google's inner workings, and a split second later, such a snapshot would be irreversibly different. Once a change is made, its effects spread before any human can review it. There is no going backward in a meganet. It moves irreversibly, inexorably forward.

A meganet is *opaque* because it is difficult and frequently impossible to gauge why the meganet behaved in a particular way. High-frequency trading (HFT) algorithms manage the stock market faster than we can observe. Forensic analysis can only sometimes explain why they made particular trading decisions, yet even HFTs are quaintly modest in comparison to the chaotic interactions within cryptocurrency markets, which blow up with distressing regularity. Meganet algorithms evolve on their own, becoming too complex for us to understand, too ephemeral for us to observe. You cannot conduct controlled experiments on a meganet because they are never in the same place twice.

Three pieces are required to create a meganet:

1. A tightly integrated set of servers and clients running software-based algorithms
2. The programmers and organizations who create and administer the software and servers
3. The participants who use and more importantly *operate on* that network, making ongoing changes to it, and who are in turn *operated on* by that network in a feedback loop

All three pieces are integral to a meganet. Most analyses of the web and internet portray them fundamentally as models of content production and consumption, in which organizations or individuals publish content, which is then passively consumed by audiences, a unidirectional operation à la television. This is fundamentally wrong. As meganets, they are ecosystems that evolve into something greater than the sum of their parts. Users are not merely consumers, nor are corporations merely administrators or capitalists. The meganet relates its components to one another organically, mutably, and inextricably, joining them so that each component constantly transforms the others, which then transform it in turn. Nothing is stable in a meganet.

TWO

NO CENTER TO HOLD

> The world of people is a world of chaos, entropy, petty passions, and egotistical impulses. . . . It is necessary to defeat in oneself the desire to see particulate individuals in this great mass, one must strive to see the mass as a singular individual, one must understand and accept this truth—that man is only a mass.
>
> VLADIMIR SOROKIN, *Telluria*

THE LAST CHAPTER DEFINED THE MEGANET AS A PERSISTENT, evolving, and opaque data network joining humans and computers. In this chapter we will examine its transformative, scattering, and unprecedented effects on human social order.

Some years ago, I was speaking with a colleague about the idea of genius and how it has seemed to have disappeared. Where, I asked, were the scientific geniuses of today on the order of Albert Einstein, John von Neumann, or Emmy Noether, all profound mathematical minds who revolutionized multiple fields of study both theoretical and practical? To my dismay, my colleague suggested Elon Musk. If he was as close as we could come today to Albert Einstein, I thought, we were doomed (and embarrassingly so).

Yet Musk does stand for our age in a different way. His larger-than-life persona has led to a larger-than-life company, Tesla, with a trillion-dollar market cap as great as all other carmakers combined. Traditional asset managers have been flabbergasted at both Tesla's size and volatility. As bets against Tesla have repeatedly failed and the stock has continued to grow, one fund manager fatalistically said of Tesla: "It's the original meme stock. . . . Tesla has been a primary contributor to destroying the credibility of active management over the past few years."[1] Musk's engagement with Twitter—will he buy it or won't he?—did little to damage his standing while devastating morale and strategy at Twitter.

Central to Musk's impact is his social media presence. A single tweet on March 24, 2021—"You can now buy a Tesla with Bitcoin"—immediately sent Bitcoin up 17 percent, while an August 17, 2018, tweet, declaring he might take Tesla private, sent the stock plummeting.[2] He has been the primary force behind the bizarre success of Dogecoin, a cryptocurrency that was started as a joke, a parody of Bitcoin.[3] Yet Musk's power, while certainly disproportionate, is highly contingent on the meganet. Such whiplash-inducing shifts would not even be possible without the surrounding infrastructure of vast networks with hundreds of millions of always online users. Musk has become a figurehead for a new, nontraditional means of wreaking chaos on the financial system.

And yet it's a bit of a case of the tail wagging the dog. Musk evidently revels in the chaos he creates, but even for the richest man in the world, his control is considerably more limited than one might imagine. He cannot necessarily predict what his tweets will accomplish: when Musk idly tweeted about taking Tesla private in August 2018, he may have had some secret ulterior motive, but he likely did not plan to make an embarrassing climb down in a PR-massaged formal public statement from Tesla called "Staying Public" a few weeks later.[4] Not that it seemed to hurt Tesla in the long run; it bolstered Musk's iconoclastic image and reaffirmed his ability to have profound market influence through nontraditional channels, as well as further upending conventional wisdom about efficient markets and the rationality of crowds.

We feel the meganet's effects most vividly in social media. That's not to say that social media is where the meganet's impact is most profound, because the financial and political implications of meganets go well beyond what one sees on social media. But when we experience the half-alienating, half-cozy feelings of being with others online, we feel most immediately and undeniably what meganets have wrought.

Social media is so familiar and ever-present that we must take a step back to see its hidden properties. We are too quick to think of discourse on the meganet as being a diminished, geographically dislocated version of offline human interaction. It is not. These persistent, evolving, opaque networks create new types of human organization and interaction. They quantify and homogenize human traits and social activity, causing our existing structure of public discourse to give way to a more fragmented, decentralized world of human interaction where groups are more important than individuals. The fundamental principles underpinning human association, decision-making, and action are different on the meganet, and without understanding those principles, we have no hope of fixing the problems of social media—or of the meganet more generally.

VOLUME, VELOCITY, VIRALITY

Consider, then, what it takes for one of Musk's tweets to have the impact that it does. It's not Musk's original tweet by itself but the chain reaction of responses, retweets, and commentary it sets off. And there are three essential components to meganet discourse that emerge in tracing that chain reaction.

First, there is sheer *volume*. From Musk's original tweet must flow thousands upon thousands of decentralized echoes of that tweet from speakers loud and small. His fan base and detractors alike don't just listen; they also participate. That participation is frequently as trivial as clicking the retweet button to spread Musk's gospel further (or attack it), but often it goes far beyond that. Musk's tweets about Bitcoin sent cryptocurrency forums into a frenzy. Musk's tweet that the government's COVID response was excessive caused antivaxxers and antimaskers to explode in jubilation from the support. Tweets about his personal life ensure attention from celebrity watchers. His initial takeover attempt of Twitter itself leveraged the backing of the angry conservative contingent that claimed Twitter was censoring right-leaning content.

Behind all this are the Musk skeptics, who ironically amplify his proclamations simply by discussing them, invoking Oscar Wilde's old principle that "the only thing worse than being talked about is not being talked about." It is not so binary on the meganet, though, where the only thing worse than being talked about is not being talked about *enough*. There is enough space online for everything to be talked about at the same time. What wins is what gets talked about *more*. Musk understands this, stoking the fires incessantly to maintain his presence in the collective consciousness, investing the existing attention on him to gain more future attention.

That collective consciousness that exists in the meganet—the sum of all the machines and people that are a part of it—is a curious beast. It is a new kind of mind, but it does not function rationally. Psychologist and economist Daniel Kahneman famously theorized that our brains can think fast or slow, with reactive judgment or with reflective consideration. The meganet's "brain" only thinks fast, never slow, because its second essential component is *velocity*. Theoretically, if Musk's fan base collectively decided that one of his proclamations was of no value, they could collectively choose to ignore it, but there is no such discussion. There *cannot* be because there is no time for it. The meganet "brain," with its millions of participants each acting independently yet in coordination, has no central inhibitor. The chain reaction (or feeding frenzy) that follows a Musk tweet requires that the surging forces powering it overtake any slower market mechanisms—by overtaking the traditional forces whereby institutional players make studied decisions and regulate collective human behavior by acting in reasonably consistent and predictable manners.

Only velocity can overcome those stabilizing forces. A large, sudden shift in investor sentiment can, as many money managers have discovered, prove impossible to debate, no matter how irrational it may seem. Were trading and online discussion to stop artificially and abruptly for a day or two following a Musk tweet, the tumult of reactivity to his words would die down and Musk's impact would be severely blunted, allowing the proverbial cooler heads to prevail. Such a pause, however, is inimical to the meganet. Velocity topples stability. It also ensures that Musk himself loses any direct control seconds after he pushes the tweet button. He sets the initial direction of the discourse, powerfully so, but after that, it is out of his hands. As the richest man in the world, he does not need to worry about the consequences; he only needs to follow his knack for appealing to the many large online groups (be they cryptocurrency enthusiasts, celebrity vultures, Twitter haters, or antivaxxers) who are liable to amplify his voice that much further.

And that amplification entails the third essential quality of the meganet, its *virality*. The volume and velocity of the meganet would only have a fraction of their power if that force did not have the capacity to build on itself. For every reaction to a Musk tweet, there follow millions more reactions. For it is not just Musk's tweet that is going out into the world and spurring a response but also those responses themselves, spurring yet more responses, building upon themselves endlessly. Many such responses are merely echoes, but others elaborate on the original or change it, and those in turn create new effects. In mid-2020, Donald Trump boosted Musk over shared opposition to COVID lockdowns, and a brief moment of explosive overlap ensued before the adherents of each man went in separate directions again.[5] Not all feedback effects necessarily continue out of all proportion; the collective will for an alliance between Musk and Trump's followers was simply not there. But in 2021, when Musk boosted the joke cryptocurrency Dogecoin by mentioning it in tweets and on *Saturday Night Live*, the chain reaction sent it soaring 4,000 percent because Musk followers overlap far more with cryptocurrency enthusiasts than with Trump fanatics.[6] What's significant, in either case, is that the combustion (or fizzling) happens before there is time for anyone, even Musk himself, to respond.

Virality has become a hot buzzword, and like most buzzwords, it's taken on a host of different meanings. To go viral often means nothing more than becoming popular online, but what I mean by meganet virality is something more particular than that. As with a real virus, meganet virality entails uncontrolled and unpredictable spread, uncoordinated simultaneous distribution, and spontaneous evolution. What is spreading might be a piece of content, a stock recommendation, a funny meme picture, or the purchase of a cryptocurrency. Our current definition of *meme* is, in fact, far too narrow. Virality is not restricted just to cat pictures and ambiguously colored dresses. Just as the most popular memes duke it out among teenagers, the same dynamic now prevails across all types of online discourse. What's common among them is that the viral spread happens in real time faster than it can be tracked, each person's reaction helping to shape the next series of reactions.

So while virality may be the more vivid term for how content spreads on the internet, the more precise term would be *feedback*. Propaganda broadcasts possess volume and velocity, but the content is static, being pushed out to a huge audience without change. Meganet content evolves spontaneously, often remaining in the same form but without the top-down control of propaganda—which ironically makes it far more spreadable, as each participant in the many chains of a viral post or meme can put his own spin on it freely, exercising a tiny piece of agency.

Those tiny bits of agency collectively surpass the agency of any single person, no matter how big. A big name like Musk or Trump may set the initial tone for a viral idea about Dogecoin or a stolen election, but even Trump could not sway his own fervent fan base to embrace vaccines. When thousands of rioters invaded the Capitol on January 6, 2021, Trump couldn't have disavowed them even had he wanted to. The narrative was in their hands as much as it was in Trump's, if not more so. Modern society has so long been accustomed to national or international figures (politicians, celebrities) who speak to silent millions that we still have yet to come to grips with the very unsettling fact that it is now amorphous groups who lead and the celebrities and influencers who follow. The most successful cybercelebrities are, in fact, those who either happen to represent an existing trend or those skilled at going with the flow on which they are carried. Those who part ways with the flow fall off the map.

So while it helps to have a big face to put on the source of meganet trends, focusing on these outsized personalities is ultimately misleading. Musk and Trump are exceptionally visible cases, but they are not representative, and they have less control over their audiences than it initially appears. (Trump's inability to get his social network Truth Social off the ground is one significant example.) Many other meganet influencers, from Joe Rogan to Jordan Peterson, have mobilized fan bases in a similarly chaotic fashion to Musk and Trump and are unable to control the aggressiveness with which their fans go on the attack against their opponents and enemies. As much as media tends to fixate on the individuals seemingly leading the charge, Musk and Rogan and even Donald Trump himself are following their crowds as much as vice versa. Just as their crowds amplify them, they too amplify what they sense in their crowds.

The sudden emergence of a wildly eccentric figure like Canadian professor Jordan Peterson, who for a time became the face of a burgeoning backlash against progressivism, speaks less to any innate characteristics of Peterson's and more to his having been in the right place at the right time while carrying enough institutional credibility to embody the collective views of an anonymous, disparate online community. Certainly what he represents is not contained in his actual writing, which in one reviewer's description holds only fleeting similarities with the views that elevated him to prominence:

> One minute Peterson is telling you to imagine who you could be and aim at that, then he's on about ancient alchemists, then discussing unwelcome letters one might receive from the tax authorities, then back to some mystic stuff about Jupiter and Mars, leading to an extended account of how the snitch in Quidditch, the game played at JK Rowling's Hogwarts, symbolises chaos.[7]

In other words, the distance between who such leading figures are and what they represent is only growing, and the most successful and enduring ones (Musk and Trump, not Peterson) go with the flow of their following rather than remaining fixed in place. And as much as an individual catalyst like Musk or Trump can amplify meganet discourse, there's nothing that requires such a public figure. Most of the time, the workings of the meganet don't revolve around a celebrity of any sort but can be triggered by a far more ordinary individual with a momentary soapbox. Musk himself is aware of this, happily jumping on already burgeoning trends and amplifying them, whether it's Dogecoin or the even more worrisome phenomenon of a "stonk."

GAMESTONK

A stonk is nothing more than a misspelling of stock, used jokingly to indicate ignorance of financial matters.[8] In early 2021, the stonk market invaded the stock market. Individual investors, loosely coordinating through the Reddit forum WallStreetBets, spontaneously organized to buy up software retailer GameStop's stock, sending it soaring 1,500 percent in the absence of any change in fundamentals. A stock that had been previously languishing at $15 shot up to $150 and stayed there for most of 2021, splitting 4-to-1 in 2022 after retaining most of that value.

The epicenter of the stonk revolution was in two opposing places: Reddit and, once again, Elon Musk. While Musk occupies a unique place with an overwhelmingly dominant voice, Keith Gill, a life insurance marketer in his early thirties with an amateur interest in picking stocks, was a fairly ordinary man who went by "DeepFuckingValue" on Reddit and "Roaring Kitty" on YouTube.[9] His working-class, outsider background appealed to a wide audience of online users who, in the wake of the 2008 financial crisis, didn't see any reason why they knew any less than the CEOs of Morgan Stanley and JPMorgan. Both on Reddit and on his YouTube channel, Gill relentlessly enthused over his GameStop investments, and through an organic process, not one of explicit manipulation, he amassed a growing army of fans and followers who among themselves bought into GameStop. That in turn sent his investment in GameStop soaring, fueling the fires and sending GameStop even higher (and sometimes lower, when some cashed out).

In terms of the efficient market hypothesis of conventional economics, there was no way to justify this increase. The efficient market hypothesis assumes that the overall market behaves in such a way that it can't be outsmarted by a coordinated group of actors. While momentary swings may occur, the "natural" order of things will prevail and markets will adjust to the levels best reflecting the available information.

Yet in sending GameStop soaring, a loose coalition of individual investors had artificially inflated an asset price not based on better knowledge or on greater farsightedness but by sheer fiat. Several hedge funds took billion-dollar losses on GameStop as a consequence. Melvin Capital lost half of its $13 billion fund and required a bailout, while White Square Capital shut down altogether.[10] The long-standing image of hedge funds as the smartest investors out there took a huge hit, and no one, certainly not a loose gang of anonymous Reddit users, took their place as the kings of investment arbitrage.

Appearing before Congress in February 2021, Gill himself seemed remarkably ingenuous and unpolished, painting himself as an independent amateur with no particular agenda and no conflicts of interest or insider information. He even joked, awkwardly. "I am not a cat. I do not have clients. My family was not wealthy. My father was a truck driver." All he had done, he said, was post on social media, the same way people talk in bars. Of GameStop, he simply said, "I like the stock."[11]

Gill couldn't have done it alone. He may have been the face of the GameStop explosion, but he was not CNBC's Jim Cramer yelling about mad money. Cramer, for all his platform, could not go up against Melvin Capital on his own because Cramer cannot create a viral feedback loop. Gill did speak the way people talk in bars, but he spoke on meganets, not in bars. It was the intensely social movement that built around Gill and grew far beyond him that allowed for the hummingbird-speed boom in GameStop. It took Reddit forums with hundreds of thousands of users all yelling at and arguing with one another. It took huge volume, high velocity, and strong virality to spread the gospel of GameStop. It took a meganet. And it's for this same reason that Gill is no permanent kingpin. He didn't control what happened, and there is no guarantee he could replicate his feat again. It was the shifting tides of meganets that happened to favor him briefly.

The closest thing to a theoretical explanation for the GameStop boom was a "short squeeze," in which the need to cover short positions sends a stock soaring, but the Security and Exchange Commission (SEC) found that theory lacking. There wasn't a rational financial explanation, the SEC concluded; it was just chaos. In an October 2021 report, the SEC plaintively bemoaned that anonymous investors in "meme stocks" had broken the unwritten laws of finance, not through unlawful connivance but merely through their very participation:

> The trading in meme stocks during this time highlighted an important feature of United States securities markets in the 21st century: broad participation. There are many different types of investors, and they buy and sell stocks for many different reasons. However, when share prices change rapidly and brokerage firms suddenly suspend trading, investors may lose money. . . . People may disagree about the prospects of GameStop and the other meme stocks, but those disagreements are what should lead to price discovery rather than disruptions.[12]

Yet the SEC had no suggestions on hand for how to prevent disruptions from such "broad participation." The report concludes on a note of powerlessness, reluctantly admitting that the self-regulating nature of markets and funds has somehow come undone.

Meganets are the mechanism that enabled that "broad participation" mentioned by the SEC. Such participation required real-time online forums (like Reddit) with huge numbers of participants who could synchronize their actions without any central authority and who did so faster than any authority could track them. In an unusually candid 2017 post, former Reddit CEO Yishan Wong, whose tenure had run from 2012 to 2014, exploded with frustration at running a company—and a website—that he simply couldn't control. He rebuffed accusations that Reddit had a political bias (left or right). No, he said in exasperation, Reddit was simply mired in trying to keep its entire network under control:

> Reddit admins don't have a particular bias. Their bias is "please simmer down, we would just like to work on adding more features." During most of the time I was there, reddit was accused by both sides simultaneously of being biased against them. We were accused of harboring horrible racist and sexist content AND accused of being controlled by SJWs [social justice warriors], because most people believe that if you enforce some rules on them, you must be supporting the other side.
>
> As a result of my experiences running reddit, I have a lot more respect for police, governors, and presidents—anyone who has to uphold a fair system in the face of multiple opposing sides, all of whom want the system to favor them because they are convinced they are "right." I tried to walk this fine principled line where we allowed free speech and just enforced actual rule-breaking, and maybe it would have worked under different circumstances.[13]

Wong had quit being CEO, he wrote, "because eventually there was just too much bullshit to put up with." I was struck by a point Wong had failed to make: that most lawful authorities do keep their communities successfully controlled, while Reddit had spiraled into total chaos, which the site's operators felt helpless to prevent. It was a frank, but unsettling, admission of impotence. Could the SEC do better than Reddit? Because of the sheer speed at which the meganet works, more people and more resources will not help. They still will not be fast enough.

Nor would shutting down WallStreetBets help. Besides the tremendous unpopularity of such a move—WallStreetBets doesn't appear by any measure to be doing anything "wrong"—its users would reconstitute elsewhere, sooner or later. When Reddit has (far more justifiably) banned its most blatantly offensive forums, like those containing nonconsensual upskirt posts or virulently racist and misogynist rhetoric, those communities have migrated to other platforms such as Gab or Parler or other shadier sites, where there is even less moderation of content.[14]

Reddit is not just a wild west of discourse; the metaphor is insufficient. The West was eventually tamed through an influx of organizations, businesses, and culture. But by giving greater voice to everyone, the meganet prevents such hierarchical organization from ever solidifying to such a degree. Smaller groups are never fully shut down but reconstitute themselves, opposing any attempt to establish or reestablish a uniform, dominant narrative. During COVID, despite all the official public health information pushed out by Facebook, Twitter, and Google in opposition to antivax sentiment, the needle barely moved in terms of public opinion, and by early 2022 even Google and New York City were relaxing their vaccine mandates.

To an elite, top-down organization like the SEC, the wild west of WallStreetBets appears to be chaos, but it is not sheer chaos as much as a new kind of order, albeit one lacking in central controls. For it was not just broad participation but *broad coordination* and *broad communication* that gave birth to stonks. It required the ability for arbitrary nonsense to be broadcasted from any of millions of random individuals to all others and for a high enough quantity of *one* kind of nonsense (about a stonk, say) to make a huge difference.

Prior to the advent of meganets, networks of communication and coordination were reserved for elite players in financial ecosystems. Individuals could broadly participate, but they could hardly coordinate, lending more predictability to the system. Once meganets allowed for diffuse but organized collections of individuals to build into significant new forces, the system became a great deal more complicated. It is more chaotic, but underneath the surface disarray, it is not pure chaos.

MIRRORING

We understand the influence of an Elon Musk or a Keith Gill because they give a face to the effects of the meganets. While they do not spearhead the online flare-ups and controversies that would arise even in their absence, they make those events easier to grasp. When it comes to truly faceless movements, without definitive leaders or spokespeople, we are far more at a loss. Yet it is here we see the distributed effects of the meganet most strongly. No leaders are needed when volume, velocity, and virality hold sway.

In February 2022, Cho Jang-mi, a popular twenty-seven-year-old South Korean personality on livestreaming platforms Twitch and YouTube who went by "Jammi," committed suicide. On her Twitch page, her uncle wrote that the cause was ongoing, yearslong online bullying: "Jang-mi has suffered serious depression from malicious comments and rumors, which led her to suicide."[15] One major trigger for the attacks was a single pinched-finger hand gesture Jammi had made in 2019, a loaded allusion implying that Korean males had small genitalia, associated with radical Korean feminist forums like Megalia and Womad. Despite Jammi apologizing twice, male-dominated communities relentlessly descended on Jammi with attacks and rumors, driving her to depression and eventually to suicide.[16] Critics attacked Lee Jun-seok, leader of the conservative opposition People Power Party, for profiting off antifeminist sentiment and tacitly sanctioning bullying like that which plagued Jammi. It was clear, though, that the bullying was not being centrally directed but was instead the outgrowth of a number of poisonous online communities.[17]

Jammi was one casualty of what has become a growing flood of online culture wars on the meganet. Most of us have had a taste of some kind of online extremism or witnessed controversies spring up over one of countless flash points. Through the forces of volume, velocity, and virality, meganets have become ground zero for an endless stream of culture wars, many of them centered around gender. A boom in fringe "men's rights" groups provides a ready stream of fodder for those who believe that feminism is causing damage to society and that the male social roles are somehow threatened. Mainstream sites, in turn, repeatedly elevate the profiles of many of these groups while purporting to critique them, inadvertently generating free publicity for them.

The ferocity of the gender wars in the United States pales in comparison to South Korea, where extremism has crashed headlong into mainstream discourse.[18] In response to a historically patriarchal society and in misogynistic troll-infested forums like Ilbe and DC Inside, female-dominated sites such as Megalia and Womad have embraced a style of online discourse termed *mirroring*, in which misogynist discourse is reversed in the most blunt, direct way imaginable.[19] While we may find it easy to condemn the misogynist communities that helped drive Jammi to suicide, the feminist sites offer a far less comfortable look at meganet discourse and its feedback-driven excesses.

Equally anonymous as the male-dominated sites, Megalia began in 2015 as an activist forum that raised funds for women's causes and lobbied to stop sales of spy cams (used to film women in bathrooms without consent) on e-commerce sites, attracting half a million users in a couple of months.[20] At the same time, the rhetoric on the site reached uncomfortable heights. From a pinched-hand logo that ridiculed the size of Korean men's penises (the same gesture used by Jammi) to posts like "Let's get an abortion if we become pregnant with a son," the tactic of mirroring misogynistic rhetoric exacerbated conflict as much as it illuminated the misogyny it was critiquing.[21] In 2016 interviews, three participants reflected on how the site progressed well beyond mirroring into outright hatred:

> When I first encountered the mirroring language, it was just funny and hilarious. But gradually, I could feel myself objectifying men. It was a fun thing to hate someone.

> It was a fun thing to hate someone. I finally realized what it was like to hate. Hatred was actually a fun sentiment. I realized why men had been enacting misogyny as a joke or a game.

> When first encountered with mirroring I was enraged, but gradually I came to enjoy it. I was startled realizing men had so much fun until now with misogyny, as I am now with mirroring.[22]

Even as the "fun" of mirroring spilled over into hatred, Megalia spilled over into popular discourse. The left-wing Justice Party was sucked into a scandal over a voice actress who posted a Twitter selfie while doing nothing more than wearing a Megalia T-shirt.[23] Other women lost their jobs after anti-Megalians exposed their participation on Megalia.[24] Even though Megalia shut down in 2017, the election of self-proclaimed "feminist president" Moon Jae-in that same year stoked the fires further, leading to the rise of antifeminist politicians like opposition leader Lee Jun-seok, who criticized the ruling party's "fixation on a pro-woman agenda."[25]

The conflict only grew. By 2021, anonymous antifeminist groups of men were pressuring companies—successfully—to take down anything that even resembled Megalia's infamous pinched-hand logo, finding government conspiracies everywhere.[26] Such pressure only radicalized the feminist side. After Megalia shut down, a far more virulent forum, Womad, arose from its ashes, inspired to action and rage by the brutal murder of a woman in the Gangnam District in 2016. Explicitly misandrist, "moralless," and advocating all-out gender war, Womad embraced homophobia, transphobia, and racism in proclaiming the struggle of women against men to be the only one worth fighting and exalted the supremacy of women as the ultimate truth:

> Progressive feminist leaders feel obliged to squeeze in a bunch of miscellanies into their pursuit of feminism, they try to include gays, transgenders, refugees. . . . But is feminism essentially progressive? No. In reality the world needs to be women-centric, this is the "law of nature." We differ from unnatural beings who want to . . . disrupt the order of nature.[27]

The mirroring grew more disturbing in 2016 when a Korean au pair living in Australia posted on Womad claiming to have drugged and sexually assaulted a minor boy, including nude images of a child she identified as her victim: "I suppose he doesn't remember anything because he played as normal the next day."[28] As with many other Womad posts, it turned out to be a prank: the images had been taken from a YouTube video, though they still resulted in the au pair being arrested and deported from Australia on child pornography charges.[29] By that point, however, the meganet had long moved on, many having processed the incident as real and reacted accordingly. There are no do-overs on the meganet.

Having spread offline, the national gender war fomented by the meganet only escalated. In 2018, three men allegedly assaulted two women at Isu Station, alleging the women had ridiculed them. The resulting tensions led to hundreds of thousands of South Koreans signing one of two petitions demanding either that the women or the men be punished by the state.[30] Though the police claimed the violence was on both sides, the women appeared to suffer far more severe injuries.[31] Two years later, a judge levied significant fines against both a man and a woman in the conflict, finding them both guilty of violence and insults.[32] Even with the existence of closed-circuit television footage documenting the incident, there was no resolution to the issue in the public and online sphere: the incident and the evidence surrounding it confirmed the existing viewpoints of all those involved in the debate. The trial was effectively an afterthought: the incident had permeated and aggravated the culture war for two years, sustained and memorialized incessantly on both the misandrist Womad and the misogynist Ilbe. Rather than one side mirroring the other, reality itself came to be a secondary reflection of what was said in online forums. "Reality" became secondary fodder for South Korea's online discourse.

Like recent racial controversies in the United States, incidents like the Isu Station conflict have always served as flash points, yet the ascension of forums like Womad and Ilbe to dominant positions in social discourse has radically changed how society processes such incidents, disempowering the legal system and the government and forcing them to play catchup with the hurried tide of online debate.

With South Korea's citizens having split into geographically diffuse but ideologically aligned factions, nearly *any* incident will only reinforce existing viewpoints. One side may be right and one side may be wrong, but much like legal judgments, moral judgments become increasingly irrelevant since there is no longer a shared space in which an authoritative moral judgment can take hold across a broad population. The immediacy of the meganet trumps the reality of the law.

That shared space of ethical unity used to be controlled by some combination of the government, a rarefied circle of public intellectuals, elite academic circles, and centralized mass media in news and entertainment. Today, that is no longer the case. As long as liberalized free discourse exists online, a hypernetworked population will self-organize into rigid ideological blocs, facilitated by meganets. To the extent that the government or mass media try to *influence* those rigid ideological blocs, they substantively fail, following them instead of leading them. Volume, velocity, and virality don't just change the nature of online discourse. They redefine the very concept of agency, absorbing individuals into larger homogeneous groups in which the autonomy of a single person is, at best, a questionable quality.

OFF THE RAILS

The typical reaction to online chaos, whether it's cyberbullying or disinformation, whether on Megalia or Reddit or Facebook, is to demand that companies just *stop it all*. If companies can't do it, critics say, then let the government outlaw it. This reaction is natural, and those who stand on principle for free speech can be forgiven for softening their attitudes in the face of thousands of anonymous online attacks. Civil liberties and tolerable public discourse can seem incompatible.

Yet the evident inability to address the toxic atmosphere does not stem from corporate greed *or* legal free speech principles but from *actual inability*. The meganet has ensured that *no one*, not even Facebook's highest executives, has the ability to control chaotic meganet discourse. Short of shutting down meganets entirely, the problems are innate to the meganets' structure. Even Facebook, the most powerful social media company in the West, cannot contravene them. Their own algorithms fire too quickly for Facebook's employees to track. This inability exists for any meganet of sufficient size, for it is not just the virtual gatherings of people that make a meganet but the lightning-speed, ever-changing algorithms that control what each of them sees.

By 2020, Facebook's overwhelming presence and influence on human affairs was center stage. Public awareness of Facebook's societal effects had only grown since the Cambridge Analytica scandal in 2016, in which a third-party app claiming to provide psychological tests to users was revealed to have harvested information on eighty-seven million Facebook users, which was then used for political targeting in the hopes of benefiting Donald Trump's campaign.[33] A former Cambridge Analytica employee ominously said in 2018, "We exploited Facebook to harvest millions of people's profiles. And built models to exploit what we knew about them and target their inner demons."[34]

What was missed in this outrage was that despite Facebook's mea culpas, Cambridge Analytica's activities were wholly typical of third-party Facebook apps and would not have raised eyebrows within Facebook. A three-year probe by the UK Information Commissioner's Office found that Cambridge Analytica and its associates had not misused the data they collected.[35] The sharing of user information and targeting of users was part and parcel of Facebook's mission and revenue model, common across all third-party Facebook apps. In Information Commissioner Elizabeth Denham's words: "the methods that [Cambridge Analytica associate] SCL were using, were in the main, well recognized processes using commonly available technology."[36] The only atypical aspect of Cambridge Analytica's methods was the particular end to which its efforts had been put: that of electing an extremely polarizing president. What was disturbing was rather how common its methods were.

Nonetheless, after the Cambridge Analytica scandal and with the surge of misinformation and disinformation during the 2020 election, only 50 percent of Facebook employees came to see their work as a positive influence on society in an internal survey conducted by the company, and only 69 percent of employees had a favorable view of the company itself.[37] This discouragement did not arise because Facebook was indifferent to the problems it faced. Facebook inarguably made efforts at moderation and control over misinformation. The evident failure of these efforts speaks to a decline in Facebook's *control* over its meganet and the growing suspicion that not even Mark Zuckerberg could steer the behemoth back on to the rails. Zuckerberg's own peculiar pronouncements only confounded Facebook's stated intentions, including a 2019 document claiming that Facebook would shift to predominantly private interactions from its present role as a public sphere.[38] Such a shift has not occurred.

Facebook endured increasing bitter criticism in 2020, driven by reports that calls for violence were flourishing unchecked on the social network both before and after the US election.[39] Facebook's own statements reveal its problem to be inability rather than indifference. In a post on September 3, Mark Zuckerberg declared a clear intent to crack down on threats and misinformation, yet his text evinced a revealing mixture of blunt measures and helplessness. In particular, Zuckerberg announced two widespread restrictions that spoke to Facebook's lack of power over its own users and network. The first measure was a blanket ban on political ads, carrying with it the admission that Facebook is unable to fact-check advertisements in real time, or even within days.

> We're going to block new political and issue ads during the final week of the campaign . . . in the final days of an election there may not be enough time to contest new claims.[40]

In the wake of the elections and Trump's contesting of the result, Facebook extended the ban into December, to the dismay of both parties, who bemoaned that they could not use Facebook for proper, on-the-level campaigns.[41] It was as though Facebook could not distinguish illegitimate and legitimate use of its platform. Facebook is permanently behind the curve of its own meganet.

The second measure, a uniform limitation on the distribution of *any and all information* through Facebook, only reinforced the impression of a company whose product had bolted from the barn. Unable to control the spread of particular misinformation, Facebook implemented an across-the-board policy to attempt to slow down a network moving too fast to monitor:

> We're reducing the risk of misinformation and harmful content going viral by limiting forwarding on Messenger. You'll still be able to share information about the election, but we'll limit the number of chats you can forward a message to at one time.[42]

Facebook director Jay Sullivan wrote, "Limiting forwarding is an effective way to slow the spread of viral misinformation and harmful content that has the potential to cause real world harm," but more than that, limiting forwarding slows the spread of *all* information.[43] In a couple years, Facebook had gone from commercializing virality to suppressing it. Facebook had gone from subtly refining feed algorithms to constraining functionality artificially.

Whatever unease one might feel about Facebook arbitrating user engagement, its tactics reveal the limitations of its power. For all of Facebook's expertise in algorithms and AI, employing some of the top machine-learning experts in the world, its ultimate approach to policing election misinformation was a combination of a blunt hammer and Whac-A-Mole—and the acknowledgment that the disorderly mass of users was too great a force for them to pin down with its algorithms.

RULES OF ENGAGEMENT

As to *why* Facebook cannot control its own meganet, we need to look closer at the nature of meganet discourse and how automated algorithms select content to show to users—and how users in turn condition those algorithms. The measure of success for meganet content, whether that content is a product, a politician, or an ideology, is summed up in the word *engagement*. Engagement is a measure of attention: How many people are interested in this piece of content? How long do they pay attention to it? How many others do they share it with?

Before social media, online life was a collection of web pages. Pages linked to other pages, and the most popular pages were those that the most people linked to. Social media turned the concept of online popularity upside down. A link on a web page began to count for less than a share, a post, or a retweet. Web pages were comparatively static entities, but once social feeds and online forums became the center of digital life, the velocity of meganets accelerated drastically. Interactions on social networks between users, social groupings, and advertisers created an incessant flood of new data about users.

By nursing and exploiting the growing mass of data created by its users, Facebook gave birth to a far more substantial and dynamic meganet than anything Facebook's predecessors had dreamed of. Facebook grew exponentially, from one million monthly users in 2004 to one billion in 2012.[44] (This thousandfold growth parallels Moore's law, though having saturated the human population, Facebook's growth subsequently slowed to linear levels, reaching over two billion monthly users in 2020.[45]) Just as exponential increases in processing power enabled qualitative changes in how humans engaged with computers, an exponential increase in users has changed the very experience of using Facebook.

While Amazon sells products and Google makes money off search results, Facebook's core content is people—or rather, digital approximations of people, presented as a grouping of demographic identifiers, consumer and recreational interests, and status updates. Facebook profiles are digital approximations of a person's entire self, a combination of demographics, photographs, videos, and words. Facebook selects status updates, photos, advertisements, and promotions from its databases of a user's friends' content and its advertisers and partners' content. In addition to what users publicly specify about themselves and their relationships to their friends, Facebook privately annotates every user profile with data it gleans from both analyses of its own data and from third-party data obtained from advertisers, apps, and other data collection networks.[46] These internal profiles massage and filter every individual user experience on Facebook. In particular, they shape the automated curation of each user's news feed.

The news feed is the heart of Facebook. Facebook has struggled with the volume, velocity, and virality of news feed content, frequently shifting its priorities in choosing what to present to users. Originally, news feed posts were ordered strictly chronologically, but Facebook has discouraged chronological ordering for years now, instead showing by default what it deems the "top" posts, ordered by a secret algorithmic sauce.

What makes a top post? There is no shortage of complaints that Facebook presents the *wrong* content to its users, but figuring out the *right* content is far from a trivial task. Here, the comment of a former Facebook product designer, Bobby Goodlatte, is illuminating. After the 2016 election, Goodlatte bemoaned the partisanship of media on all sides and blamed Facebook's algorithms for amplifying it. In a Facebook post, he wrote: "News Feed optimizes for engagement. As we've learned in this election, bullshit is highly engaging."[47] Goodlatte's implication is that like Elon Musk, Facebook is following the crowd, not leading it. This is a more profound point than it may seem because it puts Facebook in a no-win situation. If it simply chases the most "engaging" content, then all sorts of inflammatory nonsense outstrip sane and sober discourse. But if Facebook chooses to downplay some engaging content on whatever grounds, it's going against the will of its own users and dictating what users should see.

Many Facebook critics subsequently echoed Goodlatte's point that giving people what they want was frequently a very bad thing when it came to a social network. But if you do not give people what they want, what do you give them? Facebook chose to give them the anodyne. It changed its algorithms to deprioritize shared news articles across the board, even those from reputable outlets, hoping to steer people instead toward personal, apolitical content that would cheer them instead of incense them. This reprioritization led to a crash in online media in 2017 that the *Columbia Journalism Review* dubbed "The Facebook Armageddon," as online mainstays like BuzzFeed and Mashable cratered in views and profits.[48] Facebook also encouraged content providers to make videos instead of articles, only to then deprioritize such videos as well. Facebook giveth, and it taketh away.

Yet the new media Armageddon was not Facebook chasing profits. Facebook abandoned a good chunk of its content providers merely in an attempt to gain control over its own systems. Ironically, many new media critics who had long been demanding Facebook crack down on the sharing of partisan and inflammatory content got exactly what they asked for, only to find that they were included in the crackdown.

The ongoing rage at Facebook obscured the greater problem that Facebook hardly knew what it was doing. Even with its huge reservoirs of data, selecting the right posts, suggestions, and advertisements for a user at any moment is ultimately grasping in the dark. The algorithmic business of making such determinations is messy. Facebook takes its best guess based on the voluminous profiles it has amassed on its users. From those profiles, Facebook has engaged in the largest psychological modeling experiment of all time, with the goal of predicting what a user will find engaging. Facebook took the recommendation engines of Amazon, Netflix, and many others but extended them to construct a computational recommendation architecture for as much of one's personal life as Facebook could observe. Yet the complexity of such an architecture proved self-defeating because it could not be made sufficiently reliable or comprehensible. The result was not an all-knowing AI but an opaque mess of twine and tape.

From this perspective, demands that Facebook shape its feeds in one particular direction or another—as well as accusations that Facebook enforces one slanted viewpoint or another—come off as quaint. It is not that such biases cannot exist. Rather, it is that such biases emerge organically and with great complexity out of the shifting mass of weights and signals that constitute Facebook's ranking algorithms. Facebook's engineers can exert pressure on their ranking algorithms to nudge them in one direction or another, or they can make blunt moves to promote or demote a certain type of content (hate speech, for example), but the assumption that Facebook has fine-grained control over what appears in each person's feed is a fantasy. Despite employing human moderators and a top team of engineers, only a high-speed sentient AI could possibly shape the experience of every Facebook user to any fine degree—which is one reason why AI has been promoted (in vain, as we shall see) as the solution to the problems of social media.

EVERYTHINGVILLE

Around a decade ago, a strange transformation took place in people's Facebook feeds. What was once a stream of conversation and photos turned into an endless parade of cartoonish farms. The reason was that everyone, it seemed, had begun playing a new game called FarmVille. Users had a little animated plot of farmland where they could grow crops and raise animals. Many people were enthralled by this cute little landscape that they had (sort of) created. FarmVille's creator, Zynga, quickly created similarly themed clones, from CityVille to CastleVille to FishVille, all with the same basic gaming model.

How did Zynga's "free" little games, though, become responsible for 12 percent of all Facebook revenues in 2011 and a bald majority of nonadvertising partner revenue?[49] Through the meganet's combination of volume, velocity, and virality. Crops and animals did not grow on their own. A user needed to be incessantly online to make sure their crops didn't "expire," and crops and animals couldn't simply be placed freely but needed to be "earned" through a couple of methods. One method was simply waiting around playing the game on Facebook. Another was one's farm being "visited" (clicked on) by your Facebook friends, pulling them into the game. But the easiest method by far to progress in FarmVille and get more cute animals and verdant crops was by paying real cash to Zynga, with Facebook taking a cut. The games were "free-to-play," in the terminology of the casual gaming industry, but quickly gained the alternate sobriquet "pay-to-win." In FarmVille's case, it was often "pay-to-survive," as one's farm would decay if one couldn't accumulate the necessary resources. Zynga was quite stingy in allocating resources: if you did not want to see your crops wither, you needed to keep playing and paying.

The game-play formula Zynga employed looked like magic, both to Facebook and to Facebook users, who saw their feeds cluttered with endless notifications begging them to visit their friends' farms (or cities or castles or aquariums). More sophisticated variations on the FarmVille formula like Supercell's Clash of Clans provided more complicated game play while nonetheless sticking to the basic business strategy of inducing players to pay for success in the game and rewarding them for advertising the game to their friends. By 2012 Facebook was already looking less like the staid web of the early 2000s and more like the dynamic and commercialized social media world of today. Instead of seeing status updates and posts from friends, users saw their farms and their cities. And this suited Facebook just fine. With a higher volume of user engagement, the quick velocity of requiring users to be online to tend to their farms, and the virality of spreading the FarmVille gospel to all of one's Facebook friends, the innate qualities of the meganet emerged through FarmVille as they never had on Facebook before—and profitably.

FarmVille and its brethren came in for scathing criticism. Many game designers despised Zynga for appealing to the lowest common denominator of instant gratification and more or less requiring that users "pay to win" to stop their farms from dying out.[50] Game designer Jonathan Blow eviscerated Zynga for making its players suffer in the service of profit:

> When you look at the design process in [FarmVille], it's not about designing a fun game. . . . It's actually about designing something that's a negative experience. It's about "How do we make something that looks cute and that projects positivity"—but it actually makes people worry about it when they're away from the computer and drains attention from their everyday life and brings them back into the game. . . . And it's about, "How do we get players to exploit their friends in a mechanical way in order to progress?" And . . . they kind of turn them in to us and then we can monetize their relationships.[51]

Zynga was so aggressive in its exploitation of players that by 2013 it had burnt out its user base, and Facebook began to strictly limit how many notifications FarmVille-like apps could send, as the flood was clogging up user feeds and alienating Facebook users.[52] Zynga still exists to this day, but the era of its games being ubiquitous and unavoidable has ended, as more sophisticated and less annoying content has emerged to attract people and connect them with others who share their enthusiasms.

The *lessons* of Zynga, however, have persisted. The most important lesson was that Facebook's original base material—photos and status updates from friends and online discussion of such—was vastly less engaging (or, to put it more pejoratively, less addictive) than other types of content. Exactly what content was most engaging could be as much a mystery as figuring out what book might become a bestseller, but the example of Zynga stressed that volume, velocity, and virality were central to any such content. There had to be a *lot* of the content, it had to spread fast, and it had to build on itself. FarmVille was the first example of a type of content that embodied all three to the utmost, but it was far from the last.

The mid-2010s saw the rise of what was termed *clickbait*, stories published with the stated intent to be shared on social networks (Facebook and Twitter primarily). The goal was not to attract subscribers to a publication or network, as with the traditional news model, but to have content spread organically and at high speed through the online ecosystem. Wonkish analysis did not do well, but outrage, conspiracy, cuteness, and novelty did, leading to the common sentiment that the overall tone and coherency of public discourse was declining precipitously.[53] Yet even after Facebook restricted link sharing, spontaneous group explosions from Megalia to stonks have continued to occur. Facebook may profit less from these abrupt eruptions, but they are here to stay.

There is a straight line from Zynga to "listicles" (content presented in the form of a list) to Cambridge Analytica to the metaverse, and it all revolves around *engagement*, the meganet's innate tendency to promote and amplify the most voluminous, high-velocity, viral content. I want to suggest that Zynga's business model has fundamentally become that of the social meganet and that it will persist into whatever happens to fall under the rubric of the metaverse. Moreover, I want to say that Zynga, or something like it, was inevitable. As much as Zynga's shamelessness attracted opprobrium for psychological bottom-feeding, the raw fact of the matter is that someone was going to make a FarmVille, and FarmVille was going to become a hit. The meganet's combination of human nature and technological acceleration ensured it.

That combination likewise ensured that FarmVille and its brethren died out because pure exploitation has never been the most successful model of viral content. Thoughtful, reflective engagement, however, is not the most successful model either. The 2010s were a decade of Facebook and others chasing after the ideal form of meganet content, but it was also a decade of increasingly virulent forms of meganet communication emerging spontaneously. While FarmVille burnt itself out, incessant group communication around viral topics that raise one's emotional temperature (whether raising cute imaginary animals or fighting for or against feminism) isn't just a business model for the architects of meganets. It is an inevitable consequence of the meganet structure itself. Meganets thrive by keeping people online. Meganets keep people engaged. Meganets cause people to react. If Zynga or Facebook don't sufficiently fulfill that growth, other entities will, whether it's BuzzFeed, Cambridge Analytica, or QAnon.

ENCODING HUMANS

Zynga exploded in large part because FarmVille, and how people played it, were things computers *understood*. When the era of big data fell upon us, proponents frequently ignored the truth that big data was also dumb data. With voluminous amounts of data being produced too quickly for anything but a machine to process it, computers could frequently offer only the most rote sort of analysis when it came to grasping nuances of the data.

This had profound implications for Facebook in particular because it meant that its original bread-and-butter of status updates and human discourse was not especially lucrative. Having brought people together online, Facebook still lacked much understanding of what its users were actually doing. They were conversing—but about what? Facebook's lack of knowledge of its users was atypical for an internet company. Amazon and Google (as we'll see) were fundamentally marketplaces, while Facebook was not. When it came to giving people what they wanted, Amazon had users looking to buy particular products. Google had people searching for a couple of words typed into its search engine. Both Amazon and Google had very clear indicators as to how to profit off user interaction because the very nature of their sites required that users tell Amazon and Google what they wanted. On Amazon, a user is always looking to buy something. On Google, users are frequently looking to buy something. Both are wonderful marketplaces for sellers and advertisers, and Google and Amazon have become tremendously successful brokers of commerce. But one didn't go to Facebook to buy something, and so Facebook had to figure out how to monetize human interaction. The essential qualities of the meganet guided it in this goal.

As we will see in greater detail, computers do not understand the overwhelming *sense* of what people write in their posts. They struggle to identify the content of pictures and videos. Because computers, not humans, structure and monitor the vast majority of online interaction (there's too much for humans to manage, even for a huge company like Facebook), they inevitably emphasize the aspects of online interaction that they *do* easily process and understand.[54]

So when it comes to understanding online interaction computationally, simpler is better. In 2021, Facebook decided to show me a number of advertisements for a product with no possible relevance to my professional or private life, a drawing tool for making circles of various sizes. The only link it had to my life was that the product happened to bear the name of my younger daughter—but that was enough to signal to Facebook my supposed interest. It didn't know what I was saying, but it was able to pick out that word. That was the best it could do. When Facebook sometime in 2017 demographically classified me as "African American" (later updating this to my possessing an "African American cultural affinity" and finally to my having an interest in "African American culture"), Facebook recommended interests, groups, and social interactions to me in part based on that category.[55] Whatever raw data had caused Facebook to give me that classification, Facebook's recommendation algorithms now operated not based on the specific raw data but primarily on my membership in that category. Engaging with those recommendations, as always, would further reify my membership, in a now-familiar feedback loop.

Facebook—the meganet—does not understand long posts, but it understands how many likes a post gets. Facebook does not comprehend my sentences, but it knows what interest buttons I've clicked. Facebook does not understand what a user thinks about COVID, but it understands whether a user's post comes from the World Health Organization or a fringe conspiracy site. Facebook does not grasp how people feel, but it sees what they click, what they buy, and who they're friends with. Facebook does not understand what a person engages with, but it understands that he is engaging with it.

The success of Zynga and subsequent viral content signaled more than a new strategy of monetizing users. It signaled a shift toward making users more *computationalized.* Facebook encouraged users to express themselves in more structured fashions, and thus user engagement with Facebook became less textual and more "clicky," a matter of sharing, resharing, and reacting. Combined with the immense growth of mobile phones, which overtook desktops and laptops as the main medium for internet usage in the 2010s, Facebook's deprioritization of text heralded a shift from two-handed typing to one-handed clicking and tapping. It was easier for all.

When Facebook put its focus on user activities—games like Zynga included—to gain more reliable and useful data about its users, it *encouraged* those activities to grow in volume, velocity, and virality. Unlike human language, simple reactions such as likes and clicks on interests could be neatly and unambiguously represented as computationally friendly data. And they carried with them far clearer intent about their subjects: "I like this" and "I am interested in this."

In other words, the process of conditioning users to be more *computable* became a hallmark of Facebook's meganet and indeed of all meganets everywhere. Emote reactions to posts eliminated the ambiguities of textual responses. A small set of nonlinguistic, visual emoticons—like, love, care, haha, sad, wow, angry—proved far more effective for gathering sentiment information about the tenor of a post.

Facebook vice president Alex Schulz inadvertently summed up the meganet-eye view of the election when he cited what he claimed to be a cheering statistic:

> One point I found heartening in preparing this data was this quote from one of our data scientists. Following the announcement of a winner, "Americans applying heart reactions on political content were off the charts, while angry reactions were closer to baseline." It's possible to have a spike in positivity without having a corresponding spike in negativity.[56]

Facebook (the company) judged the emotional measure of a national election by reaction emojis. This is how a meganet sees elections and how a meganet sees the world. As a result, it is increasingly how *we* see the world. Facebook asks its users to sort themselves, their thoughts, and their reactions into data-friendly categories, simultaneously crowd-sourcing its data analysis while shunting users into a narrow, discrete, and computationally friendly set of choices. This too is a hallmark of the meganet: the blending of human and computational languages to make them more compatible with each other. Meganets tread the line of preserving a sufficient amount of human choice while sharply limiting the form such choices can take, conditioning people to be more computable in their behavior.

Yet this trend away from nuance and toward blunt categorization goes far beyond Facebook. Everywhere you go online, whether it's Reddit or Twitter or Megalia, people are self-sorting into like-minded groups with shared hobbies, opinions, affinities, and so on. This happens even in the absence of a profit incentive because it is what meganets do. Any online space of any meaningful size requires some way to organize and select its content for each participating person, and only computers can perform this task at the required scale.

Consequently, the limits of a computer's understanding determine and constrain the very structure of online existence. Any online space that tallies up the popularity of content falls prey to the same kind of simplification and filtering that occurs on Facebook. And because the meganet produces such a glut of data that filtering *must* occur in order to present it to humans, a meganet always brings with it a computational sorting of human activity, usually a very primitive one.

Overwhelmingly, the idea of "engagement" prevails. We go online to be engaged. We give primitive indicators of what might best engage us, and the meganet shunts us toward like-minded people and sympathetic content. It promotes the most engaging content to us. What is the most engaging content? It is that which is generated and shared in the greatest volume, spreading at high velocity, and building on itself in a feedback loop of virality. It is that which the meganet determines to be engaging, based on our cues. This is the crux of the meganet's unique joining of humans and computers: how humans are encoded to computers and how we increasingly come to see ourselves as defined by those encodings.

Well beyond a "filter bubble," this is a feedback loop, in which public and hidden information both contribute to directing users further in whatever direction the loop points.[57] Among the users, tech companies, third parties, and the sheer opacity of the underlying algorithms, there is no one dominant controller. The meganet's feedback loop, containing both human and machine parts, takes on a life of its own, and its superhuman size and lightning speed ensure that it cannot be controlled. Facebook's dynamics play out elsewhere, on YouTube, Reddit, Instagram, TikTok, WeChat, Snapchat, LinkedIn, Pinterest, and hundreds of smaller networks. Just as Elon Musk guides but does not control the trends he amplifies, social networks are frequently bystanders to the fervent activity on their platforms, albeit profit-reaping bystanders.

NO CENTER

A meganet computationalizes its users. Based on simple identifiers (demographics, hobbies, politics, emojis, etc.), a meganet invariably draws people of shared values together. From what we like, we find others who like the same thing—even in places where there is no "like" button. And in the meganet, "like" attracts like. The resulting groups possess a strong unity that, as we saw in the case of Megalia, tends to feed back on itself and amplify its extremes.

Social groups on the meganet are unusual both in size and character. They are *stratified, homogeneous* social groupings, geographically diverse collectives of extremely like-minded people. The meganet ensures that their like-mindedness becomes even more like-minded. As people engage with content deemed to be most engaging for their group, the meganet filters out less engaging content. These processes occur automatically: there is too much data for there not to be a filter, and our natural tendencies toward community and agreement result in us being sorted into homogeneous strata wherever we go. Facebook can be charged with capitalizing on these tendencies, but it neither created them nor controls them.

The tendency to blame Facebook arises, I argue, from the hesitancy to see how much the underlying nature of socializing has changed on the internet. The meganet has devastated and nigh obliterated not one but *two* modes of human social existence—private and public—in favor of a set of semipublic, medium-sized associations. The unit of online identity is no longer the individual but the group. The meganet is all about numbers, and so even an Elon Musk or a Donald Trump is no one without a vocal, active group of fans and acolytes behind him—or, just as often, in front of him. We carry these groups with us, on our phones and in our minds, and we are frequently closer to them than we are to our surrounding physical communities.

In 1980, cultural critic George Trow wrote that decades of centralized mass media had devastated social consciousness in the United States, resulting in life being reduced to two contrasting contexts of opposing size, "the grid of two hundred million . . . and the tiny, tiny baby grid of you and me."[58] To Trow, small, community groupings had become obsolete because we were either paying attention to celebrities and the national news or else withdrawing into our own private lives.

By drawing individuals into homogeneous online groupings that can easily ignore dominant, top-down narratives, the meganet has unexpectedly reversed Trow's account. Both the individual context and the mammoth context are fading as our always-on meganets cause us to "belong" permanently to the small groups that Trow had thought lost. Such groups have reemerged in radically different form, however, as they are now virtual and geographically spread out. Ironically, they are *less* diverse than before, since such groups no longer form by the happenstance of geographical proximity and daily routine but through a computationalized process of like-minded people being thrown together and reaffirming their similarities.

To anyone who doubts the loss of the larger context, the observations of frustrated elites are telling. "It's time for the elites to rise up against the ignorant masses," trumpeted a *Foreign Policy* column by journalist James Traub in June of 2016, in response to the Brexit vote.[59] The self-contradiction was apparent: true elites do not incite one another to action in published columns, even in rarefied magazines like *Foreign Policy*. Traub blamed cynical members of his own elite class for inciting the "citizen revolt" through fearmongering, but he left one crucial question unanswered: How did the citizens revolt so effectively that even their elite enablers "lost control" of them? How was it that the hoi polloi were now running the show?

The answer was meganets, empowering groups of hoi polloi while disempowering any and all central narratives. Volume, velocity, and virality destabilize and fracture any larger consensus while solidifying the smaller affinitized groups created on the meganet. The problem of bringing order and consensus to an entire meganet is that *there is no center* from which to exert control.

Letting go of the idea of a center is not easy. Traub was bemoaning Brexit, but one could easily imagine his sentiment applying to half a dozen subsequent crises, from the 2016 American election to global warming to COVID misinformation. Traub predicted that Donald Trump would lose the November 2016 election and that a "reformed center" would emerge of pragmatic globalists. This did not happen. Trump won against a background of willful and accidental misinformation spread through shadowy sites as well as through Facebook. Pizzagate and QAnon rose up as massive conspiracy theories despite having no buy-in from even the officials of the Republican Party, the party QAnon believers overwhelmingly support. COVID brought with it a dazzling array of misinformation spreading like wildfire, against which elites were left literally offering to pay people to get vaccinated.[60]

Clearly the rules of how ideas spread—whether those ideas are political beliefs, misinformation, or memes—have changed, dislodging the elites from a stable, authoritative perch. Equally clearly, the internet and its flood of information had a great deal to do with this change. But what was so difficult in figuring out how to control this spread?

The difficulty was in recognizing that the whole (the meganet) was far greater than the sum of its parts. Like the weather, a meganet's constituent parts act upon one another incessantly, pushing the system in chaotic and unpredictable directions. Like tectonic plates, the borders of its pieces scrape and push against each other, reshaping themselves. Like evolution, a meganet provides a hothouse incubator in which the "fittest" and most "viral" views and narratives triumph over more prosaic competitors. With little human intervention, the most powerful and provocative views and narratives on the meganet turn viral and spread with ruthless efficiency through a hyperconnected world. That is where we have arrived. To understand how to move forward, though, we must first better understand how we got here.

THREE

DISCOVERING THE MEGANET

There are two ways of losing oneself: through confined segregation in the particular or by dilution in the "universal."

AIMÉ CÉSAIRE, letter to Maurice Thorez

IN THE LAST FIFTY YEARS WE HAVE UNDERGONE SO MANY TECHnological minirevolutions, from mainframe to desktop to mobile to cloud, that we frequently forget how far we have come. The transition from the advent of the home computer in the 1980s to the full-on datafication of society in the 2010s has been momentous, yet oddly unobtrusive. One cannot fully grasp the severity of this change without having progressed, as I did sheerly by accident of birth, from having no internet at all to dial-up to broadband to social media to today.

In my twenties, I wound up working at two pioneers of these developments. At the turn of the century, I worked at a middle-aged Microsoft and then at Google at its moment of ascendancy, a paradigm shift in and of itself. I had been working on Microsoft's internet offerings but going to Google was like going to sleep and waking up a decade later. Microsoft had wired and computationalized homes and offices. Google, more than any other company until Facebook, was wiring the world.

It was a time of extreme optimism and, more than that, seeming empowerment. At both companies, employees worked with the confidence that their products helped (and sometimes vexed) hundreds of millions of people. As the software industry migrated from shipping disks and CDs in boxes to building websites and servers, it went beyond simply offering products *to* consumers and started to take something *from* them: their data. Data flooded into Google, Microsoft, Amazon, and Facebook, and the employees at these companies were left with this immense, messy, potentially lucrative pile of information to dig into. That was my very first reaction on joining Google: *look at all this data*. I had been using computers since playing with an Apple IIe at age six, but this was something very different and very new: this was *humanity* in the form of data.

Ironically, though, *the data didn't matter* to us software engineers. This is a crucial point to which I will return repeatedly. Certainly, it mattered in the sense that we needed it for the business to make our products successful, and we needed to write programs to react to it appropriately, but the underlying content of the data—what it meant to our users—was ultimately irrelevant. We cared about the different forms and subforms that data could take: weird cases that could trip up our programs and hidden structures that we could use to better organize it. But not the ultimate meaning of the data.

It was that *way* of looking at data, and what we did and did not care about, that cryptically augured the future. We—or at least I—had no idea that the computational view of human data would come to *shape* human life. I thought we were just sorting data to make it more easily accessible, the web being the biggest pile of disorganized chaos ever to have confronted humanity. But in fact, we were inadvertently writing the rules for how people would come to construct their own online identities.

SHOOTING THE MESSENGER

Microsoft struggled to conquer the internet. In the late 1990s, Microsoft was still resolutely focused on the Windows desktop model. Even though Bill Gates wrote in a "Pearl Harbor" memo in the mid-1990s that Microsoft would embrace the internet, in practice Microsoft was determined to subjugate the internet to Windows, a doomed effort from the beginning.[1] Microsoft's "hawks" chose a strategy that was fundamentally about protecting Windows' primacy, attempting to tie the internet as closely as possible to the operating system. Against that background, Microsoft nonetheless made tentative independent advances on to the internet. The purchase of Hotmail instantly gained Microsoft hundreds of millions of online users, and Microsoft made other attempts at internet services (MSN, NetDocs, Passport, HailStorm), though most were ultimately unsuccessful.[2]

I was assigned to one of Microsoft's internet projects, its instant messenger service, when I joined the company in 1998. It had the unwieldy name of MSN Messenger Service (Messenger for short) and had begun as a competitor to AOL's Instant Messenger. Messenger had the advantage of inheriting those hundred million Hotmail users and so began with a thriving user base. I was quickly entranced by the internet side of things and ended up becoming a server engineer and eventually a manager of a server team. It was, from today's perspective, a very simple application: a small program with a list of contacts, with whom you could exchange messages. More significantly, it had a *server*.

Microsoft, like most software companies of the time, was not accustomed to running servers that did much more than administer websites. Servers were something Microsoft sold software for, not machines the company typically operated itself. Messenger itself merely ran on dozens of servers, not thousands. Those servers were housed in a single location in Silicon Valley, and they had nowhere near the degree of standardization, automation, and robustness that you will find in any large server farm today. For a titan like Microsoft, this was still something new. Today, twenty years later, it is rare to run a piece of software on a computer or a smartphone that *doesn't* talk to a server. That too is a measure of how far we've come. Today there are millions upon millions of machines in data centers around the world, each containing tens if not hundreds of thousands of servers doing the work of administering our websites, email, streaming, and more. Most of those data centers sprang up only in this century, long after the internet and many years after the birth of the web. Those data centers require not only the infrastructure of the internet and the fundamentals of computer science but also the ongoing exponential increase in processing power given to us by Moore's law. Back when my team created Messenger, what is ubiquitous today was new territory even for Microsoft.

COMING TOGETHER

Messenger released in mid-1999, but the full import of what we were doing only presented itself on September 11, 2001. On that day, after the Twin Towers fell and cell phone networks were overloaded, Messenger passed three million online users simultaneously. And it didn't just pass that metric: it shot through it, as people ran to it to find some avenue of communication that worked. Messenger held up.

All of us working on Messenger realized that the project was something different than what we had imagined. It wasn't just that a previously recreational form of communication had abruptly become essential, though that was surprising enough. Rather, it was that the service was taking on a life of its own. Back then, servers primarily performed static tasks: serving up web pages, routing emails, and grinding through analyses of data. On that day, however, Messenger felt much more like a living, breathing entity. In response to a catastrophic, unprecedented event, people rushed online to communicate news to one another, and from there a cascade took place as more people logged on to spread the news further.

Messenger was a communication network, but it was more than that. Everything that happens across a telephone system or cellular network is transient and (mostly) unobserved. People's words translate into electrical signals and back into sound, traveling across wires, and then are forgotten forever. But Messenger's communications were different: every single bit of activity was going through a few dozen servers in Silicon Valley. Telephone networks do not cohere; they are bits and bobs shot from one place to another, with no memory and no possibility of coalescence. When a computer network transmits data, it does more than carry that data from one place to another. It processes it, analyzes it, and learns from it. The network can store it, compare it against other data, and change it arbitrarily. Unless someone goes out of his way to record it, what you speak into a traditional telephone disappears forever. By default, what you transmit through a server belongs to that network forever.*

Before the rise of commercial internet services, however, many networks just threw out that data. Prior to the rise of Gmail, even large email services like Hotmail and AOL acted as no more than supercharged post offices, sending and receiving virtual letters to millions of other distribution centers. Communications were point to point, from one person to another, not broadcasted one to many like television and other mass media.

But all of Messenger was unified in a single geographical location. Even if the Messenger servers had been distributed across multiple data centers, Messenger still would have possessed a centrality that telephones and emails lacked. We were able to observe the system handling its traffic in the system in real time. We weren't peeking at people's messages (unless something had gone wrong and we were debugging), but they were all there in one place, which Microsoft owned.

That coherence was only possible because computers had by the late 1990s attained enough speed and capacity to host an entire communications network on a unified set of servers. That in turn enabled such a network to possess a persistent, evolving *state*—a state that changed not just in response to code alterations made by the programmers but also in response to the activities of the users. Messenger was my first encounter with that central, defining feature of the meganet: a service's users can have as much of an impact on how the service behaves as the people who built the service and run it.

* Hence, much online activity is now encrypted for large parts of its journey, so that intermediaries cannot eavesdrop on it.

LOSING CONTROL

Another Microsoft offering around that time, the chat-room service NetMeeting, offered a more lurid hint of what was to come. Here the surprise lay not in the chat rooms themselves but in NetMeeting's online directory, where users could locate one another before entering chat rooms together. NetMeeting was a very primitive predecessor to the social media of today, a way for people to register themselves on a central server so that everyone else connected to that server could see them. There was no way to broadcast content to everyone else on the server. NetMeeting was intended more as a directory service for locating people, not a public or semipublic forum.

As we've seen in the years since, however, the urge to broadcast one's thoughts to a large audience can be quite overpowering, and many people will leverage even the slightest opportunity to grab a bigger platform for themselves. That very human urge drives so much of the benefits and pitfalls of Facebook, Twitter, and Reddit today. NetMeeting held nothing like the possibilities of those services, but it did offer one little avenue of public expression. Anyone with a NetMeeting account could set a custom display name for themselves. If my NetMeeting account was "dauerbach351@hotmail.com," I could also choose (and arbitrarily change) a display name for myself, whether it was "David Auerbach," "David A.," "AuerbachsKeller," or anything else. Everyone else on the NetMeeting server would then see the latest name I had set for myself.

The purpose of the display name was only to make one more easily identifiable, but there were few restrictions on what users could choose for their monikers. Profanity was banned, but at any given time the directory was blanketed with all sorts of wacky and obviously fake names. It was a form of personal expression to an anonymous audience and mostly a harmless one. It hardly seemed like the antecedent to the deafening displays of public buffoonery and obnoxiousness that would come to define Twitter. There wasn't enough space for such behavior.

One day, however, a clever user figured out that the NetMeeting directory software would not just publish people's display names verbatim but would also format them according to whatever HTML markup tags they contained. For instance, if you changed your name to `David <bold> "The Yellow Dart"</bold> Auerbach`, it would not show up as that text verbatim. Instead, NetMeeting's software would understand the boldface HTML tag `<bold>` and display the text as:

David **"The Yellow Dart"** Auerbach

But NetMeeting would render not just HTML formatting tags but also embedding tags. One such tag is the `<IMG>` tag, which instructs HTML rendering software to fetch and display a particular image. The NetMeeting software, it turned out, respected this tag, so if you were to change your display name to `<img src= https://media.gettyimages.com/photos/bigeyed-naughty-obese-cat.jpg/>`, NetMeeting would not see this just as text but as a coded instruction to fetch the image at that URL, a fat cat. So whenever any user scrolled by you in the NetMeeting directory, her computer would fetch and display a picture of a cat, pasting it over other names. Users could not prevent the pictures from displaying because the NetMeeting software did it automatically. If fifteen users all embedded `<IMG>` tags into their display names, each linking to some image somewhere else on the web, the NetMeeting software on your computer would fetch those fifteen images, whatever those images were. In other words, any single user could now control what appeared on the screens of everyone else logged on to NetMeeting.

This bug's potential for performance and chaos was irresistible to some portion of the NetMeeting user base. Some people might be apathetic, while others might ethically choose not to mess up the experience of other users, but there will always be a nontrivial number of people who cannot resist causing chaos. It was, in a restricted way, a form of human creative expression. You could choose a funny picture and surprise everyone else with it. Or you might also just want to annoy people with a disgusting or obscene image. That antisocial instinct, which defines the all-too-common creature called the internet troll, suffuses a significant percentage of humanity to one degree or another.

As images spread virally across people's computers through NetMeeting, more users realized what was going on and more decided to join in. The knowledge of this trick flooded through the system, leading to a flood of images through the directory and onto the screen of every person using it.

Microsoft employees noticed. "Look what showed up on NetMeeting!" exclaimed a coworker. We looked at the directory display on his client. It wasn't just one image but a nonstop cascade of overlapping images. Soon after the first person had made the discovery, others had quickly figured out the secret. But more than just expressing themselves, the kooks and trolls who were exploiting this trick were actually *engaging* with one another. A pornographic picture would appear, summoned by one troll, only for some other righteously minded user to embed an image of Jesus that covered up the first obscene image. The troll would then change his own display name to embed a different porn image, causing that image to appear again on top of Jesus, and the fight would go on. A dialogue (of sorts) was taking place between users, in pictures rather than in words, as they embedded images into their display names in response to the images other users were embedding in theirs. A directory had turned into a real-time conversation, albeit an obscene and rancorous one.

The origin of this entire phenomenon was a bug that was quickly fixed, but what occurred was far more than a bug. The entire directory server had turned into a proto-Twitter, with users *broadcasting* data—images, specifically—to one another and in turn reacting to one another's broadcasts. Microsoft can, and did, shut down the servers, but the entire company and its employees were bystanders to this chaotic, pornographic symposium. Microsoft's employees had coded the software and ran the servers, but the NetMeeting directory and its users had become greater than Microsoft's creation: they had become a meganet. The feedback loop of user interactions had outstripped, momentarily, Microsoft's ability to control the network.

In Messenger, this feedback effect was comparatively minimal next to what was to come on Facebook or Google. It manifested itself when we added the ability for users to set status messages, the little phrases or jokes next to your name that are broadcast to everyone on your friends list. These status messages are fundamentally different from instant messages. They aren't transient communications from one person to another. They are persistent pieces of data semipublicly attached to your username and visible to your entire friends list—or possibly to everyone on the network. Friends would see their friends' statuses and then change their own, and the feedback loop would continue. In such small loops was online "virality" born, as the popular overwhelms the unpopular.

This sort of persistent, many-to-many broadcasting, impossible with a phone, changes the fundamental nature of a communication network. Now, networked users can react to one another and contribute to the enduring, evolving state of that network. To do so, the network must make all users potentially available to all other users, and it must do so in real time. At that point, the network takes on a life of its own. Users respond to other users' messages, and what was once a simple service for delivering electronic messages from one person to another becomes a network that represents (albeit very partially) a *community* of people. That representation constantly evolves in reaction to the actions of its participants, and it does so without requiring any intervention from its creators. It is a persistent, evolving meganet.

Our small Messenger team only half realized this development. We saw that we had created a space for a new form of social organization that went beyond email and chat rooms by bringing millions of users together in such a way that they could theoretically all interact with one another simultaneously. In Messenger, at least, the degree of interactivity was comparatively limited. The same was true for NetMeeting, where the sudden explosion of creative virality was due to a bug giving users more power than they should have had. But far from being an unusual circumstance, the bizarre NetMeeting incident is increasingly representative. On our gigantic social meganets, unforeseen interactions are now the rule rather than the exception. This is due not to bugs, however, but to the nature of the meganet itself. When a program on a PC exceeds its intended parameters, the worst consequence is a crash and a reset. But on a meganet, unintended consequences don't result in a reset to the system; they cascade.

NetMeeting was a small-scale meganet, and it took a bug to cause it to explode into an uncontrolled feedback loop of cascading images. Yet in that moment, we see the fundamental origin of so much of our loss of control today, even if it merely seemed like a laughing matter at the time. As the broadcasting of human expression across the internet became more central, that kind of chaos became the norm.

THE GOOGLE INDEX

The next, far greater stop on the path to today's meganets was Google's search engine. Google was born in 1998 as an internet company, and its outlook was fundamentally different from Microsoft's from the very beginning. Where Microsoft saw its fortunes in the sale of its software, Google positioned itself as an organizer and broker of the information that was freely available on the web. I had only had the smallest taste of what a meganet was at Microsoft, but at Google I saw such systems far more clearly and at vastly greater scale, even if they were still nascent.

The heart of Google then was its search engine. At their inception, search engines seemed to be *observing* the internet rather than engaging with it. As passive observers, they wouldn't qualify as meganets. But Google in particular discovered that the way to make a search engine better was to pay far more attention to how users and websites interacted with its search engine. That development turned the search engine from a passive observer into an active meganet.

Search engines prior to Google, from AltaVista to Yahoo, failed to make Google's crucial jump, which was to view the raw data of the internet as *valuable to the company itself*, rather than as merely a means to lure users to click on banner ads. Google ranked websites by Google's own assessment of their importance, and in turn website owners redesigned their websites in the hopes of garnering more attention from Google. And as websites changed, user behavior gradually changed as well: people searched for different things. And so the feedback loop essential to the meganet began. Google went from being an observer to being a broker of website content, and the calm control of Google's early days was replaced with an increasingly anxious dance. The *index* at the heart of its search engine—the carefully assembled database of the entire web and rankings for the relevance of each page along countless axes—became not a passive thing to be consulted but a war zone between Google and the web itself.

To see how this shift happened, it's necessary to look at the problem Google intended to solve. As it ballooned in size, the web presented a huge problem to anyone using it: how to locate the information for which one was searching. In the 1990s, the web was a diffuse environment without much in the way of hierarchy, a stark contrast to today, where established companies host highly institutionalized websites that make up the dominant resources for most online engagement. Underneath, however, the same problem remains, even if its locus has shifted: If there is too much information for humans to curate and administer, how does one filter it to select that which is most relevant and most important?

The crux of the problem was that the web's data was not *computer-friendly* but *human*-friendly and computer-*unfriendly*. Prior to the web, data that was stored on computers was overwhelmingly in highly structured, primarily numerical form: spreadsheets, financial records, statistical classifications, hierarchical databases. *Human*-oriented data, such as language and images and videos, were primarily offline. When such data was entered into a computer, it was usually intended purely to be stored and nothing more. My 1980s word processor helped me format, edit, and print text, but it performed few operations on the text itself beyond spell checking. Computers did far more with the computationally friendly numbers in spreadsheets. The internet turned this state of affairs upside down. Within a very short time, the internet was dominated not by structured, numerical data but by human-readable data with no obvious explicit structure. Data was no longer just numbers; now it was primarily words.

As we will see later, computers do not do well with words. Computers are fundamentally number-crunching machines. CPUs do nothing more than execute primitive orders to store, retrieve, and do simple arithmetic on numbers. Programmers must figure out how to turn words into numerical representations that can be manipulated computationally. The science of information retrieval originated and grew in the late 1990s as a means for managing the data flooding the web. It was not a science of *understanding* this new strange human-oriented data but only of trying to extract structure from it. Even if a computer could not understand human language, it could take human language and analyze it in fairly simple ways, counting which words were on which pages and performing quantitative analysis on it. Human language may not have obvious structure, but certain *implicit* structure could be garnered from it.[3] To take a very simple example, a web page talking about cats will likely mention the word *cat* far more than pages that don't talk about cats, so it is a reasonable bet for a search engine to classify that page as a "cat" page. In turn, a user who types in a search query for "cat" is more likely to find those cat pages interesting. Given the messy petabytes of data on the web, information retrieval asked how a search engine could build a computationally friendly *index* of those pages.

Information retrieval birthed the search engine, the first major paradigm for organizing the flotsam and jetsam of the web. For a search engine, the fundamental question was which web pages were *most relevant* in relation to a set of search terms (or a query). If I were interested in finding all pages about jaguars, or all pages that mention "jaguars" *and* "cars," how could a search engine quickly provide results for any such queries in a timely way? The raw data was not good enough. Search engines transformed that raw data of the web into an organized and efficient index which could be easily and quickly consulted.

The result, in the case of Google, was the greatest vacuum cleaner and processor of information the world had known to that point. To analyze and make use of the web, Google first made a full-on copy of it. Google tore through every web page on every site in order to amass copies of all the pages on the web, as well as refreshing any of that content as soon as Google predicted it to have changed. This mission translated into the fetching of billions of web pages per day.

With this snapshot of the web in hand, Google's servers then created an *index* of the web, which held billions of web pages in the early 2000s and holds hundreds of billions of web pages today. The word *index*, however, understates what is being created. The index of a book is selective, highlighting a curated set of topics and names that function as lookups into the main text of the book. A search engine index is not such an index. A search index could better be termed a *metatext* or a *supertext*—something greater than the text itself, rather than a reduction of it. Google, like many other information retrieval projects from Facebook to the NSA's internal databases, does more than just make a copy of the raw data that it collects. It does more than create lookup tables and annotations of that data. It creates a new and greater version of that raw data that overtakes the original data, organized and annotated in such a way that it can be computationally processed and queried.

A book index lists subjects and categories already specified, implicitly and explicitly, in the main text. A search index *infers*, *selects*, and *creates* categories out of independent, unrelated texts produced by millions of independent authors, categories that unify previously unrelated texts. This sort of categorization is closer to the Dewey decimal system than a book index—it is a cataloguing system. Unlike a book index, a search index does not selectively exclude subjects and categories of lesser importance. A search index is not selective but exhaustive. As much as is possible, every word, every phrase, every name, and every subject are placed into the search index, and the search engine then marks up the index with additional tags and statistics that may help better gauge the priority or structure of a particular word or set of words. Some pages might have high priority for "car," some for "jaguar," some for both, and all three sets of pages are different and important. A search index is not interested in abridging or selecting but in ordering and ranking. Ultimately, the search index becomes bigger than the "text" itself. When we send a query to

Google, we are not searching the web per se but instead are searching this new hybrid.

Such algorithmically enhanced, computationally comprehensible copies are so fundamental to the workings of meganets that they require a unique name. Some have suggested the name *digital twin*, but that suggests too much similarity between the original and the copy, when in fact the copy is distorted and enhanced.[4] Rather, these copies are *mirages*: idealized, phantom forms of people, products, social groups, and everything else that they come to represent. They are a key contributor to how meganets subsume reality as we previously knew it.

Like the web itself, the resulting search index changes over time. A search index is a growing, enduring thing, reactive to the changes in the billions of pages it analyzes—and capable of itself causing changes in the original sites it crawled. That persistent, evolving quality makes it a meganet. When Google achieved dominance in the 2000s and became the main driver of traffic to websites, webmasters altered their sites to encourage Google to direct more users their way. New sites sprang up with the express intent of obtaining traffic from Google. Not only did the web determine the index, but the index also started to influence the web as well. The feedback loop of the search engine meganet was in place.

THE FINANCIAL INCENTIVE

On top of the feedback loop between the Google index and the websites Google crawled, there arose a faster and far more lucrative loop centered around advertising. At the dawn of this century, Google discovered, as no one had to that point, how to monetize a search index through the sale of targeted advertisements. If Google's original role as impassive observer of the web had slowly faded as websites evolved to better please Google's search rankings, Google's AdWords program supercharged its shift from observer to influential actor and arbiter. The search index was about organizing information and determining relevance; advertising was about using that information to drive revenue. The unpredictable bidding wars that Google triggered, melding humans and network services in previously unseen ways, became the indirect antecedents of today's decentralized cryptocurrency booms and busts.

AdWords, which became the lucrative revenue foundation that created the Google of today, remains one of the most profitable innovations in the history of computing. Utilizing an elegant auction system, third-party advertisers created text advertisements and then placed monetary bids on Google search keywords that they wanted their advertisements to appear under, specifying how much they would be willing to pay for a single advertising click. The bids could range from pennies for the most uncommon terms to hundreds of dollars per click for especially prized search terms like *mesothelioma* and *asbestos*, which were bid up by law firms searching for potential clients.[5] Google's profits from these advertisements were staggering and single-handedly boosted Google for years to the position of the unquestioned internet kingpin. Atypically, this targeted advertising was not based on any modeling of users, demographically or otherwise. Google presented advertisements to users purely based on the search queries that users had just entered into Google—queries that very frequently indicated something users were looking to purchase.

All subsequent forms of internet advertising struggled to replicate AdWords' simple model with far less success, leading to increasing levels of user tracking and consumer profiling in the hopes of pinning down advertising targets.[6] Fortuitously for Google, user search queries turned out to be one of the few scenarios where a company can gauge what a user is interested in buying without knowing anything else about the user. There are precious few situations in online or offline life where people actually tell companies what they want right at that very moment, and Google had, somewhat serendipitously, taken its place at the center of one of them.

The innovative simplicity of Google's advertising revenue model belies how byzantine such advertising meganets could (and would) become. As such, AdWords serves as a revealing model of the workings of the automated and *autonomous* meganet. While Google's web page rankings became increasingly opaque as their ranking algorithms grew in complexity, the placement of AdWords advertisements did not: it remained primarily a function of (1) how successful an AdWords advertisement was in compelling people to click on it when it appeared, and (2) how much third parties were willing to pay for clicks on those ads. While the workings of AdWords were still humanly derivable in individual cases, thanks to this simplicity, there was almost never any human intervention in the selling and displaying of the ads. The search-advertising ecosystem evolved on its own, advertisements percolating to the top and sinking to the bottom in accordance with the algorithms Google had set out. Google had to do additional work to prevent outright fraud, but there was overall a wonderfully self-organizing aura around the AdWords system that showed human and machine working together in remarkable and profitable harmony. Advertisers who bid the most on keywords had the most prominent placement on Google's search for those keywords. Advertisers could set their own limits on spending, which, if exceeded, would allow lower bidders to take their place on results pages. For a system built around the disorganized mass of the web, it was strikingly beautiful—to me and to many other software engineers who witnessed it. That it was also profitable enough to turn Google quickly into a titan of technology seemed almost a miracle.

Initially, AdWords was an example of the long-gone optimism of the early 2000s, which arose from the functional and healthy interactions among the engineers, servers, website publishers, and advertisers that constituted Google's meganets. Success came all too easily. What was most remarkable was how Google had engaged so many third parties (content providers and advertisers) to work symbiotically with its own business model, automating the process of forming small but lucrative business relationships. It appeared that Google had not only understood the internet but had also seamlessly integrated the humans and human-run companies into its systems.

That would not last. As it turned out, this simplicity, elegance, and harmony was highly atypical. There were even indications at the time of impending decay, as Google's search engine gradually sank into greater opacity and complexity—as all successful meganets invariably do.

RANKING AND RELEVANCE

Here is where things fell apart. Here is where Google lost control of its wonderful beast. Initially tame, it became wild. Even as Google's AdWords raked in voluminous revenues, Google's ranking algorithms for the search results themselves grew ever more byzantine. Crucially, the *human* element became increasingly integral to the search engine's effectiveness, and as that human element grew more labyrinthine, more populous, and more fungible, Google's ability to control and understand its own systems declined.

As we saw, judging which advertisements to place on search results is a comparatively simple process: whoever bid the most got the top placement. Advertisers had to duke it out among themselves, but Google could be a detached, neutral arbiter and allocate the ad space neatly based on who was willing to pay the most. But money didn't determine how to sort the actual search results. If I were to search for "mesothelioma," the top advertising result would be a law firm that was willing to pay the most for that spot, but no such bidding impacted the actual search results. The top search result should be the most *relevant* web page to the term *mesothelioma*. But how is relevance defined, and how do you calculate it?

Debates over relevance, I would argue, were the next step in the emergence of meganets as the central entities of online life, a step toward how Facebook and similar meganets judge "engagement" today. Everywhere we look today, there are contests in engaging users. What memes will spread most virulently? What political candidates and positions will achieve dominance across the internet? What opinions will appear sufficiently popular that others are influenced to share them? These dynamics are all a consequence of the meganet, with computers amplifying and accelerating human social behavior to unheard-of speeds. Just as NetMeeting gave a taste of the high-velocity interactions fueled by network technology, the relevance of web pages in Google's search engine was the first large-scale appearance of meganet engagement disputes.

But uncontrolled and dynamic chaos was hardly Google's intent. Google's original innovation in search, circa 1998, was the algorithm Google's founders termed PageRank.[7] In PageRank's original formulation, a "popular" page that was linked to by many other pages was deemed more useful and more important than one that was linked to by fewer pages. This popularity contest reiterated itself. A popular page's links counted more toward making other pages more popular. PageRank's core idea was that the web needed to be analyzed not just by its content but by its *structure*. Not all pages were created equal. *Popularity*, as gleaned from the link structure of the web, was a good proxy for the *relevance* of a page to people looking for useful information on the web. Relevance implied engagement because people would be engaged by what was relevant to them.

Perfect "relevance" became the theoretical ideal for which Google reached. The goal of the search engine was for its top results to be those the user was most likely to click on, that being a proxy for where the user's interest truly lay. At its inception, PageRank allowed Google to return far better results than competitors like AltaVista, AskJeeves, and Yahoo, whose ranking algorithms ignored how pages linked to one another and returned results almost entirely based on what appeared on the web page itself, so one eccentric's page about *Casablanca* could gain as high a placement as that of any more "authoritative" and well-connected source like IMDb or Wikipedia's page.

PageRank, nonetheless, only delivered a crude approximation of "relevance" because the popularity rankings it used to calculate relevance were hardly a perfect proxy for actual relevance. The greatest resource on *Casablanca* may well be some brilliant eccentric's single page, besting IMDb and Wikipedia, but Google had little way of knowing that until other humans had discovered that page and populated the web with links to it. Google was already depending indirectly on the collective, distributed, and disorganized human labor of creating and maintaining web pages in order for its algorithms to do what they needed to do.

There was a greater problem, however, in the very definition of the holy grail of relevance. No quantifiable (or algorithmic) definition of relevance existed—or can exist. There is no set formula by which one can magically calculate the most relevant search result for a single person at any particular time. Perhaps the best possible page for a search term exists but hasn't been discovered by enough other people yet for enough links to tip off Google. Or maybe I simply entered search terms that didn't make it sufficiently clear what exactly I was looking for—maybe I entered "casa blanca" searching for the Casa Blanca lily, but Google thought I had simply mistyped the far more popular movie. All of these ambiguities cause problems, but it is the inability to perfectly gauge human intent that makes it impossible to attain a perfect assessment of relevance. What's more relevant for me might be less relevant for you. I may want that lone eccentric's page about *Casablanca*, while you may want IMDb's list of cast and crew, and Google then, as now, has no direct way to determine that it should show us different results. For the most part, Google still shows everyone the same search results, albeit with some broad customization depending on preferred language, geographical location, and a handful of other factors.

The entire quest for relevance was a quest for the good enough, not for the perfect. It was the quest for an algorithm that would produce acceptable results for most people most of the time. The wonderful property of Google's search engine was that unlike its predecessors, its results very frequently *were* good enough. Especially in its early days, PageRank frequently led you to where you wanted to go, or some place useful enough. The trouble was in maintaining that standard. Without constant updates, refinements, and tests of the ranking system, today's good rankings would become the obsolete and irrelevant rankings of tomorrow. Worse, the humans who had contributed so much to Google's skill at ranking ceased to cooperate so conveniently.

DANCING ABOUT ALGORITHMS

Google knew full well that relevance was a subjective ideal rather than a reachable goal, something that was fundamentally in the eye of the beholder (or of millions upon millions of beholders). Google saw the web changing out from under it in response to its own search engine. It knew it had to keep up. Google's beleaguered ranking engineers tested changes to the ranking algorithm more through trial and error than through proof of concept.* Unlike the automated internal tests that ensured that the server infrastructure continued working as expected, Google subjected potential ranking changes to "experiments," meaning that a small subset of users inside and outside the company were exposed to the new ranking formula, and Google assessed the new formula based on user behavior in response to the clicks. If, under the new ranking changes, users tended to click more frequently on the highest-ranked search results, the ranking was deemed better. If users clicked less frequently on the top search results, the ranking was deemed worse. In other words, "relevance" was defined after the fact, experimentally, rather than in advance. Only informed guesses could be made of how a ranking change would fare.

And so it was not just Google's engineers who determined the workings of its search engine but also the users who input search queries and indicated to Google what terms were more or less common and important and then helped Google judge relevance by choosing which results to click on. Alongside them were the website creators themselves, who looked to Google to drive revenue and struggled to follow its lead. The pursuit of higher rankings led website creators to engage in search engine optimization (SEO). As Google became the central force of the web instead of a mere detached accumulator of information, websites small and large restructured and tweaked their content with the intent of influencing (or tricking) Google's ranking algorithms into placing their content higher in search results. SEO became a profession as a flurry of experts rose up to advise webmasters on how to raise their Google rankings.

* This was the primary reason I personally chose to work on Google's server infrastructure rather than on ranking, so that I would have blessed precision in my goals.

SEO was an ongoing, iterative process that revolved around the so-called Google dance. In one sense, it was merely people learning how to game Google's system. As website operators gleaned how Google was ranking sites, they adjusted their sites to try to raise their rankings. Google, in turn, readjusted their algorithms to prevent this gaming. But from another perspective, the Google dance revealed both Google losing control over its own system as well as shifting from an observer of the web to a participant in it. It wasn't just the search results that were dancing, however. All the participants and constituent pieces of the Google search-advertising meganet were dancing in response to what every other component was doing, resulting in a dynamic and unstable network that could not be pinned down and was not under any ultimate authority.

Three groups—Google's engineers, users of the search engine, and website creators engaging in SEO—collaborated to construct the "special sauce" that was the Google ranking "algorithm." The term *algorithm* is misleading in the case of ranking because the term algorithm suggests an orderly, static, and humanly comprehensible series of steps for a computer to execute, like a recipe you would follow while making dinner. The pre-Google search engines of the 1990s, like Lycos, Excite, AltaVista, and Northern Light, had algorithms in this classical sense. These search engines applied a prebaked set of algorithms to every web page in turn, rather than looking at the web as a whole.

While Google's more advanced algorithms were initially fairly elegant and comprehensible to humans, the meganet's feedback loop sent Google's algorithms tumbling into vastly greater complexity and constant evolution. Google's search ranking became neither orderly nor static, nor humanly comprehensible. Much like meganets more generally, these sorts of algorithms are ever-shifting, voluminous entities that do not stay in one place long enough to be precisely observed. While their overall direction can be estimated and charted, such "algorithms" violate the spirit of the term if not the letter.

The "algorithms" of a meganet evolve not only in response to the data on which they operate but also in response to *their own outputs.*

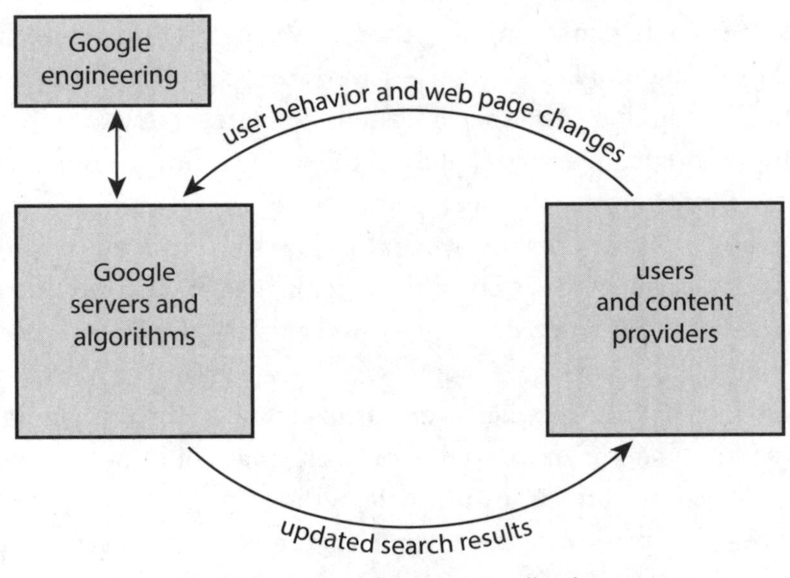

The Google Search Engine Feedback Loop

Google's search rankings cause web pages to alter their content in the hopes of higher ranking, and in turn those changes cause Google to alter its ratings. In other words, Google's past search rankings help determine what the next iteration of its search rankings will be.

At the dawn of Google, the effects of this feedback loop were minimal. The ranking of sites was done through fairly static indicators, chief among them being the PageRank algorithm, which assessed the importance of pages by analyzing which other pages linked to it and what anchor text was used in the link. But PageRank—the analysis of links to determine the importance of a particular page—lost prominence as more and more inputs were placed into Google's special ranking sauce and, in particular, as more of these inputs arose from feedback caused by Google itself. The feedback from Google's search engine—the effects Google had on the web and on its users—became as important to determining Google's rankings as the original content Google had crawled. Google, in other words, had to play catchup with itself, struggling to track the changes its own search engine was causing across the wider web. Google—and perhaps the entire web—effectively began chasing its tail. That feedback-driven loss of control—by which Google was struggling to keep reins on the extraordinarily successful system it had built—heralds the meganet.

At its founding, Google nominally stood outside the web ecosystem it was meant to analyze, throwing pebbles into an ocean to judge what ripples they made. Within five years, Google might as well have been the moon, controlling the tides. SEO specialists, both established and shady, steeled themselves for the next iteration of the Google dance, and in turn, Google steeled itself to make further changes as the web reacted to its last set of changes.[8]

RUNNING TO KEEP IN THE SAME PLACE

These feedback-driven cycles are integral to meganets and cannot be avoided. Google's search engine came to *require* the human element, integrating it into its workings inextricably. Google could not automate the process of testing changes to ranking algorithms because humans were needed to evaluate the success or failure of a change. PageRank paled in importance next to a different measure: How often did users click on one of Google's top search results instead of leaving Google in frustration? *That*, rather than PageRank, was an indisputably meaningful metric. If users clicked on a search result, they must have found *something like* what they were looking for.

But relying on such metrics meant that Google could not determine the relevance of a web page without the active, ongoing participation of humans. The human element became an integral and necessary part of the development of ranking algorithms. Ranking required *ongoing* feedback to remain successful because there was no constant, objective measure of the quality of search results—only the evolving opinions of hundreds of millions of users. Gathering data and approximating humans' overall preferences—and adjusting when those preferences changed—became the bread and butter of Google as well as Amazon, Facebook, and many other networks that followed in Google's wake. Such user analytics vividly illustrated the persistent, evolving opacity of meganets.

Introducing human contributions at this scale and degree entails a loss of control; it also defines the meganet. Once humans become an essential part of a system such as Google's search rankings, there is little hope of removing them and just as little hope of understanding them. Too many people want too many different things. The hope is that the system can manage the diversity and chaos, but managing is far from controlling. A small number of engineers will never be able to quantify the entirety of all humans' preferences into algorithms. Recently, many have suggested artificial intelligence and deep learning as ways to automate the process of deriving and honoring the preferences of hundreds of millions of users, removing the tedium of endless trial and error on the part of software engineers so that algorithms like search-result ranking automatically improve themselves. These AI-based approaches have yielded, at best, partial success, as we shall see later.

But if we can't make the algorithms complicated enough to honor the diversity of choices, there is another possibility. We can try to make the human element more predictable: to condition users so that their behavior and desires are more standardized. If human behavior becomes more uniform and less diverse, then a user's personal criteria for the best possible search result will vary less and become easier to model by computers. Restricting or corralling user choice can make the problem more manageable as well. Instead of letting users choose what to search for, algorithms can gently (or less gently) recommend what they might be interested in and what it would be algorithmically simpler for users to be interested in.

So as the initial glory of PageRank faded and human intent remained difficult as ever to glean, the age of recommendation engines and conditioning of human choice began. YouTube began as a Google-like search engine, but its focus has shifted to its recommendation engine, which shepherds users from one video to the next based on YouTube's opaque, internal models of which videos are likely to appeal to the same groups of people. Amazon has downplayed customer reviews in favor of its own recommendations.

Netflix now promotes its own content overwhelmingly rather than gauging much in the way of an individual's preferences.

Human homogeneity is the great algorithmic simplifier, and meganets have gained the presence and sway to encourage such homogeneity. Recommendation engines require that users *sort themselves* into homogeneous interest-based categories, the better to help YouTube and Amazon group videos and products along such categorical lines. While this could be considered a form of unpaid labor, it is also a decentralization of authority onto a collective of users. Every user now possesses a small, nondecisive but still consequential form of control over the behavior and results of a meganet, control that Google or Amazon or Facebook do not have. At the same time, however, the feedback loop conditions *us*, the users, to behave more predictably and uniformly.

Technology companies and software engineers never intended to cultivate homogeneity in human behavior so explicitly. Neither did they intend to shepard human behavior in a particular direction. It was merely the path of least resistance. Algorithmically, it mattered less *how* human beings became more homogeneous than simply *that* they became more homogeneous. More homogeneity, in any direction, meant better algorithms. Meganet companies had little interest in micromanaging their content. In theory, companies like Google and Amazon could go in and muck about with search results to produce certain results. Occasionally, as with Google's deranking of racist and disinformational search results, companies do perform such manual intervention, but such intervention is generally reactive and highly selective, made in response to public controversy.[9] It's simply too much trouble otherwise.

Today, for better and for worse, *we* make ourselves more computable to meganets, simply by engaging with them. The human-machine feedback loops that constitute meganets have, intentionally and unintentionally, been accelerating the molding of human behavior into more simplified and regularized—and sometimes more predictable—forms.

THE LESSONS OF THE MEGANET

Google's search engine was the first *significant* example of a new kind of entity—an enormous, dynamic network operated on by millions upon millions of people—which slowly slipped out of the control of any of its participants, even as all its participants retained some ability to influence it. Website owners and advertisers felt acutely at the mercy of Google's opaque ranking changes, even as they themselves influenced those changes. Users, of course, had no insight into the ranking and simply reacted to whatever Google presented to them, scanning the top results and top advertisements in the hope that they would find what they were looking for—not realizing that they too were influencing Google's rankings.

Yet on the inside, Google too felt an increasing loss of control to those outside forces. There were website owners jockeying for increased prominence in search results. There were advertisers trying to game the system and piggyback off of Google's success. And there were the users, whose feedback was increasingly crucial to Google in determining what results were the best results because Google *needed* users to tell it, constantly, how good a job it was doing. But to make users the arbiters in such a broad, disparate, and partially opaque way required that Google cede the control that it appeared to have gained.

Once ceded, the control didn't go to any one place. Rather, bits of control spread to every piece of the online ecosystem, with no single entity gaining enough to influence the system decisively. Each user, engineer, or executive has some control over pieces of a meganet, but when everyone has a little bit of control, no one has full control—and frequently, no one has *enough* control.

This dislocation and loss of centralized control has only accelerated. Google's search engine did not clean itself up or return to simpler times. Once it was out there scouring and ranking the web, the web grew, as did Google, and there was no turning back. The search engine gave way to social media, but the loss of control remained, and more and more people came to feel the brakes come off.

A successful meganet like Google becomes increasingly out of control—not because it has a central will of its own but because it becomes increasingly independent of its owners and operators. When a meganet grows, it in turn influences the actions of the individuals who contribute to it, building a dense feedback loop. Over time, the feedback element will inevitably dominate, as the loop of user response to a meganet's evolving data accelerates and outpaces humans' ability to control it. Microsoft and Google provide two examples, but we shall see many more. A meganet grows in size and relevance by accumulating users, data, and connections. As it grows, its internal feedback structure must also grow, its components acting upon one another with increasing speed and complexity, until more and more of its evolution is determined from within rather than from without. A meganet that fails to grow is a failed meganet. Increasing feedback and increasing complexity are inevitable.

As this feedback acceleration occurs, software engineers and the algorithms they program lose authority over the feedback loop. Rather than controlling a simple windup toy, it becomes like trying to write a program to administer the human body. There are too many interlocking pieces, dynamically affecting one another, for static, concise algorithms to perform faultlessly or even satisfactorily. The same piece of code cannot control an ear, a liver, and a heart. The meganet sprouts new organs constantly even as its existing ones mutate.

A meganet's code and algorithms are either so general that they overlook this variety and work only partially, as with the case of PageRank, or else they are targeted fixes designed to address a single problem or task in the meganet without any intended larger effect, as with the targeted banning of unacceptable derogatory epithets and explicit language. Despite such interventions appearing to outsiders as the heavy hand of omniscient technology companies, they are actually ad hoc tweaks made without full knowledge of a meganet's organization and workings. When Facebook claims to crack down on hate speech or conspiracy theories and there appears to be no measurable effect, or when TikTok claims that it is banning misgendering even as it displays content encouraging teen girls to expose and starve themselves, there is a blatant disconnect between companies' purported actions and the effects of those actions—or, more often, the lack of effects.[10] It is an endless series of attempted brain surgeries performed with boxing gloves on.

The meganet is not a carefully maintained machine but an evolving, semiautonomous system over which its operators only have limited control. Amazon is at first glance a far more tightly constructed meganet than Google or Facebook, based as it is around comparatively static products whose listings evolve slowly if at all. Instead, Amazon's feedback loop arises from a constant influx of new product listings and reviews for existing listings. Amazon's recommendation engine is yet another feedback mechanism, seeking to reinforce existing recommendations by clustering products into implicit groupings and displaying those clusters to browsing shoppers, thereby further encouraging their combined purchase. In uniting disparate data sources from many third parties and users, Amazon follows a similar feedback loop to Google and Facebook, even if in somewhat diminished fashion. The loss of control, however, is still there.

For one, Amazon's listings are littered with more errors than they can fix. Different books are combined under a single product heading; products are chronically miscategorized; and pages for discontinued (or nonexistent) products often endure for years. Third-party sellers enter blatantly wrong information and charge absurdly inflated prices, to the apparent indifference of Amazon—whose employees are themselves overwhelmed by the sheer number of *things* sold on the site.[11] With hundreds of millions of products being offered by millions of third-party sellers, how *could* Amazon proactively police its listings in any but the simplest of ways?[12] The most hilarious errors do get noticed and fixed, but only when enough users draw Amazon's attention to them. A series of trade market reports by the Fresh, Chilled and Frozen Horse and Ass Meat Research Group was incorrectly parsed by Amazon as being by three authors: "Chilled the Fresh," "Frozen Horse," and "Ass Meat Research Group."[13] These authors endured for five years before being fixed, and then only as a result of garnering enough online attention.[14] Today, books about Shakespeare are credited to Shakespeare himself, while books that were never published linger on as Amazon product pages.[15] I have waited more than five years for Amazon to notify me of an available copy of Grigol Robakidze's novel *The Snake's Skin*, supposedly published in 2015, but I will never get that notification because the book's Amazon page is in reality a tombstone for a book that never existed.[16] The product, like many of its listings, is simply too marginal for Amazon to have noticed the error.

Despite regularly sweeping its store for contraband and illegitimate merchandise, Amazon has proved unable to crack down effectively on fake products *or* fake reviews.[17] As with Google, there is an "Amazon dance" in which scammers and disreputable entities work around Amazon's imperfect policing mechanisms. Birkenstock announced it had stopped selling on Amazon due to Amazon's inability to crack down on counterfeits, while products under Amazon's own brand names (like AmazonBasics) actually suffered from fake imitations themselves, once more indicating Amazon's inability rather than indifference.[18] A glance at many sorts of popular products, whether laptops or batteries or USB cables, often reveals thousands of obviously fake reviews planted to inflate ratings.

Despite their obvious differences, Amazon and Google's meganets still display the same large-scale phenomena of inaccuracy, fraud, and, above all, feedback. All three problems stem from the same underlying structural issues. Only once we understand this structural similarity across meganets—the recurrence of the same structures and problems—can we have any hope of addressing the problems. Targeting hate speech on Facebook, fake products on Amazon, or spam websites on Google has no effect; a problem common to Google, Facebook, and Amazon will not be resolved by a Facebook-specific solution. Nor will targeted solutions work for the lesser-known but burgeoning meganets that are coming our way under the name of the metaverse.

FOUR

THE MEGANET AS GAME AND COMMERCE

> Make no mistake about it: Computers process numbers—not symbols. We measure our understanding (and control) by the extent to which we can arithmetize an activity.
>
> ALAN J. PERLIS, "Epigrams on Programming"

SOCIAL MEDIA IS THE MOST VISIBLE MANIFESTATION OF THE meganet today, but it is not the most influential. While social media has tremendous power in shaping popular discourse, it is only indirectly connected to flows of money and commerce. That will change as the metaverse (or whatever the next iteration of online life ends up being called) comes into being. In the coming years, monetary value will become the measure of online activity as never before through the wide-scale deployment of cryptocurrency-like technologies across multiple meganets.* With that deployment will come new ways of *valuing* online activity monetarily, turning far more of our

* While present-day cryptocurrencies and cryptocurrency algorithms may or may not serve as the underlying infrastructure for tomorrow's online currencies, the idea of a purely virtual currency common across different online services is here to stay.

lives, online and offline, into commercial activities. These commercial activities will most often take the form of games. Online life feels tremendously unreal to us because of the computational artifice around it all, but the meganet drives that unreality into all parts of the world. The meganet turns life into a game.

THE METAVERSE STRATEGY

The entrepreneurial goal of bringing money and financial transactions more directly into online life has been slow to arrive. Every internet company seeks to monetize some aspect of online existence, but the regulation and complexity of credit card infrastructure made it difficult for websites to access users' wallets; you can't give cash to a website like you would at a grocery store, so some third-party guarantor for the transaction has to be involved. Amazon has succeeded in placing purchases at the absolute center of its business model, but Google and Facebook found their revenue models through advertising, acting as brokers rather than selling products or services directly to consumers. But those veins are running dry, having been thoroughly mined by these three companies.

When Facebook became Meta in late 2021, it signaled a reorientation toward new sources of revenue—but from where? Meta did not have an easy answer, though Facebook's restlessness had been evident for some time. In 2019, Mark Zuckerberg said the age of public social media was over and the future lay in encrypted, private chats.[1] What he didn't say was how Facebook would make money from them—and evidently that answer never did present itself. A terrible earnings report in early 2022 sent Meta's stock plummeting to almost half its peak, losing $200 billion in market cap—the largest one-day decline of any stock in history.[2] Facebook's user base was failing to grow, its existing users were losing interest, and Meta was sinking tremendous amounts of money into its speculative bet-the-company metaverse strategy.[3] In total, it painted a picture of a company admitting the decline of its existing revenue sources and turning to an untested one. Meta seemed far less a titan and much more a moonshot.

By that point, Meta's turn to the metaverse as the company's salvation was clear. *Metaverse* became a wildly lucrative buzzword in 2022, with, as noted earlier, JPMorgan, Morgan Stanley, and Goldman Sachs touting it as a multitrillion-dollar opportunity, even in the absence of a clear revenue strategy.[4] Meta's description of its social VR platform Horizon, "a social experience where you can explore, play and create in extraordinary ways," is so generic as to verge on parody—metacommentary on the metaverse, if you will.

Metaverse promotions focused on virtual reality headsets bringing more "real" experiences to online users. But behind the flash of VR, the metaverse is not a revolution. VR technology itself continues to provide increasingly realistic experiences, but it is not a game changer in the way that the internet itself was. An online house that I can walk around in 3D still isn't one I can sleep in (even if I can sublet it). In the metaverse, people will do things together online—just as they already do. VR will make it increasingly immersive, but all the talk of immersive online experiences belies the fact that we are already well and deeply immersed in online life. Anyone visiting our present time from 1985 would find a world of people glued to their devices, listening to streaming music or talking to people across the country, unable to disconnect because technological threads sustain far too much of their daily existence.

For all of the metaverse being just the same except more so, the real difference is that there will be many more things to buy and many new kinds of things to buy and therefore more money to be made. Since Amazon already dominates the market of offline products, the companies in the metaverse will be marketing online products. The closest analogy here is to online gaming—which is why Microsoft bought the video game company Activision Blizzard as part of its metaverse strategy. Players sell and trade virtual goods in games like World of Warcraft and Pokémon for significant amounts of real-world cash, goods like extremely powerful weapons or digital pets that follow you around. Some gamers have invested thousands to purchase spaceships for the online game Star Citizen, even though the game has yet to be released—the virtual spaceships are themselves funding development of the long-delayed game.[5] All these goods were created out of nowhere by fiat, their value originating purely from their role in a particular online social environment. The metaverse business strategy is to expand these sorts of in-game transactions into the wider online world and thereby merge them with the offline world. The financial key to the metaverse lies not in VR but in gaming and money. In the metaverse, cryptocurrency will provide the money, while global, multiplayer games (or game-like activities) will provide the contexts in which buying and selling will take place. When Microsoft bought Activision Blizzard in early 2022, it did so chiefly to obtain its online gaming network World of Warcraft. CEO Satya Nadella was explicit that gaming would become the heart of the metaverse, not a sideshow. In an interview, he said:

> Metaverse is essentially about creating games. . . . You and I will be sitting on a conference room table soon with either our avatars or our holograms or even 2D surfaces with surround audio. Guess what? The place where we have been doing that forever . . . is gaming. Being great at game building gives us the permission to build this next platform, which is essentially the next internet: the embodied presence. Today, I play a game, but I'm not in the game. Now, we can start dreaming [that] through these metaverses: I can literally be in the game.[6]

Yet traditional online gaming by itself is not sufficient to add up to Goldman Sachs's $8 trillion vision. Just as Google commoditized web pages and Facebook commoditized friendship and shared interests, the emerging vision of the metaverse stakes its financial bet on the commodification of human association itself. This is a step forward from Facebook, which managed friend networks and brought people together in threads but limited their interactions to socialization and apps. In the idealized vision of the metaverse, the basic activities of human existence become commodified so that social groupings of all kinds gain some kind of monetary valuation—enabled through cryptocurrency infrastructure.

Technologically, online gaming and cryptocurrency have little to do with each other. Earlier, I observed that a concept like the metaverse, by encompassing both, became so amorphous it held very little concrete meaning. And if we are limiting ourselves to the technologies underlying online life, that remains true. But while cryptocurrency and online gaming lack a shared technological base, their combination does have very real *financial* consequences for the meganet. Taken together, they allow for the commodification of human life to a far greater scale than has yet been seen.

Both cryptocurrency and online gaming only arose when real-time, massively connected data networks—meganets—had already integrated a huge percentage of the world's population. Grafting cryptocurrency *and* gaming onto the meganet turns the real, global economy into a massively networked game. Through the free-flowing capital of cryptocurrencies, games can now impact and disrupt the world's economy and labor flow in real and significant ways, for better or for worse. The massive crash of cryptocurrencies in mid-2022 was as surprising as their rise, and though many of the particular cryptocurrencies in the crash will die off, the underlying technology of distributed and decentralized virtual money is here to stay, hopefully in less volatile forms. The "metaverse," or whatever we call the next iteration of online existence, will supercharge the meganet's pull on our larger economy. And as always with meganets, the effects of these new economies will not be under our control.

The growth of online fantasy games like World of Warcraft into cryptocurrency-backed mediators of economic and social life is one more story of the inexorable growth of meganets and of the slow loss of control. Online games are meganets as much as Google and Facebook are. The same goes double for cryptocurrency. Turning meganets into real economic entities requires giving up control to them, just as we have already seen with Google and Facebook. But because we will be tying trillion-dollar economies to meganets, the risks will become far greater. Online and offline economies will become indistinguishable, and the unpredictable effects of cryptocurrency—already a hugely volatile market—will resonate strongly in the entire global economy. Everything will be a game.

KNOWING THE SCORE

We normally don't place quantifiable, monetary value on our everyday interactions with others. We don't think of chatting, going for coffee, or attending concerts and sports events as actions that can be assessed in terms of financial value. Consequently, we lack clear metrics to agree on the value of our activities: Is my going to a Spoon concert more or less valuable than your watching a game at Yankee Stadium? But there is one area of activity in which ranking and valuation already exist, whether or not real money is attached to it, and that is games—of all sorts. Games by their nature rank, sort, and assign value to human activity within them. Games set the values by which all players abide; people must agree on them simply to play the game. And that in turn makes it simple to turn those shared values into quantities of money. Turn something into a game, and you can turn it into a market.

That is what the metaverse aims to do. The union of cryptocurrency and gaming in the metaverse is the culmination of existing trends within meganets. Without changing the underlying structure of the meganet, the metaverse will foreground *games* and *money*, with the goal of creating new trillion-dollar economies. In that light, the metaverse is already here, though most people in North America and Europe have yet to feel its pull. But in the third world, where national currencies are less reliable, the online combination of game and money is already in full view.

In the Philippines, septuagenarian convenience store owner Lolo Silverio spent much of the pandemic playing games on his mobile phone for money. When COVID restricted his movement and kept customers from his store, he discovered a Pokémon-like game called Axie Infinity on his mobile phone, which mysteriously promised that he could make money just from playing. By third-world income standards, he earned enough to pay for his medications, and so playing Axie Infinity became his job, consuming hours of every day.[7]

Hundreds of thousands of Filipinos did the same as Silverio, competitively raising and breeding cute digital pets for profit. Axie Infinity's wrinkle is that the whole game is built on top of a Bitcoin-like cryptocurrency (called Smooth Love Potion) earned by playing and winning battles. Smooth Love Potions have exchange value with real currencies, whether US dollars or Filipino pesos. Merely by playing Axie Infinity all day, many Filipinos made more money than they would working overseas in wealthy nations—something that became considerably harder to do in the age of COVID—even if there was no guarantee that Smooth Love Potion would retain its value next year or even tomorrow. In fact, the boom is already over. In the cryptocurrency crash of May 2022, Axie Infinity's cryptocurrency dropped catastrophically from a peak of $0.35 to $0.004, or effectively nothing.[8] While skeptics celebrated the crash and cryptocurrency boosters maintained a punctured optimism, the crash did nothing to invalidate the unsettling truth that these hypervolatile cryptocurrencies are now an integral part of the world economy and are here to stay.

The bizarre phenomenon of third-world workers earning a living by playing games all day on a mobile phone would hardly have made sense twenty years ago: people making real money by playing a lightweight game with no concrete rewards. Such injections of money and commerce into even the most unlikely aspects of online life will only increase. Money's intrinsic universalizing force ensures that.[9] Money and the meganet were made for each other. The forces of volume, velocity, and virality, the exponentially increasing computational power at our disposal, and the natural human urge to acquire and compete not only made cryptocurrency inevitable, but they also invariably bring us dodgy "play-to-earn" games like Axie Infinity.

Games are serious business; today the gaming industry is larger than Hollywood. No longer solo endeavors on individual computers as they were in the 1980s and 1990s, the most successful games today join together players in real time and often in real life. Later in this chapter, we will examine Axie Infinity and its ilk far more closely, but first we must pull back and look at both the nature of games and the nature of computation, and why money grafts so easily onto both of them. That will explain why it is that soon our own online lives will be gamified and commodified, just like that Filipino store owner who briefly earned a living playing games all day.

THE GAME OF MONEY

Computers are brilliant with numbers. In human terms, that translates into the maxim that computers are brilliant at *keeping score*. Any measurement we care to make is recorded, preserved, compared, and republished many times over by the meganet. Measurements do not have to even be made numerically for them to be computer-friendly. Simply restrict the options to a well-defined list—whether it's a list of hobbies, movies, genders, races, Pokémon, or so much else—and computers will prove perfect at tracking, comparing, and cross-referencing people and things across an endless variety of metrics.

Keeping score is something we do while playing games. Keeping score is also something we do in our occupations, in our personal relationships, and in our finances. Computers have quickly taken up scorekeeping tasks across all these arenas of life. Yet for all the different ways of measuring people and things, only one form of measurement comes even close to being universal. Pokémon combat ratings are obviously only meaningful to the Pokémon players, but broader measurements and categories aren't necessarily good for scorekeeping either. Race or gender, for example, make for poor metrics. As much as we talk about race and gender today, there are no uniform, agreed-upon ways to make comparisons within each of those two categories—quite the opposite, as incessant, endless debates prove.[10] Rather, the one store of measurement that has unstoppable, universalizing force and forces reconciliation even when there is disagreement is money.

The human urge to compete impels people to do things for no clear reason other than getting ahead of others. The human urge to play impels people to do things for no clear reason other than fun. When a storm hits in Caracas, Kyoto, or Peoria, a handful of people will run out into the storm following an alert from their mobile phone. They aren't being warned about the storm. Rather, the storm has triggered their phones to lead them to a particular spot where they can catch a cute animal that they badly want, cute animals that only come out in especially bad or unusual weather. These aren't real animals, of course, but virtual pets deployed by the servers of the mobile Pokémon GO game. The Pokémon mantra, "Gotta catch them all," sends millions of players dashing around in rain and snow to collect rare Pokémon, which the players then train to fight other players' pets. Cryptocurrency, as Axie Infinity discovered, neatly ties this competitive gaming to an economic model that is truly part of the "real" economy instead of a walled-off play economy. Win the game, and you are winning at life, and quantifiably so.

The meganet's unmatched capacities for quantitative assessment, tracking, and ranking pushes its participants toward two kinds of activity: commerce and games. Both translate human activity into data that represents some kind of uniform statistical *valuation*: revenue, profit, points, views, followers. While AI has achieved astonishing feats of reading facial expressions and recognizing visual objects, this work is almost always in the service of reducing complex inputs into a well-ordered, ranked taxonomy, translating analog reality into digital classifications and statistics. The meganet thrives on that digital information: once shorn of the complexities of deep learning (the field of AI that attempts to find buried patterns in less-structured data) the meganet's algorithms overwhelmingly operate on transmitting, securing, and comparing information that is essentially numerical or categorical.* Sometimes these comparisons are piled on top of one another to the point of being incomprehensible, as with Google's or Facebook's ranking algorithms, but the inputs and the outputs are nearly always simple statistics or rankings. The meganet has turned games into commerce and commerce into a game.

* If it is not explicitly numerical, the information is simple enough to be represented and compared numerically. The outcome of a sports game is two scores that can be numerically compared. A product listing is a set of metadata identifiers that categorize it along dozens of axes.

ONLINE CURRENCIES

As it transforms play economies into real economies, ignoring geographical and temporal boundaries, the meganet joins virtual worlds to real ones. It collapses the barriers between home, work, and play. Herein lies the history of how games turned into reality, and how two threads of the meganet—multiplayer *games* like World of Warcraft and multiplayer *economies* like Bitcoin—combined to form the metaverse. Such games are the prototypes for online life in the future.

We already read how Microsoft bought Activision Blizzard, the creator of World of Warcraft, to form the basis of its metaverse strategy, and Facebook has long profited off more casual games. Fortnite and Minecraft have become staples of adolescent and preadolescent life, supplanting television as the talk of schoolyards. Mobile "casual" games like Clash of Clans, Pokémon GO, and Candy Crush Saga, which all bring their users together in social competition with one another, have become billion-dollar gold mines for their creators and permanent aspects of people's recreational landscapes.[11] Such mobile games grossed over $100 billion in total in 2021.[12] With almost three billion people playing mobile games in 2021, these games are not just a sideshow; they are as essential to online (and offline) life as social networks and an ever-increasing part of the global economy.[13]

These games are also more profitable than traditional social networks, which is why the distinction between a social network and a game will be increasingly blurred in forthcoming years. Such games will become the fundamental substrate of online life, and their economies will be anything but a game. Online life will exist alongside offline life as a basic driver of the world economy, and this life will increasingly take the form of games of one kind or another. Some games will be recreational; others will be status oriented. And some, like the "game" of cryptocurrency trading and boosting, will be far more important than that. The obsessive players of the past are the everyday citizens of tomorrow. Online life will look more like a game, but as money increasingly becomes the means of keeping score, these games will feel increasingly real.

While money has been slow to enter online life, it is not for lack of effort on the part of entrepreneurs, who have diligently tried to yoke payments to online activities. When it came to online financial transactions, logistical and regulatory difficulties slowed the path to an outcome that now seems to have been inevitable. Money came late to the internet (and thus to the meganet) because paper money could not be exchanged virtually; it took two decades for the infrastructure for authorizing credit card payments in a distributed and secure manner to be constructed. Venmo and Zelle have finally allowed people to send money to each other virtually without too much hassle, more than twenty years after the birth of internet commerce.

Historically, websites and web services have only had access to the wallets of a minority of visitors. To collect money directly from a user, it was usually necessary to create an account, give a credit card number, or introduce some intermediary responsible for setting up financial transactions (and taking a cut). The dream of "microtransactions," in which a user could pay a website a small tip for a piece of content, fell prey to overhead and the inefficiencies of small-scale transactions. As for that majority of users who could not pay for content, sites monetized them indirectly through advertising. For many years, advertising was the preferred way to make money from websites, with a large middleman like Google or Facebook taking a chunk of the profits in exchange for administering and policing the advertising infrastructure.

With the online advertising market now saturated, Google, Facebook, and Amazon can no longer obtain exponential gains in revenue year over year. Worse, diminishing returns and increasingly pushy ads led to the rise of ad blockers, and Apple and Google have significantly restricted the ability for advertisers to profile and target users by allowing users to opt out of activity tracking.[14] Facebook's near-50 percent stock price crash in early 2022 was by far the most significant indicator that online advertising had passed its peak.

Behind the rise and stagnation of online advertising, new "currencies" began to arise over the last twenty years, but ones that were not convertible into cash—at least not directly. Reddit Gold, for example, is awarded by users to other users who make especially well-liked posts. Twitter likes and retweets are nothing if not currencies of attention. Their cash value, however, is dubious. Views do not equate to revenue, and seeing an advertisement does not equate to a sale. There is no substitute for legal tender, or at least not for quantifiable commodities that have explicit exchange rates with actual money. Where most newspapers and magazines once put up their content for free online with the hope that attention would net them revenue, Facebook by itself was able to trigger what one media analyst termed a media "apocalypse" merely by adjusting its news feed to deprioritize news stories.[15] Today, nearly all big names in news (from the *New York Times* to the *Economist*) gate the majority of their content behind paywalls, and even free sites like the *Guardian* intrusively ask for donations. Subscriptions and direct payments have become more viable for content providers than advertising. Sites like Patreon and OnlyFans allow artists, charities, and sex workers to set up personal pages for soliciting recurring donations. Trusting Facebook or Google to translate "free" activity (users viewing content) into hard cash turned out to be neither a safe nor reliable revenue model.

Having finally begun to suffuse the virtual world instead of being localized to large commercial sites and services like PayPal, money will never leave it. Oddball ideas like Bitcoin originate all the time, but most of them do not involve the creation of a new asset class. Bitcoin's novel decentralization of financial transactions has turned it into a meme and a virus at the same time, spreading easily without any *apparent* need for centralized advocacy or management (though there are, as we will see, some wrinkles here). But the development of new, online-only economies began long before Bitcoin in the realm of multiplayer gaming. It was there that entire economies—"toy" economies that worked just like real ones—blossomed, awaiting connection with the real world. It is there we see most clearly what meganets will bring us once the metaverse is in full swing.

FARMING GOLD

Online gamers have known for twenty years what the rest of us are only learning now: once real money enters a virtual world and people invest their own wealth in the evolution of a game world, a meganet gains a new sphere of influence to spread its chaos. Money more than anything else connects these once-isolated realms of play to the greater economies of the world, and once those play realms grow to sufficient size, a game like Axie Infinity can exert as much force on our world as a small nation.

Today World of Warcraft (Warcraft for short) is one of the most venerable online role-playing games (to be precise: a massively multiplayer online role-playing game, or MMORPG), and it remains one of the most successful. In 2005, Warcraft was the most popular MMORPG in the world, with six million subscribers spending anywhere from several to hundreds of hours a month running, fighting, and questing with their online avatar inside a 3D fantasy world.[16] In 2022, Microsoft saw enough promise in it to purchase its parent company Activision Blizzard (Blizzard for short) as a key element of its metaverse strategy.[17]

Warcraft is built around measurable objectives of progress. A character, with race (in the sense of an elf, orc, human, etc.), gender, and skills chosen by the player, begins at level one, then, via completing quests assigned by the in-game universe, advances by acquiring experience points (XP) across the fantasy land of Azeroth, exploring dungeons, killing bosses, and grabbing treasure. With greater XP comes increase in player level, though the growth in required XP is exponential rather than linear: while a player can progress from level 1 to level 10 in hours, the progression from level 50 to level 60 (the maximum in 2005) can take weeks of play.

Warcraft has its own internal currency, "gold," used for buying and selling in-game items either directly from in-game merchants run by Blizzard, or from other players via an in-game auction house. Gold is not easy to come by in large quantities. Players must devote hours of play to repetitive "grinding" tasks to accumulate enough gold to afford various perks, like a fast-traveling animal mount, or to purchase rare equipment from other players. Extremely rare, "epic" weapons and armor drop from enemies only a tiny percentage of the time and so draw significant prices in auction. With many players desperate for such items to make their characters that much stronger, obtaining sufficient gold can appear an interminable task—unless you were to pay someone else for it, with *real* money. Officially, Blizzard has always banned the purchase of gold with real money, but policing such transactions is difficult: if I happen to hand you 50,000 gold in Warcraft, who is to say whether you sent $500 to my PayPal account, which is otherwise completely unconnected to Warcraft? Perhaps I was just feeling extremely generous.

Blizzard did not intend for Warcraft gold to have any real-world exchange value. It was purely an in-game mechanism of keeping score, like XP. Yet meganets by their nature seek to grow, spread, and merge, and Blizzard's self-contained economy spilled outside of Warcraft's fantasy world of Azeroth. With many, many such gold-purchasing transactions taking place, real-world money flowed into Warcraft's toy economy without Blizzard seeing a penny of it, a true laissez-faire system. Warcraft's economy merged with the real world. In practice, there was now a genuine exchange rate between Warcraft gold and US dollars (and thus any other real currency)—not exactly fixed or stable but indisputably real.

All this gold needed to come from somewhere. The easiest way to obtain it was through literal "mining" within the game: holding the mouse button down while standing in front of a yellow-veined rock in order to generate gold—tediously but steadily. That repetitive task made real money—not enough for a first-world worker as a full-time job but more than enough to pay overseas labor to sit in front of a computer, clicking on Warcraft rocks. "Gold farming" became a lucrative industry, particularly in China, where wages and the cost of living were far lower than in first-world countries and workers could earn a living sitting in front of a computer and mining gold for over twelve hours a day. This was as real a job as any other, more profitable than working in many factories and far safer given the absence of heavy machinery and workplace accidents.

Researcher Ge Jin interviewed some of these gold farmers for his documentary *Gold Farmers*, many of whom seemed grateful just to have a job, though others bemoaned the sweatshop-like working conditions:

> Actually this job is not easy. You have to sit there every day, even if you are in a bad mood. You still have to be glued to that computer.[18]

In 2008, researcher Richard Heeks estimated that four hundred thousand people were engaged in gold farming, the overwhelming majority of them based in China.[19] Gold farm owner Tie Tou in Shanghai observed that selling farmed gold to Americans was "the same as transmitting Chinese labor, virtually," an unregulated globalization of the Warcraft economy in which Chinese labor was sold to American players.[20] This globalized commerce and lack of regulation mark gold mining as a precursor of cryptocurrency.

Despite lacking the decentralized freedom of cryptocurrency, miners and buyers were ingenious in creating an intra-Warcraft economy without the involvement of Blizzard. The business of gold mining became attractive and prestigious enough to draw the attention of future Trump administration Svengali Steve Bannon. Internet Gaming Entertainment (IGE), a Hong Kong–based company, had been founded in the early 2000s by the twenty-something Brock Pierce, a former child actor who had moved to Hong Kong and employed a hundred Chinese workers to play Warcraft eighty hours a week for meager wages.[21] In 2007, then investment banker Bannon hooked up with IGE after leaving Goldman Sachs, negotiating a $60 million investment from his former company and joining the board of IGE.[22]

Blizzard, needless to say, had little to no control over these developments, nor did they even profit much from them beyond collecting subscription fees from gold miners. The company subsequently cracked down on gold farmers, shutting down thousands of accounts and more or less killing IGE in the process, but gold farming survived

Blizzard's policing, resulting in in-game inflation that continues to this day.[23] Their meganet was spinning off on its own.

It wasn't just the internal economy of Warcraft that shifted in unexpected directions. The unregulated currency transfers and performance of remote labor, even in a toy currency like Warcraft gold, appealed to desperate workers outside China as well. When Venezuela's political crises, economic depression, and hyperinflation reached fever pitch in 2017, citizens there also turned to farming currency in Warcraft-like games such as Runescape because those unregulated virtual currencies were more stable than Venezuela's own national currency—at least initially. In turn, Venezuelan-based mining triggered hyperinflation in those virtual economies and the ensuing rage of players, who railed against Venezuelans in online forums.[24]

These virtual economies don't merely globalize unregulated labor; they also globalize inflation. As there is no limit to the amount of gold that can theoretically be farmed, the influx of farmers led to chronic, long-term inflation within the Warcraft economy. Blizzard had little control as the most elite and rarest swords, axes, helms, and gloves soared in price on the Warcraft auction house. Blizzard couldn't limit new gold generated, or else it would create artificial scarcity and favor rich players over poor players. It couldn't revoke gold from players who had bought it, lest those players quit and depress Blizzard's user base. And identifying gold miners in the first place was an endless game of Whac-A-Mole. Once trading gold for money had started, Blizzard's failure (or inability) to put a stop to it caused the problem to grow to the point that no fix short of turning back time could undo the growth of a black-market economy Blizzard had never intended. Blizzard's world had escaped its control. Whatever gains Blizzard saw through its meganet's economy bleeding into the real world were negated by the problems the meganet caused for Blizzard, problems over which it had no more control than Mark Zuckerberg does over extremist postings on Facebook. As a meganet, Warcraft could not be reversed or reset.

Inflation continues to plague Warcraft twenty years after the initial boom in gold farming. It has led to an explosion of amateur economics among Warcraft players. In 2019, a player writing for Warcraft fansite Blizzard Watch put the problem simply: "How would you soft reset World of Warcraft's in-game economy?"[25] In other words: How could you undo the hyperinflation in Warcraft gold while preserving the meaningful differences in status and assets among existing players? To put it yet another way: How can you eliminate gold generated by farmers without eliminating the gold obtained through proper "fun" playing?

When phrased in that final form, the problem reveals itself as insoluble. Liquid currency does not carry a sticker on it detailing how it was obtained. Blizzard does not have sufficient omnipotence within its virtual world to track all gold acquisitions and eliminate only the farmed ones. Since much of that gold has been laundered through multiple transactions, many players don't even know that they may possess farmed gold that contributed to hyperinflation. Worse, gold farmers themselves can simply launder gold into other commodities, like expensive player gear, that wouldn't be touched by any crackdown on gold. But players, expecting that a game should be *fair* and *controlled* in a way that real life isn't, understandably object when their escapist entertainment falls prey to real-world economic landmines. This wishful thinking is on full display in posts on the official Blizzard forums, such as this one from early 2021:

> We need a fresh restart instead. And a GM [Game Master] team that does nothing but ban bots all day. And actually, they shouldn't outright ban, just move them to a prisoner island server. . . . Then anyone who buys gold should be also transferred to prisoner island server where they can swipe their credit card to their heart's content but it won't break other servers' economies.[26]

Other players immediately pointed out how such proposals were both unworkable and unhelpful. The author of this post wanted to treat the economy as a collection of individual actors, punishing the bad ones while benefiting the good ones. But the very nature of an economy is that it cannot be controlled in such a way: beyond a certain level of complexity, there is little evidence of central planning actually working. And no doubt Blizzard's economy of millions of players had reached that level. But the author of this post went beyond that and also wanted to start from scratch, unaware that resetting an economy would inevitably be grossly unfair to most participants in that economy. Yet one can forgive this player for wishing that Blizzard could simply *fix* the problem by turning Warcraft into a police state where all individual transactions are monitored and players are disciplined not just for explicit breaking of the rules but also for any sign of suspicious "ungamer-like" activity. We have all idly wished for a reset button on this or that, to go back to before things were so bollixed up. You can reboot a computer, or reinstall the operating system. But you cannot reboot a meganet.

The question the author implicitly asks is why Warcraft can't be more of a *game* and less of an *economy*. A game is fully controlled; an economy is an organic system. A game can be reset or restored to an earlier point; an economy can't. Warcraft, like Facebook, Google, and all meganets that interact with commerce, can be influenced by both administrators and users, but the system itself has taken on an autonomous existence. No one, not even Blizzard, controls the flow and price of Warcraft gold. Blizzard retains the nuclear option of forcefully redistributing gold among players or even resetting or eliminating it as a currency, but these tactics would be so disruptive and unpredictable that as many players would revolt as would welcome them. As with Facebook and Google, Blizzard is stuck with the meganet it has created, and we all are stuck with the impact of this meganet's toy economy, which turns out not to be a toy at all. The Warcraft economy's impact on the greater world economy is comparatively small—but it need not be.

PANDEMIC

Gold mining and virtual inflation reveal one way a meganet can get out of control, impacting both its own realm and the greater world through the distributed actions of many players. But an equally strong risk of destabilization exists from the inherent instability of complex and imperfect meganets. A meganet does not need a bug to get out of control, but the right bug can accelerate the loss of control millions of times over. A meganet's noneconomic chaos can compound its economic chaos, leading to a perfect storm.

In 2005, long before COVID, a deadly plague killed tens of thousands of people, only to kill them again and again after the dead repeatedly resurrected. It threw a world into chaos—just not our world. The plague was called Corrupted Blood, and it remains one of the most infamous events in the history of Warcraft. The plague, wholly unintended by Blizzard, rendered the game so nonfunctional that Blizzard was forced to briefly shut down its servers completely, an ugly and desperate move.

From early on in Warcraft's history, keeping veteran players engaged with new challenges and content was one of Blizzard's top priorities, alongside attracting new low-level players to the game. Veterans and "noobs" (new players) also had to coexist in reasonable peace, so high-ranking players could not simply ride by and idly slaughter dozens of newbies for fun. Areas of the game were assigned difficulty ranks describing roughly how powerful a character had to be to have a chance of surviving. A level 1 character with 100 hit points would lose not only a fight with a level 60 character with 6,000 hit points but also a fight with any monster that the level 60 character would be likely to encounter.

In late 2005, Blizzard introduced a new elite dungeon (termed a "raid") called Zul'Gurub, presided over by a very difficult and very nasty boss, Hakkar the Soul Flayer. Twenty top-level players were required to enter the dungeon for a try at defeating Hakkar. Hakkar had a spell, Corrupted Blood, which would infect players fighting him like a disease, causing the infected characters' hit points to drop by about a thousand over four seconds.[27] Uniquely, Corrupted Blood was *contagious*, meaning infected players could pass it on to other players nearby. Four seconds was not enough time for players to carry the plague out of Zul'Gurub and into more generally populated areas, so the contagion could not spread beyond the twenty players in the dungeon.

Or so it seemed. A loophole, not known to Blizzard, existed. Corrupted Blood could infect player pets as well—cute creatures that followed players around and sometimes did battle alongside them—and pets had the unique ability to be summoned and dismissed at any time. When dismissed, a pet was effectively put in suspended animation, freezing its condition at that time. That meant that whenever it was resummoned, the pet would be in exactly the same state it was when it had been dismissed. If it had been infected with Corrupted Blood during a fight with Hakkar and dismissed within four seconds, the pet would still be infected for a few seconds when resummoned. And if a player resummoned an infected pet in a heavily populated area, such as one of the hub cities of the Warcraft world, those few seconds would be enough time for the pet to infect dozens of others.

A number of malicious players, termed "griefers," did exactly this, aggressively spreading the plague across the entirety of Warcraft.[28] Once the infection was out in the wild, the effect was catastrophic. Lower-level players died instantly. Higher-level players survived, only to pass along the infection to others and then get reinfected. Characters resurrected, only to then be reinfected and die again. Immortal, computer-controlled non-player characters (NPCs) were continually reinfected and didn't die, passing along the virus to everyone who happened to walk by.[29] Dead bodies filled the streets of every city.

For four days, World of Warcraft was utterly changed and well-nigh unplayable. Select players retreated to isolated areas, only to find that there wasn't much left to do. High-level healers tried to mitigate the damage, fighting a losing battle. One player commented:

> There are three things you can do: infect people, die, and watch other people do the first two. There's no way to rush for a cure; there's no way to stop the plagued idiots from coming in, there's no quest, no change, no nothing.[30]

Thanks to the efforts of only a handful of people, the game had transformed utterly in less than an hour's time. At first, Blizzard attempted to contain the plague by asking players to quarantine themselves and restarting servers where infection had gotten out of hand, but griefers continually reintroduced the plague. The plague spread faster than Blizzard could clean it up, with overwhelming volume, velocity, and (literal) virality.[31] Eventually, Blizzard modified the code to restrict Corrupted Blood to Zul'Gurub and restarted every single server.[32] It took four days—an eternity in online time—for Blizzard to fix the issue for good.

In the wake of COVID-19, researchers have debated whether or not Corrupted Blood could serve as a viable model of a real-world pandemic.[33] Whether it does or not, Corrupted Blood certainly models the out-of-control feedback effects of meganets. The entire Warcraft economy was uprooted during those four days, with most players unable even to access the auction houses that lay in the plague-ridden cities. Both the system *and* the players were racing ahead of the company that had birthed the system but no longer controlled it. In the hours after the pandemic exploded, self-organized groups of players were better able to mitigate the spread than Blizzard itself. As economist Peter C. Earle put it:

> The player-coordinated response to the pandemic, hours (and perhaps longer) before World of Warcraft's game managers got involved—perhaps before they even understood the dimensions of the virtual disaster—was voluntary, emergent, and with small groups of survivors gathering in the distant wilds of World of Warcraft, arguably effective.[34]

Even in their spontaneous, collective response, players only exerted very partial control over the course of the pandemic. Yet it was not the code itself racing out of control but the larger situation of buggy code when it was deployed on a huge network with users exacerbating and accelerating the unintended consequences of the buggy code. Whether those users were taking those steps intentionally, as the griefers did, or unintentionally, as with anyone who happened to log on and got repeatedly infected, the chaos arose from the interaction of the meganet's three necessary components: the programmers, the networked servers, and the users. The result was a mess that neither its programmers nor its users could control until the whole world was shut down and rebooted.

It is tempting to see the Corrupted Blood incident as a funny lark in an imaginary world, a quirky bug specific to the domain of online games. But meganets throw these kinds of plagues at larger systems as well, and sometimes they cannot be reset. As long as a game remains firmly isolated within its own virtual world, the opportunity frequently exists for the operators of the game to play god and partially reset the system, undoing unexpected damage. As we saw with gold farming, however, once money and financial transactions enter the picture, the scope for action is far more limited. The distance between Corrupted Blood and a global financial meltdown is smaller than you think—the right combination of currency exchanges, sudden shocks, fraud, and theft could destabilize larger markets, especially as institutional players come to invest more heavily in cryptocurrencies, making the cryptocurrency crash of mid-2022 seem like a minor blip. Short of a total collapse of faith in the very idea of cryptocurrency, these new kinds of assets will only grow in influence, bringing with them the meganet's loss of control and its associated risks.

POKÉMONEY

In hindsight, the integration of gaming and cryptocurrency on the meganet was inevitable. Players get intensely invested in games like Warcraft—emotionally and financially. The closer one's "scores" in a game get to actual real-life money, the more meaningful that investment becomes. Microsoft bought Activision Blizzard in the hopes of placing gaming at the heart of the internet, while Facebook has always sought to gamify its existing social interactions. While these moves have been termed "metaverse plays," they are in fact amplifications of existing meganet trends, just as the metaverse more generally is.

In the 2000s, meganet economies were largely restricted to the biggest corporations and corporate MMORPGs like Warcraft and EVE Online. The subsequent explosion of virtual economies began before cryptocurrency, with the rise of "pay-to-win" games, in which players are heavily encouraged to pay money above and beyond the purchase price of a game (which is usually free) so they can progress much, much faster in the game. FarmVille, as we saw earlier, is the classic example of such a game. Having seen how much money gold farmers made, it's little surprise that game developers decided that they would cut out the unexpected middlemen and sell their own currency direct to users. Even as cryptocurrency loomed in the background, these in-game currencies showed what uses cryptocurrency could be put to. The two threads were not yet joined, but they were approaching each other.

The lure of the cute pet creatures of Niantic's wildly popular mobile game Pokémon GO (part of Nintendo's mammoth Pokémon franchise) attracted 150 million users and $1 billion in revenue in 2020, with further growth expected.[35] Pokémon GO is an augmented reality mobile game in which players must go to real-life locations indicated by the game app in order to "catch" wild Pokémon to train and also meet other players with whom to do battle. Niantic controls which Pokémon creatures get deployed in its game world, as well as where and how frequently, with the most powerful and unusual creatures appearing only rarely, depending on variables like the weather and time of year. By combining an obsessive collector mentality, adorable anthropomorphic creatures, and the competitive instinct innate to humans, Pokémon GO keeps its players glued to their phones, running around their neighborhoods. It is as though a meganet has extended its tendrils into real life.

Once caught, Pokémons must be trained to have the best chance of beating other players' Pokémons in battle, and here is where money enters the picture. The process of training one's pets is long and tedious, but it can be ameliorated with the use of special items bought using the in-game currency, PokéCoins. Like Warcraft gold, PokéCoins are used to buy in-game items, but unlike Warcraft, Niantic will gladly sell you PokéCoins themselves, for about one cent per PokéCoin. While it's possible to obtain PokéCoins in game with some effort, it is vastly more efficient to purchase them. Because PokéCoins speed up the rate of game progression drastically, this makes Pokémon GO one of many "free-to-play/pay-to-win" games, like FarmVille, Clash of Clans, and Runescape, in which the cost of playing is minimal or even zero, but where spending money can give a player a leg up on other players as well as making play far less tedious. It's not that the game is unplayable without spending extra money, but judging by the revenues of the companies making such games, the incentive to spend more is certainly powerful.

The PokéCoin economy is comparatively small, more of a toy economy than a real one, but there's nothing necessarily keeping it that way. PokéCoins, like Warcraft gold, have a rate of exchange just like real currencies, and their buying power increases and decreases in relation to economic developments. PokéCoins *can* generate real-world value, albeit indirectly: Pokémon GO accounts with especially valuable items can sell for thousands or even tens of thousands of dollars.[36] What's bought and sold is nothing more than the ability to play in different ways, but that is sufficient for Pokémon GO to possess a legitimate economy.

Like Warcraft gold, PokéCoins are not so different from real-world money—even more so, since Niantic intended PokéCoins to be in-game equivalents for real-world money. Warcraft gold was intended to be a within-universe measure of value with no use or meaning outside Warcraft's servers. Niantic, on the other hand, sets an explicit and fixed exchange rate for PokéCoin and dollars, though they cannot enforce the rate outside its own store. (Though Niantic attempts to position itself as the only seller of PokéCoins, third-party apps and sellers do indeed exist, selling PokéCoins at a discount in exchange for the risk of the buyer being banned or scammed.) In setting an exchange rate, though, Niantic immediately ran up against real-world economic problems. Because the cost of living varies so drastically among countries in which Pokémon GO players live, Niantic varies its exchange rates between PokéCoins depending on what currency they are bought in, effectively making PokéCoins drastically cheaper in many foreign currencies. Savvy players engage in what is effectively currency arbitrage by tricking the Pokémon GO mobile app into thinking that their phone is in a different country, one with cheaper PokéCoin costs. Though technically against the rules, this kind of deception has become popular enough to have its own Reddit forum, PokemonGoSpoofing.[37]

All this financial manipulation is not in the service of profit, since the easiest way to profit would simply be to stop playing Pokémon GO entirely, but for the players' fun and competition. However much Niantic loses to the arbitrage, it's surely only a small percentage next to what it still rakes in from selling currency that the company itself mints. Nonetheless, Niantic still runs the long-term risk of the sort of inflation Blizzard saw in Warcraft because meganet economics ensures that even with its own currency, Niantic still has less control over its economy than it thinks.

PokéCoins and other such currencies are the next step to our ultimate destination: cryptocurrency. It was only a matter of time before someone put two and two together and realized that Pokémon and Bitcoin bore some very significant similarities. Both create valuable virtual commodities out of thin air, relying on the enthusiasm of their communities to grant real-world financial value to those commodities. Cryptocurrency, however, attempts to turn the meganet's fault into a virtue, by exerting control not centrally but algorithmically—with only partial success.

SMOOTH LOVE POTIONS

The drive to monetize every aspect of life—to turn game scores into the real score of money—has increased rapidly with the spread of cryptocurrency. What better way to attract noncryptocurrency aficionados into the world of the blockchain than to turn the quasi-game of acquiring, mining, staking, and trading cryptocurrencies into a full-on game. Placing cryptocurrency at the heart of a game-like activity—as the metaverse aims to do—will further open the real economy to gaming's toy economies, bringing the meganet's chaotic forces with them.

Cryptocurrency is already a shadowy yet huge part of the global economy. Beyond Bitcoin, Ethereum, Tether, and other popular coins, the oddest cryptocurrency yet might be Smooth Love Potion (SLP), the cryptocurrency backing the casual multiplayer game Axie Infinity. Axie Infinity, created by Vietnamese developer Sky Mavis, is no more and no less than Pokémon crossed with Bitcoin. The spectacular rise and equally abrupt fall of Smooth Love Potion gives us a small glimpse of what the metaverse might look like when its twin poles of games and cryptocurrency are looming over all of online (and part of offline) life. When combined, the two can have profound effects worldwide—effects over which, as now should be expected, we will have only limited control.

Here is Sky Mavis's vision, set out in the Axie Infinity whitepaper:

> We believe in a future where work and play become one.
> We believe in empowering our players and giving them economic opportunities.
> Most of all, we have a dream that battling and collecting cute creatures can change the world.
> Welcome to our revolution.[38]

Despite the inflated rhetoric, the nature of cryptocurrencies combined with the magnifying power of the meganet puts Sky Mavis's vision unsettlingly close to reality.

□□□

CRYPTOCURRENCIES LIKE BITCOIN and Ethereum are intrinsically worthless. Like money, they only gain inherent utility after being exchanged into something else. Sky Mavis's insight was that just as PokéCoins and Warcraft gold have value within their artificial worlds, so could a cryptocurrency. To avoid dreaded regulation and legal liability, game companies need to keep legal tender out of their artificial worlds. That restriction does not apply to cryptocurrency, which is not (yet) legal tender. So cryptocurrency can be the native store of value for a game *and* have all the properties of a cryptocurrency outside of the game at the same time.

Axie Infinity grants one very particular in-game usage to its own cryptocurrency: like PokéCoins, Smooth Love Potions can be used to win a game—or at least, win more often. There are actually two levels of cryptographic assets in Axie Infinity. First, there is Smooth Love Potion (SLP), the cryptocurrency itself, which functions akin to a typical cryptocurrency like Bitcoin or Ethereum. Second, there are the Axies, the game's Pokémon equivalents, which are unique cryptographic tokens (also known as non-fungible tokens or NFTs) rather than a currency. Axies, like all NFTs, are distinct, individual objects that are assigned indisputable ownership through the distributed consensus mechanism of the blockchain. We will be discussing Bitcoin and the blockchain in the next chapter, but the salient point here is that the blockchains ensure that everyone playing Axie Infinity agrees on who owns which Axie, just as they agree on how many Smooth Love Potions everyone has, and not even Sky Mavis can arbitrarily or unilaterally revoke that ownership. Where Blizzard could potentially reset the Warcraft economy, even if it would be extremely damaging and unwise to do so, Axie Infinity's economy can *never* be reset.*

The economic cycle of Axie Infinity takes place with Smooth Love Potions as the currency and Axies as the assets. To get started, a player needs a team of three Axies. Three entry-level Axies currently will run you about $1,000 and serve as a buy-in cost to the Axie economy.[39] (The most expensive Axies have sold for over $100,000.)[40] Like Pokémon, your Axies then fight with other monsters and other Axies to improve their skills and win Smooth Love Potions, which is where the Axie economy kicks into high gear.

Unlike Bitcoin, which is held and traded more than it is spent, Smooth Love Potions have one easily accessible and popular use, which is that they allow you to breed new Axies from existing ones—which in turn can be sold on the marketplace to players looking for new or better Axies. If this has the whiff of a pyramid scheme, in which a stream

* As we will see in the next chapter, this isn't entirely true, but it is vastly truer than it is for any nonblockchain game economy. Even the smallest reset is extremely painful in a blockchain system.

of new players is required to generate profits for old players, the rarity of elite Axies goes some ways to legitimizing the Smooth Love Potion economy. New players keep the prices of low-grade Axies afloat—but old players are equally willing to bid far more for those rare, elite Axies. Axie Infinity does not have the structure of a pyramid scheme. If Axies still *feel* like a pyramid scheme, it's only in the greater sense that the entire world is a pyramid scheme, in that our very notion of monetary value is dependent on the ubiquitous expectation that some potential buyer exists to pay an established price for some thing or service or fuzzy little digital asset—even if no such buyer ever appears.

Meganets remove these circles of value and expectation that much further from concrete reality, revealing their artificiality more baldly. And Axie Infinity is undoubtedly a meganet: it algorithmically joins people who act in real time and respond to each other. The parent company mints its own cryptocurrency but can only loosely control its exchange rate with real money or other cryptocurrencies. Collective player action can send prices soaring or plummeting without any recourse. Even if Axie Infinity is not a pyramid scheme, its economy is nonetheless extremely unstable and can come crashing down at any time, by internal or external causes.

Which is precisely what has happened. As of this writing, the Smooth Love Potion economy has collapsed from a mid-2021 high of 35 cents to a current all-time low of half a cent. The rise had been as meteoric as its collapse. In April 2021, Axie Infinity had fewer than 50,000 daily users, but by August the game had ballooned to 900,000 daily users, while Smooth Love Potion wandered between a market cap of $100 to $200 million.[41] Axie Infinity caught on in the Philippines in particular, whose citizens currently contribute half its user base. Gabby Dizon, a Filipino evangelist for the "play-to-earn" model, described Axie Infinity's rapid growth when COVID abruptly cut off worker mobility:

> Axie Infinity exploded in the rural Philippines last year during the first wave of Covid-19 lockdowns. People were stuck at home with no income, looking for ways to earn money to live. Most people never knew that you could earn from gaming.[42]

Cryptocurrency observer Luis Buenaventura theorized that the revolutionary thing about Axie Infinity was allowing Filipino workers to pull in first-world level income without having to emigrate out of their home country to become Overseas Filipino Workers (OFWs).

> The average player can earn 4,500 $SLP a month, so if we assume that about a third of those Pinoy players are playing at the optimal level, they are collectively going to earn 222,750,000 $SLP this month. How much is $SLP in peso terms? Well, as of this week, it's over 9 pesos each, which means that these kids are cumulatively going to be raking in around 2 BILLION PESOS this month. To put that into perspective: 2 billion pesos is the average amount of remittances that ALL the OFWs living in Hong Kong send back home to the Philippines each month. But there are 800,000 of them stationed there! And don't even get me started on how exploitative their living conditions are. Meanwhile, these Axie gamers are playing from their own bedrooms 3-4 hours a day, and making 4x as much.[43]

Yet in 2022 this entire economy evaporated in days. At present prices, Axie Infinity is no longer viable, but there's nothing preventing the next Axie Infinity from coming along and mobilizing another country's economy in some wild, unpredictable direction. Even the events that spurred the SLP crash were geopolitical. On March 23, 2022, hackers compromised Sky Mavis's blockchain and stole over $600 million worth of cryptocurrency, including Smooth Love Potions.[44] The US Treasury Department identified the hackers as the Lazarus Group, a large group of hackers working to steal funds for North Korea's regime, as cryptocurrencies are both rich targets for theft and effective ways to get around sanctions.[45] Smooth Love Potion is not just a game but also a significant facet of a new meganet-driven web of multiplayer games and cryptocurrencies integrated into globally significant political and economic activity.

In the wake of the crash, Axie Infinity and its currency have crashed into nothingness and seem likely to stay there. It does not matter.

Future games will avoid Sky Mavis's mistake, and Axie Infinity will have already made its mark. Smooth Love Potion's successors will rise and fall, sometimes with even greater impact. However unstable the SLP may be, it grew before crashing to a size where it exerted a monumental effect on a country's economy—and, from there, on the world economy. In economic terms, the game is not only real, but it is also uncontained. Play and real economies are no longer distinct things. The meganet has tied them together, severing our control over both.

LUDENS EX MACHINA

The metaverse, ultimately, is just a new name for what meganets have already brought us with systems like Warcraft and Axie Infinity. Meganets have already begun integrating gaming and money into online life. All online economies, whether cryptocurrencies or in-game currencies, gain value and relevance by being part of a *game*, and the meganet is bleeding these games into reality. The meganet has blurred the distinction between playing World of Warcraft and trading cryptocurrencies: the reality of what's underneath the game (if there is indeed anything at all) has become increasingly irrelevant.

To the question "Why does online life appear so unreal even as it consumes more and more of offline life?," meganets give an answer: meganets *make themselves more real by consuming reality and turning it into a game*. The distance between gathering gold in World of Warcraft and garnering retweets on Twitter is not so great: both are games of status and acquisition, whether you are acquiring attention or powerful weapons. The young, cavalier operators of the Potemkin village FTX cryptocurrency exchange acted more like they were playing a game than running a business, only for its bankruptcy to ripple through the greater economy.[46] With cryptocurrency putting monetary values on all sorts of online activity (whether virtual clothes, virtual real estate, or virtual events), the monetary value of all online activity will become increasingly more explicit.

Tech entrepreneur Packy McCormick wrote a 2021 essay called "The Great Online Game," in which he enthused over this gamification of the world. "The Great Online Game," he wrote, "is *free to play*, and it *starts simply: by realizing that you're playing a game*. Every tweet is a free lottery ticket."[47] The meganet turns social capital into actual capital, and cryptocurrency gives it the financial juice to create a real economy out of it. But there is a darker side to McCormick's vision—a vision not far off from that of Meta and Microsoft in their metaverse plays. Most games balance strategy and chance, but the Great Online Game is far closer to Chutes and Ladders than chess, a nebulous game that doles out rewards by dint of fortune. Instead of dice, though, we have the meganet as an inhuman and inscrutable referee. Rewards in the metaverse will be allocated arbitrarily and unfairly, and the meganet's chaos will restrict our ability to even the score.

A crypto entrepreneur and former webcam model who goes by the name of Aella has written extensively about the psychology and economics of online sex work, conducting extensive surveys and research in order to lay out the ecosystem of online sex workers. She presented the fierce competition for attention and revenue among camgirls as yet another game.

> Men want a few things, and probably one of the biggest is *winning a competition*. You see, you're not just trying to get a guy to pay you—you're trying to get a guy to pay you *in front of a bunch of other guys*. This is a super key. A man wants to feel attention from an attractive woman *on him*, and this is made even more satisfying when it's *to the exclusion of those around him*. The most profitable thing I ever did was have a "war" with another camgirl, and it became my tipping members vs. hers. Competition is bread and butter. Competition is love. Competition is life.[48]

She may as well have been talking about Warcraft, Pokémon GO, or Axie Infinity—or about cryptocurrency. The importance of money to Aella's game also makes it predictive of what meganets will look like once cryptocurrency adds value to most online activity. It's still a game but with realer stakes. Despite the difference in content, there is *structurally* not much difference between playing McCormick's Great

Online Game of gaining social influence and webcam models strategizing to increase their revenue. Every webcam performance is, like every tweet, a lottery ticket, but saturation occurs quickly, there is a long tail, and lottery "wins" can be quite elusive and even arbitrary.[49]

The competition among webcam models and Pokémon collectors replicates itself with far higher financial stakes in the crypto community. McCormick's celebratory essay is atypical, and accurate, in emphasizing the *gaming* aspect of meganet sociality, whether in business or leisure.

> People in crypto seem to understand better than anyone that this is all a game. The right meme can send a random coin to the moon and make people legitimately rich. But beyond that, *crypto is in-game money for the internet*. It rewards participation directly.[50]

Where McCormick slips is in believing this game to be immune to busts, painting it as a rising tide that lifts all boats, albeit at different rates. Many, not least the SEC, find the prospect of a meme upturning the world economy to be more frightening than exciting. As with the stock market, and as with all economies, rewards will be doled out and revoked unfairly and unpredictably, with no more warning than there was for the 2008 financial crisis—or, for that matter, for the Corrupted Blood pandemic in World of Warcraft. The meganet increasingly turns life into a meticulously and obsessively scored game, but it is still ultimately life as well, and losing in life is far more serious than losing a game.

The metaverse makes explicit what has long been implicit: commerce and games (the two are increasingly interchangeable) are the languages in which humans engage with meganets. It just is not always clear what game is being played, nor who (or what) is running the game. But as is the rule with meganets, the answer is that everyone is running a little bit of it, and no one is controlling it in total.

FIVE

MAJORITY RULES

To some men I will bring harm and to others benefit
as I herd the wretched tribes of men about.

Homeric Hymn to Hermes

In the previous chapter we saw how players can pull online game economies out of the control of their operators, pushing their algorithms in unexpected and uncontrollable directions. We touched on how cryptocurrency is multiplying this instability by joining the toy economies of online games to the real-world economy.

There is far more to say about cryptocurrency, however, as it is a meganet taken to a logical extreme. Cryptocurrencies themselves allow for decentralized, verified ownership of virtual tokens of value—Bitcoin, Ethereum, and the like. The blockchain technologies underlying NFTs likewise enable universally recognized ownership of purely virtual assets, making them impossible to clone. Both technologies introduce artificial scarcity into what was previously a realm of unlimited abundance. In much the same way that each Bitcoin is assigned indisputably to a single digital wallet, NFTs assign digital "assets" to individual owners. Two people may have identical-looking designer dresses for their avatars, but only one of those dresses is "signed" by the designer, and NFTs guarantee the authenticity of the real one, relegating the other to the status of a knockoff.* The speculative NFT market exploded in early 2022 only to crash alongside cryptocurrencies months later, but great plans for the technology remain in the conference rooms of Facebook, Google, and many other companies.[1]

Underpinning all cryptographic assets is a blockchain-driven meganet. When we say that ownership of crypto assets (currencies or NFTs) is indisputable, it would be more accurate to say that *ownership is indisputable as long as enough people don't dispute it.* Blockchain technology—which underpins cryptocurrencies and NFTs—relies on *consensus-based* mechanisms in which all participants in the currency must agree on the legitimacy of each and every transaction. The blockchain algorithms automate such agreement, but they do not guarantee it because ultimately each and every crypto and NFT owner can choose to take his ball and go home, refusing to join in the consensus. If one person does so, nothing of consequence happens. But as we've seen in other meganets, when enough people act in unanticipated and chaotic ways, algorithms can drastically amplify the spontaneous behavior of groups, joining them together in new and chaotic ways.

Blockchains and cryptocurrency are the apotheosis of the meganet: they guarantee that no centralized control can ever be total and that spontaneous revolts, if large enough in size, can shake the underlying system with no recourse. With that in mind, we can turn to Bitcoin itself, the original cryptocurrency that everyone first laughed at before it invaded the economy and exploded into corporate dreams as the future foundation of the metaverse.

THE GAME OF BITCOIN

Take away the explicit "game" of Axie Infinity from the underlying cryptocurrency backing it, and what's left is still a game. Crypto-

---

* Whether this distinction is actually meaningful is up to the owners of the dresses and the communities in which they exist.

currency is a different sort of game, however, both cooperative and competitive, in which people work together to help give value to a nigh-imaginary asset. The game is only about those assets. Bitcoin is the biggest game of all: gotta catch those coins, all $400 billion of them (Bitcoin's market cap as of this writing). Dan Conway, a middle-aged manager at a San Francisco media company, got addicted to the thought of being set for life and sunk his family's life savings into the Ethereum cryptocurrency, the second-most popular cryptocurrency after Bitcoin, with a $200 billion market cap:

> When I checked my phone, I'd be up another 6 figures since the last time I looked. I couldn't resist stopping whatever I was doing to pump my fist and shout, "YEESSSS!" But other times, ETH [Ethereum] would dip, and the value of my stack would plummet by more than $1m in less than an hour. The "orgasms" were replaced by brutal withdrawals. The volatility was a narcotic, shooting up my brain with boosts of dopamine and serotonin.
>
> The coins consumed me and changed my entire persona. When ETH stopped going up or had a mild dip, I'd get snappy with the kids. I donned a hoodie and stared into the void for hours, my mind enslaved to the promise of Ethereum and its price variations. I was fired from my job of 6 years. In the midst of a particularly volatile week, I found myself in the emergency room, struggling to breathe. The doctor diagnosed me with a panic event. "Is anything making you anxious?" he asked.[2]

Conway was lucky. He sold all his Ethereum near a record high and secured a financial future for himself, his wife, and their three children. Many have not been—or will not be—so lucky. But for Conway, as for many of the other players of cryptocurrency, the game is as meaningful as the money—and there is little difference between them while one is playing:

> Today, I've settled back into a normal life. Crypto no longer consumes me. But every now and then, after the kids are asleep, I

> lie awake thinking back on the rush of the market. And I miss it like hell.[3]

What sort of game is this? I get the same question time and again whenever someone asks me about cryptocurrency: *Where does all this money come from?* The answer is the same as where dollars or pounds or yen come from: it's created out of nothing, albeit in a peculiar and unprecedented fashion only made possible by meganets. When exchanged into traditional currencies, the money paying for cryptocurrency comes from the same place a casino payout or hedge fund money comes from: *somewhere else*.

Vitalik Buterin, known today as the creator of the second-biggest cryptocurrency Ethereum, put it bluntly (probably more bluntly than he would today) in 2011 when describing Bitcoin:

> A currency is similar to a pyramid scheme—its value is based on the expectation of it having a value in the future, but it can last forever since it relies on trade and not expansion to generate wealth. The value of a currency does not depend on its value as a good, it depends only on its value as a currency itself, in a circular loop.[4]

Buterin's defense is conditional: Bitcoin may lack intrinsic value, but its users and society assign it value based on the expectation of it continuing to have value. If this sounds like a castle in the air, no more real than Warcraft swords, it is in fact no worse than the very nature of all currencies and economies, real or toy. National currencies work on the assumption that they will remain reasonably stable in value, and doubt in that will cause currencies to crash. Cryptocurrency may *seem* less real, but that is because cryptocurrency just adds several more complicated redirections to how that money transforms itself. There may be less reason to believe a cryptocurrency will continue to remain stable in the absence of a backing government and central bank, but that does not make it less real than a traditional currency.

Most cryptocurrencies are created through a computationally and electricity-intensive process called "mining"—the connection to

Warcraft's gold mining is only metaphorical, though still telling. The algorithms that underpin Bitcoin and Ethereum award newly created coins—out of a strictly limited maximum—to those miners whose arrays of computers perform enough mathematical calculations of certain kinds to win a virtual lottery that takes place whenever it is time for a new coin to be created and awarded. That new coin is instantly worth however many hundreds or thousands of dollars the cryptocurrency is trading at. In the process of coin creation, huge amounts of electricity, on the order of the total consumption of several small nations, are spent performing useless calculations that do nothing except create those lottery tickets.

To those outside its strange fever-dream world, it seems literally incomprehensible that hundreds of thousands of processors are grinding away, performing difficult, electricity-consuming, and intrinsically useless computations, to generate immaterial yet inviolate tokens of Bitcoin or Ethereum. It's even stranger that these tokens have taken on great (though highly volatile) real-world value, with the sum total of all cryptocurrencies surpassing $2 trillion in value in early 2021 and retaining over $800 billion in value even after the 2022 crash.[5] True, paper money and its virtual equivalents have no intrinsic value either, but they are backed by governments, banks, and sheer ubiquity. Any intrinsic value a cryptocurrency may possess has been conjured out of thin air; at best, its value originates solely from the peculiar new sort of thing a cryptocurrency is: it is valuable sheerly by virtue of being cryptocurrency.

Cryptocurrency is a controversial subject, attracting vicious skeptics and wide-eyed optimists. At first glance, cryptocurrency may appear to be the biggest, most ephemeral economic bubble of all time. But like high-frequency trading and overleveraged hedge funds, cryptocurrency has far more connections to normal currencies and "real" economies than it initially appears. As investment banks like Goldman Sachs and Morgan Stanley dip heavily into cryptocurrency trading, their investments tie cryptocurrency prices to the larger economies in which those banks play a major part.[6] The trillion-dollar market cap of Bitcoin is enough to make it a major component of the larger financial system, enough to swing and sink major funds as they turn to investing in cryptocurrency. In addition, so-called stablecoins like Tether (the third-biggest cryptocurrency after Bitcoin and Ethereum) and TerraUSD (whose unexpected collapse helped trigger the 2022 cryptocurrency crash) create shadier links between the mysterious new asset class and the traditional liquid currencies on which we all depend.

In the last chapter, we explored the early-2000s boom in Warcraft gold mining. Today when a group of Chinese entrepreneurs controls an unregulated currency by transmitting "virtual labor" internationally, one thinks less of Warcraft's gold and more of Bitcoin, where a huge chunk of the world's mining power was centered in China until the Chinese government started cracking down in mid-2021.[7] In fact, the two cases are similar. Just as Warcraft's economy is more real and out of control than it appears, so is Bitcoin's. Bitcoin, Ethereum, and other cryptocurrency ecosystems bring with them the same loss of control that Blizzard experienced with Warcraft gold.*

How does decision-making take place on a meganet? Specifically, how do those with a stake in a meganet exercise their far-from-total control over its direction? Earlier, I hinted that the internals of corporate-operated meganets were nowhere near as neat and tidy as they pretended to be: the executive leadership of Facebook and Google are not the tyrannical CEOs of old. With cryptocurrency, the devolution of decision-making to the collective goes considerably further. Unlike most meganets, this decentralization is intentional, part and parcel of the anarcho-capitalist vision of Bitcoin's creators and cryptocurrency's advocates. Yet while technologically ingenious, cryptocurrency meganets, encompassing both the underlying network and its users, do not make decisions in the way one would expect. When a cryptocurrency meganet flies out of control,

* One notable difference, however, is that most cryptocurrencies are architected to prevent hyperinflation by strictly limiting the amount of a currency that can ever possibly exist.

only massively coordinated action can bring it back in line, and even then the meganet places limits on how much control can be exerted.

CRYPTO HYPERINFLATION

Microsoft, Google, Facebook, Blizzard, Reddit, and other companies all lost control of their meganets despite their best efforts. With cryptocurrencies, that loss of control is baked into the very algorithms that drive the currency, in a bold attempt to make a virtue out of necessity. While indisputably successful enough to turn cryptocurrency into a major new asset class, this willful anarchy has triggered a series of crises from Bitcoin's very beginning.

On August 15, 2010, with Bitcoin just over a year old, the currency suffered a sudden, unexpected, and catastrophic bit of hyperinflation, now called the "value overflow incident."[8] To guard against inflation, Bitcoin was architected to have a strict and unchangeable number of total coins, making it algorithmically impossible to mint more than the 21 million coins, a number set when the system was first released. In 2010, however, some anonymous hacker took advantage of a bug in the Bitcoin source code to instantly mint almost 185 *billion* Bitcoins and deliver them to two Bitcoin wallets in a transaction immediately validated by the rest of the network.[9] The Bitcoin community, small at the time, was horrified. But since no one controlled Bitcoin by its very nature, and since the transaction was already recorded permanently in the immutable ledger known as the blockchain, what could be done?

Before answering that question, we need to examine the structure of a cryptocurrency. Cryptocurrencies like Bitcoin are odd beasts. At first glance, they are less currencies than they are commodities, rarely used for actual monetary exchange (sketchy black market activities being one significant exception) but rather for investment and speculation.[10] Yet as a commodity, cryptocurrencies have no function: Bitcoin cannot *do* anything beyond being held and exchanged, yet that is enough for the cryptocurrency economy to place significant monetary value on these virtual tokens. Too intrinsically useless to be a commodity, yet too nonliquid to be a currency: cryptocurrency could be termed a pseudocurrency.[11]

Bitcoin, like most cryptocurrencies, stakes its value on decentralization. By design, it cannot be centrally regulated. Any transaction requires an effective consensus among all participants on its network. All participants in the Bitcoin network—to mine or hold Bitcoin is to be part of the network—must jointly agree that the ongoing blockchain ledger of Bitcoin transactions is valid. By continuing to participate in the single, growing blockchain of transactions shared among Bitcoin users, each user endorses that list of transactions as legitimate. The network holds together by virtue of its participants all using software that commits them to sharing the same view of Bitcoin's reality: *these* particular transactions are valid, and *these* holdings belong to *these* people.

Without this joint consensus, the network falls apart. If for whatever reason some large percentage of the Bitcoin community chose to validate a *different* version of the singular blockchain, the blockchain would split (or fork). It would be as though half the country started calling the sky red instead of blue. The stability of Bitcoin and all other blockchain applications (not just cryptocurrency) requires that consensus to function. Because it is in the self-interest of cryptocurrency and blockchain users to maintain exactly such a consensus, the thinking goes, such a consensus will consistently prevail.

Yet with that hyperinflation bug in 2010, the automated consensus suddenly became unacceptable. The bug had caused the software used by the community to agree on what everyone in the community (save the hacker) considered to be a *wrong* version of the Bitcoin reality. The community took quick action. Within five hours, a new version of the Bitcoin software had been rolled out, endorsed by pseudonymous founder Satoshi Nakamoto. The new version fixed the bug but also invalidated *all* Bitcoin transactions that had taken place after the hack. Like all blockchains, Bitcoin's blockchain is a strictly linear and sequential set of transactions. Once the Bitcoin network recognizes a transaction, it is immutable. Any and all subsequent transactions are only valid if all previous transactions are also valid. To erase a transaction from the blockchain, the entire Bitcoin community had to travel back in time before the hack and reset the system, erasing the bad transaction but also everything after it. Anything that had taken place in the hours after the hack was erased from existence. Having rewound time and undone the problematic transactions, the community then forked to a different version of the past in which the hack didn't and couldn't take place.* Once the new fork of reality exceeded the old fork in number of transactions, it became authoritative, even to older clients.[12]

A successful fork, however, relies on the community agreeing that such a fork must happen. Theoretically, if all the members of the Bitcoin community (those mining and holding Bitcoin) had not upgraded their software, the hyperinflationary transaction would have remained valid. If only half the community had upgraded, Bitcoin would have forked into two realities, one hyperinflationary and one not. In practice, no one but the hacker wanted those 185 billion Bitcoins to exist, and so the community took their lumps and resigned themselves to losing a few hours of transactions. But such quick and unanimous action isn't a given, even if everyone's incentives are aligned, and the rapid response was only possible because of the small size of the Bitcoin community in 2010. If such a bug were to arise today, Bitcoin's fundamental integrity would collapse due to the size of the disruption.[13] A community of hundreds can undo their collective

* There are two types of fork, a "hard fork" and a "soft fork." A hard fork requires all clients to upgrade before they can continue to follow the blockchain, while a soft fork does not and so creates a backward-compatible blockchain. This distinction is not particularly relevant for the discussion here. In both cases, two different realities are created. In the case of a hard fork, two different blockchains actually exist. In the case of a soft fork, only one blockchain continues to exist, but clients will see it differently and acknowledge different transactions as valid or invalid. In either case, reality forks. The value overflow fix was in fact a soft fork, but most of the other forks discussed will be hard forks.

activities and cope with the disruption, but a community of millions cannot. Once Bitcoin, like any meganet, reached a certain size, resets become impossible.

Bitcoin's value overflow incident was not so different from the Corrupted Blood incident in World of Warcraft, which we saw in the last chapter. In both, unintended bugs in code led to a chain reaction in which bad actors poisoned the well of the collective reality inhabited by all the system's users. In both cases, the fix required resetting the meganet: shutting it down and losing some amount of information so that the underlying code could be changed and restarted. In both cases, the *rules of the world* had to be changed for the plague to be eliminated.

Both stories are ultimately heartening: a unified community coped with massive disruptions to its world until the world could be rewritten and fixed so those disruptions were no longer possible. Compared to today's meganets, however, the Bitcoin network of 2010 and World of Warcraft are toys. The growth of meganets makes forks or resets increasingly untenable. Can you imagine, for example, Visa or Mastercard invalidating all credit card transactions over a five-hour period and asking their customers just to perform them again? If an algorithm was found to misclassify people as terrorists due to a bug, can you imagine the government rolling back an FBI database to before the bug was injected into the system? Rollbacks and resets are a luxury only allowed to those operating at a certain remove from reality. The closer a meganet comes to managing *our* reality, not some play or virtual realm, the less it is possible to undo or reset the meganet because *our* reality truly is immutable and permanent.

CONSENSUS?

Cryptocurrency bugs embody the meganet's decentralized volatility: an unexpected and unwanted problem that *requires* the coordinated action of many disparate individuals to solve, a problem for which no centralized solution exists. The blockchain requirement for "consensus" is in fact a requirement for an extreme form of the decentralization that all meganets bring, a consequence intended by Bitcoin's creators. Such requirements are not necessarily negative. Cryptocurrency's explosive growth, whatever reservations may exist (and there are many), does show that the innate qualities of the meganet can achieve *something* significant and significantly different from what has gone before. Those achievements can be remarkable and can enmesh themselves with our lives inextricably. We could not easily do away with Amazon, Facebook, Google, and their brethren, despite their downsides. But it would be naïve to ignore that with those meganet-driven achievements come equally necessary downsides. Cryptocurrency's amplification of the meganet's essential tendencies will likewise amplify the meganet's negative qualities, which is why subsequent forks in the Bitcoin community have been less reassuring than the value overflow incident.

In 2013, the Bitcoin software forked again, this time by accident. Very late on March 11, 2013, Bitcoin users noticed that the new software version 0.8 had unexpectedly and wholly accidentally created its own fork of the blockchain, so that everyone who had upgraded to version 0.8 was adding to one fork and everyone still on 0.7 was adding to another.[14] Instead of one good fork replacing the other defective fork, as had happened with the value overflow fix, both forks this time were equally fine—just separate. In the value overflow incident, the "correct" blockchain was obvious: the one without the 185 billion new Bitcoins. No one needed to be told which blockchain to follow, nor which version to use: everyone upgraded. This time, neither blockchain was problematic, but the community needed to pick one.

Vitalik Buterin, the creator of Ethereum whom we heard from above, wrote up the ensuing debate and decision, stressing the sheer logistical difficulties of gaining community agreement in the absence of an undisputed central authority:

> With the fork in progress, the Bitcoin developers had a choice: do they support the 0.8 fork or the 0.7 fork? Ultimately, there could

> only be one; a monetary system cannot function if there are two different databases of how much money each person has. . . . The developers quickly settled on 0.7, and the community set to work on the next task: notifying major miners and mining pool operators of what they need to do.
>
> Over the next few hours, nearly every major Bitcoin developer and mining pool operator joined the bitcoin-dev IRC channel. Major mining pools that were using bitcoin 0.8 shut down, downgraded to 0.7, and switched back on. Merchants were also notified; most large businesses, including BitcoinStore, BitPay, SatoshiDice and MtGox, shut down deposits to protect themselves from double spend attacks. . . . At 06:19 both chains converged to the same length at block 225454, leading to nearly all remaining miners abandoning the other.
>
> This incident will go down in history as one of the closest moments that we have come to the underlying Bitcoin protocol actually failing.[15]

In less than twelve hours, the entire Bitcoin community had chosen which of the two blockchain realities would match up to *our* reality. Compared to the 2010 incident, the scope of action was larger and so were the losses. All miners on the rejected 0.8 fork lost their mining income during that time: twenty-five Bitcoins, which were worth around $1,000 then and would be worth on the order of $1 million today.

Yet contrary to Bitcoin's decentralized image, a handful of community members ultimately made the decision for the rest of the community. It was then implemented in large part thanks to the operator of the BTC Guild, a mining pool in which many individual miners yield autonomy and ownership of their mining efforts to the operators of the pool in exchange for proportional rewards allocated by the pool operators. Less than an hour after the accidental fork was discovered, BTC Guild's operator, who happened to be available, told Bitcoin developers Pieter Wuille, Jeff Garzik, and Gavin Andresen that BTC Guild had enough power to choose, unilaterally, which tine of the fork would prevail:

> **23:43 BTC Guild** I can single handedly put 0.7 back to the majority hash power I just need confirmation that thats what should be done
>
> **23:44 Pieter Wuille** BTC Guild: imho, that is was you should do, but we should have consensus first
>
> **23:44 Jeff Garzik** ACK on preferring 0.7 chain, for the moment
>
> **23:45 Gavin Andresen** BTC Guild: if you can cleanly get us back on the 0.7 chain, ACK from here, too[16]

In this case, consensus turned out to be not a consensus of all Bitcoin community members but of one pool operator and the central brain trust of Bitcoin development—a handful of people. The rest of the community then *had* to follow. Princeton computer scientist Arvind Narayanan, writing two years later, pointed out that it was the centralization of decision-making among a small number of Bitcoin mavens that allowed Bitcoin to survive the crisis with comparatively little damage.[17] In contrast to the meganets we've previously examined, such as Facebook and Google, which are operated by centralized corporations yet too complex to control properly, the supposedly vigorously decentralized Bitcoin network could be steered, it turned out, by a small set of community elders—or at least it could in 2013.

Not that the Bitcoin community minded this de facto centralization: the quick action benefited them. Rather, the troubling aspect of the story was the ongoing *requirement* for immediate, centralized intervention by humans to prevent the supposedly automated, decentralized system from failing. Such centralized action could still be possible today: pro-Bitcoin journalist Jamie Redman expressed concern in 2019 that five mining pools could coordinate to take control of the Bitcoin blockchain.[18] Contrary to Narayanan's observation that centralization was needed, the Bitcoin community still sees any such concentration of power as a danger.*

Yet even if Narayanan's sentiment is accurate (and at least in 2013, it seems to have been), inertia is on Redman's side: for better or for worse, the extent of centralized control is dissipating due both to the increasing size and speed of meganets. The real irony is that in fixing such problems through a handful of dominant players, Bitcoin mavens were fighting against the very nature of their own beast. Over time, they lost, and the meganet prevailed.

As Bitcoin grew, forks ceased to be resolved so neatly, creating schisms rather than resolutions. Community elders could no longer steer the entire community into a single consensus, as required by the Bitcoin protocol (and all blockchain-based protocols). By 2017, debates about reforming Bitcoin's inefficiencies were spilling into long cold-war conflicts, resulting in over one hundred hard forks with separate blockchains. Some of these forks became their own cryptocurrencies, with names like Bitcoin Classic, Bitcoin Gold, and, the most successful, Bitcoin Cash (which itself subsequently forked into Bitcoin Cash ABC and Bitcoin Cash SV).[19] Most of these cryptocurrencies fell by the wayside, but Bitcoin Cash ABC, now simply Bitcoin Cash, has achieved significant presence. Its success signals that forking decisions—at least ones that don't involve the dubious manufacture of 185 billion Bitcoins—no longer lie solely in the hands of a small, mostly unified elite but rather in a larger collective of what journalist Laura Shin describes as four main stakeholders: "tech-focused core developers, the profit-driven miners, the business-oriented startups and the users, who range from immigrants sending remittances back

* In theory, if a set of Bitcoin miners possessing the majority of mining power choose to recognize a fraudulent transaction, the rest of the community could not reject the fraudulent transaction without forking Bitcoin. Consequently, Bitcoin mythologizes the ideal of a set of independent participants, most of whom are honest, so that a minority of malicious actors cannot subvert the honest brokerage processes. In practice, mining power is considerably more concentrated, though this sort of fraud is comparatively rare. It is far easier, it appears, simply to hack exchanges like Mt. Gox and steal Bitcoins directly, rather than going through the difficult process of taking control of the blockchain.

home to the 1% wanting in on this new digital gold rush."[20] These amorphous masses of people have supplanted the community elders, placing power across a wide collective instead of within any individual authority. As was inevitable, the meganet won—the blockchain had even stacked the deck in its favor.

In 2019, after the large cryptocurrency exchange Binance was hacked to the tune of $40 million worth of Bitcoin, its CEO Changpeng Zhao provoked general outrage when he proposed that the community roll back the blockchain to before the hack took place.[21] Zhao evidently thought it feasible to gather enough major mining players to control 51 percent of Bitcoin mining power, then exploit that power to roll back the blockchain by fiat. Bitcoin enthusiasts, by and large, believed such a move would destroy Bitcoin's reputation and tank its value, and Binance ultimately did not attempt such a rollback.[22] Even if the possibility of a centralized consensus still exists, the reputational costs of *doing* anything with it have gotten so high that, short of another value overflow incident, "consensus" has been replaced with schisms.

Now, step back and imagine the possibilities when such distributed (lack of) consensus intersects with the real-time high-speed chaos innate to meganets. In 2010 and 2013, the entire Bitcoin ecosystem shut down for the hours during which uncertainty reigned. The currency could no longer be traded or used, as though one's credit or debit cards and actual cash lost all purchase power and value for the duration. Imagine such a crisis in which quick consensus could not be reached. Imagine, perhaps, being in World of Warcraft as Corrupted Blood spread, except that the bug could not be fixed because (1) the community could not agree on how to fix it and no consensus could be achieved and (2) even if consensus were reached, the costs of shutting down the system and rolling back to an earlier, preplague state would be prohibitive. If we look at Bitcoin as a kind of virtual world akin to World of Warcraft—a competitive game in which participants must cooperate in agreeing on the rules before competing against one another for rewards (whether better weapons or virtual coins)—then the potential effects of losing authoritative control are quite unsettling.

In any such crisis, the community will self-organize to the extent possible, but it will increasingly lack the will or even the ability to come to a quick, unified consensus about what to do. Bitcoin users vote with their feet, so to speak, by choosing which blockchain to follow, but the sort of intimate, rational discussion that informed the handling of the value overflow incident has become impossible. The high priests of Bitcoin may speak, but as the community and the meganet grow, the high priests will be drowned out by the musings, complaints, and rants of Bitcoin users across message boards everywhere, in English, Chinese, and other languages. In the place of coordinated decision-making, there are the opaque actions of unspeaking mobs, not so different from the fracturing we see on social meganets. *This* is the self-organization of the meganet.

This self-organization functions better than one might expect. The abandonment of rational discourse still leads to remarkably stable systems—most of the time. Yet when instability takes hold, the result is inarticulate panic. Systems like Bitcoin, then, are designed to put a rubber band around such momentary panic by raising the bar for action higher than uncoordinated mobs can manage. In the case of Bitcoin, as long as 51 percent of the stakeholders do not agree on a single course of action, the blockchain will go along as it has been, for better or for worse, allowing for the periodic schism. And this is fine and well until the status quo proves unworkable because of a bug, a hack, or some other catastrophic issue. At that point, unless some small group of Bitcoin elites can convince enough major stakeholders that their chosen solution is the way to go, the status quo and its problems will unravel the entire system.

Again, imagine that the Warcraft software engineers needed buy-in from 51 percent of Warcraft players before rolling out their Corrupted Blood fix. Imagine that there are multiple groups of software engineers, each proposing *different* fixes for the Corrupted Blood plague. And imagine that no matter what the fix, the cost of shutting down the system to deploy the fix will be astronomically high, amounting to millions or possibly even billions of dollars. In such a situation, the structure of the meganet, as well as the high bar to implementing a universal change to its rules, makes it overwhelmingly likely that no course of action will prevail.

CONTRACTUAL OBLIGATION

Without direct, top-down control, cryptocurrency's workings become an organic process like the weather or evolution, one that can be described (approximately) but not controlled: a meganet process. Such processes are growing in size and importance. From Warcraft's imaginary world, we have now reached a point where some of the least controllable meganets—blockchain-based cryptocurrencies—have enormous pull on the entire financial system.

Bitcoin was just the beginning. The cryptocurrency network Ethereum is a bit like Bitcoin on steroids. While Ethereum, like Bitcoin, also uses a decentralized blockchain as an underlying architecture, Ethereum also allows for "smart contracts," applications that can be built on top of the basic Ethereum framework. These smart contracts cause the Ethereum network to perform transactions in Ethereum's currency (Ether) in an authenticated, automated, and distributed fashion. In other words, Ethereum theoretically allows financial contracts to be executed in the absence of a legal system for enforcing contracts and adjudicating disputes. Every time a streaming platform plays a song I wrote, for example, a smart contract could trigger a deposit of Ethereum into my own account. My rental of a property could be recorded in Ethereum's "virtual ledger" by validating monthly rent payments. In effect, all Ethereum participants agree by consensus on a ledger for all the world's transactions, and the Ethereum network acts as a virtual escrow for funds, guaranteeing the funds will be released when a contract's conditions are fulfilled.[23] Ethereum's contracts are immutable once implemented, so a contract's parties can't welch, and no middlemen are needed as guarantors for transactions. The Ethereum software and blockchain does that automatically. So goes the theory, at least. By rejecting guarantors and legal enforcement, Ethereum participants entrust the technology and network to adjudicate disputes—ideally by removing the possibility of disputes in the first place. While vastly more powerful than Bitcoin, Ethereum's smart contracts are also vastly more complicated, requiring an entire *computer language* in which contracts can be computationally encoded. And with complexity come bugs.

And with bugs come exploits. On June 18, 2016, an anonymous hacker stole almost 3.5 million Ether (about $50 million at the time) from The DAO, a platform built on top of the Ethereum network. The DAO (which stands for "distributed autonomous organization") was intended to be a distributed venture capital network in which anyone could invest money. Participants in The DAO could then submit proposals requesting seed financing from The DAO. If enough investors approved, the proposal's author would automatically receive financing through an Ethereum smart contract. Unfortunately, The DAO's code contained more than one significant security hole, holes loosely analogous to the value overflow incident.* After the attacker had leveraged those security holes to steal The DAO's Ether, the ill-gotten Ether was sanctified as legitimate by the entire Ethereum network. The Ethereum meganet, running away on its own, had already legitimated a massive financial transaction against the will of nearly all of its participants. Volume, velocity, and virality, all entirely automated without a backstop.

That same day, an open letter, purportedly from "The Attacker," deployed the anarcho-capitalist rhetoric of cryptocurrency enthusiasts against them:

> I am disappointed by those who are characterizing the use of this intentional feature as "theft". I am making use of this explicitly coded feature as per the smart contract terms and my law firm has

* The technical nature of the attack on The DAO was entirely different, but in both cases an undetected bug in the code led to a massive exploit by a single anonymous user, which was then enshrined as legitimate by the underlying blockchain ledger. Peter Vessenes explains the bug and the poor programming practices beneath it at https://web.archive.org/web/20180227201011/http://vessenes.com/deconstructing-thedao-attack-a-brief-code-tour/.

> advised me that my action is fully compliant with United States criminal and tort law. . . . A soft or hard fork would amount to seizure of my legitimate and rightful ether, claimed legally through the terms of a smart contract. Such fork would permanently and irrevocably ruin all confidence in not only Ethereum but also . . . in the field of smart contracts and blockchain technology. Many large Ethereum holders will dump their ether, and developers, researchers, and companies will leave Ethereum. Make no mistake: any fork, soft or hard, will further damage Ethereum and destroy its reputation and appeal.[24]

The Attacker rubbed the community's noses in their own idealism: if the whole point of blockchain cryptocurrencies was to remove the fallibility of human and legal adjudication, then whatever the code did should not be overruled by human intervention. Otherwise the entire purpose of cryptocurrencies would be defeated, and they would just be particularly unstable fiat currencies managed in a particularly disorganized fashion. The Attacker also had a more practical motive. The illicit transactions took twenty-eight days to settle, and so The Attacker had not yet obtained the $50 million. The community, luckily, had a good amount of time to decide what to do. Ultimately, a choice was posed: either do nothing and let the bug-exploiting transaction settle, or perform a hard fork of Ethereum into two realities, as had been done with Bitcoin in the cases above.[25]

This time, however, a hard fork would be even more egregious because it did *not* rewind time. Ethereum was far larger than Bitcoin had been at the time of its earliest forks, and too many Ethereum transactions had already taken place since the hack for such a rewind to be feasible. Rather, an Ethereum hard fork would have to cancel the problematic transaction ex post facto, by changing the underlying laws of Ethereum in a very specific way for one single case.* The

* In this, the hard fork recalled the Supreme Court's decision in *Bush v. Gore* (2000), which implied a nonprecedential nature to the decision by declaring: "Our consideration is limited to the present circumstances."

hard fork, as proposed, entailed writing into Ethereum's code (its "constitution," so to speak) a very special, singular clause that would reassign The Attacker's gains from the bug-exploiting transaction to a new, special account. Users of The DAO could withdraw from this special account in accordance with their original contributions.[26] This transfer would take place before the twenty-eight-day settlement period, so by the time The Attacker's own contract settled, The DAO's original accounts would be empty, so there would be nothing available for The Attacker to steal. In other words, it entailed taking Ethereum's code, which treated all transactions as sacrosanct, and rewriting it to say: "All transactions are sacrosanct, except that in the middle of June 2016, all money from these accounts magically transfers into a different account."

Philosophically and structurally, this hard fork was hideously ugly, but it was the simplest way to reverse the hack without canceling transactions and contracts that had taken place after the hack. The question was, would the community agree to it, or would it refuse? As befitting a meganet, the community did both. By one estimate, 89 percent of Ethereum holders voted for the hard fork, deciding that the abstract principle of immutable transactions was less important than undoing the work of a blatantly bad actor.[27] The remaining community members chose principle over practicality and enshrined The Attacker's gains as legitimate. The hard fork took place, and two Ethereum blockchains continued from that point on.

Which blockchain won out? In truth, both did, to varying degrees. Cases like Bitcoin's value overflow incident or its accidental 2013 fork, in which the community unanimously and with quick coordination chose one fork, are now a distant memory. The majority Ethereum blockchain, which had undone The Attacker's hack, continued on as Ethereum (ETH). The minority blockchain continued on as Ethereum Classic (ETC). Since, aside from the hack, the blockchains were identical, holdings were duplicated across both blockchains. If you held 1,000 ETH before the fork, you now held 1,000 ETH *and* 1,000 ETC. (The economic meaning of such schisms remains unclear.) One meganet became two.

In the worlds of both Ethereum and Ethereum Classic, however, The DAO collapsed. Having lost all trust and most legitimacy, major cryptocurrency exchanges delisted The DAO tokens by the end of 2016, and in 2017 the SEC actually ruled that The DAO tokens qualified as securities, and in offering them publicly, The DAO and its token holders had violated securities law.[28]

Ethereum and Ethereum Classic both continued on. Ethereum Classic, the smaller community, fell prey to a number of "51 percent" attacks in subsequent years, as attackers gained enough power to rewrite the blockchain unilaterally—by single-handedly controlling 51 percent of all of Ethereum Classic's computing power.[29] Despite this tremendous loss of prestige, Ethereum Classic still participated in the cryptocurrency boom in early 2021, jumping from $10 to $100 in the span of months, having never before passed $20, before once again trending downward and falling back to under $20 after the crash of 2022.[30]

It is likely that Ethereum Classic will eventually die off and Ethereum will prevail. One could even argue that cryptocurrencies inhabit a Darwinian ecosystem in which the most popular, most robust, and most secure cryptocurrencies will outcompete the Ethereum Classics and Bitcoin Golds, as crashes like that of 2022 violently prune the set of viable cryptocurrencies to a manageable number. What one cannot argue, however, is that this process of weeding out is anything but chaos: a clash of meganets emerging organically from the actions of millions and under the control of no one. When the consequences of blockchain-related bugs become irreversible and community votes generate schisms by their very nature, it is clear that no one, not even the collective cryptocurrency community, is in charge of what is occurring.* No Rousseau-esque "General Will" emerges from the bugs and forks. Instead, the roiling valuations increasingly push up against the larger, noncryptocurrency economy, destabilizing it as well.

* Ironically, the only time there is clear control over the process is in the case of a 51 percent attack—that is, when the intended process of decentralized consensus and decision-making has failed pathologically.

TETHER UNLEASHED

If cryptocurrency had remained a niche indulgence for a small group of speculators, the risk it posed to the larger economy would be minimal. But meganets by their nature grow and connect. Outside the internet, doomsday preppers and back-to-the-landers are marginal groups that persist without ever reaching a critical mass, small communities that welcome newcomers without particularly evangelizing themselves. Such an equilibrium is far rarer on the meganet, where survival of the fittest is the rule, and the high-velocity, virally driven interaction forces groups to either grow or be eliminated. With the lubricating force of money in play, cryptocurrency never stood a chance of remaining a small fringe group as it was in 2010. It would either die out completely—which in retrospect seems fairly unlikely—or it would explode into other areas.

For a time, cryptocurrency's appeal appeared to lie mostly in dubiously legal transactions. As cryptocurrency's owners were difficult to trace, it quickly became the preferred method of exchange for darknet transactions involving drugs and ransomware demands. Hackers could demand ransoms be paid to an anonymous Bitcoin wallet far more easily than they could establish anonymous bank accounts into which ransoms could be deposited. And for a time, such associations stigmatized Bitcoin, even as Bitcoin's market capitalization approached $1 trillion and Ethereum met with similar success.

But only for a time. By 2021, Morgan Stanley took a decisive step by offering Bitcoin funds to its investors, albeit only those clients with at least $2 million already invested with Morgan Stanley and only up to 2.5 percent of a client's total net worth.[31] While likewise stressing its volatility, Citigroup also embraced cryptocurrency in a 2021 report. Against the charges of its being valueless, a report from Citi Global Perspectives & Solutions (Citi GPS) stressed two properties of Bitcoin and other cryptocurrencies that made it more than a worthless asset. First, cryptocurrency was a censorship-resistant (and border-resistant) store of value, distributing the cost of authenticating and securing transactions across a network of participants rather than laying it at the feet of a financial service provider. Second, cryptocurrency possessed guaranteed scarcity, making it invulnerable to inflation (though not to crashes).[32] The combination of these two factors, to the Citi GPS analysts, positioned blockchain-backed cryptocurrencies as both a hedge against inflation and as a cost-efficient global transaction mechanism resistant to protectionist policies and tariffs. Citi GPS summarized the advantages:

> Bitcoin may be optimally positioned to become the preferred currency for global trade. It is immune from both fiscal and monetary policy, avoids the need for cross-border foreign exchange (FX) transactions, enables near instantaneous payments, and eliminates concerns about defaults or cancellations as the coins must be in the payer's wallet before the transaction is initiated.[33]

In other words, Citi GPS saw cryptocurrency as providing an avenue to attaining the deregulated, laissez-faire world that global finance wished for, a means around the obstacles put in its path by uncooperative governments and international organizations like the WTO and the World Bank. In particular, Citi GPS stressed the growth of cryptocurrency in Africa among migrant workers and small businesses, reaching over half a billion dollars in transactions in 2020. The intrinsic security and global reach of cryptocurrency allowed for technology to do an end run around the local, inefficient, and frequently corrupt institutions that controlled flows of money in Africa and other third-world nations.

Citigroup's optimistic scenario, however, relied on one particular breed of cryptocurrency, called a stablecoin, acting as a dampening force on the wild swings of cryptocurrency meganets. Stablecoins, in theory, act as a bridge between cryptocurrencies and the state-backed money (termed *fiat currency*) that we use every day. There is an old saying in linguistics that a language is a dialect with an army. Analogously, a currency is an IOU with an army: the validity of the money ultimately depends on the ability of the government to enforce the value of that money—one way or another. The weaker the government's financial security and clout, the weaker the currency. The absence of *any* such guarantor in cryptocurrencies is one of the many reasons why they are so volatile and risky, feeling more like an asset than a currency.

The concept behind a stablecoin is that a nongovernmental guarantor provides backing in a traditional currency in order to ensure that the stablecoin cryptocurrency has a fixed exchange rate with that traditional currency, say the US dollar. This was what the third-most popular cryptocurrency Tether promised when it emerged in 2014. Tether was a cryptocurrency with a difference. Though it was built on top of Ethereum and Bitcoin, its owner, Tether Limited (a Hong Kong–based company closely linked with cryptocurrency exchange Bitfinex), architected Tether to be considerably less decentralized, placing itself at the center of the Tether ecosystem. For one, Tether Limited guaranteed from the beginning that any Tether coin (termed a USDT) could be traded in for $1 USD at any time. To control this exchange rate, Tether Limited took control of the supply of USDT. Unlike Bitcoin and Ethereum, Tether was not mined through virtual computational lotteries but minted out of thin air. Only Tether Limited can mint coins, but it can do so with complete freedom. The company can increase the supply to produce inflation or withdraw coins from circulation to create deflation to keep the exchange rate in line with 1 USDT = $1 USD. In effect, Tether Limited set itself up as both the Federal Reserve and the FDIC (Federal Deposit Insurance Corporation) for Tether.

Tether met with immense success. By mid-2021, Tether Limited had minted over $60 billion in Tether, putting it into the top five cryptocurrencies by market cap, with several other stablecoins in the top twenty.[34] Citi GPS's report described the obvious appeal of stablecoins:

> Moving money between the traditional fiat currency-based economy and this emerging on-chain landscape has been difficult, relying on traditional payment rails and networks that often place limits on the extent of user activity. Stablecoins are a newer offering

> providing a more efficient mechanism that acts as on and off ramps between the two domains.
>
> Fiat currency stablecoins are collateralized vehicles that can be used to move large sums of money from the off-chain into the on-chain ecosystem and allow those coins to circulate like any other cryptocurrency within blockchain-based ledgers and digital wallets. These coins are effective for use within public network blockchains, but they also provide a template for private networks.[35]

For Citi GPS, stablecoins were the best of both worlds of currency: they offered nonstate guarantors for cryptocurrency transactions exempt from traditional financial regulation, while still converting easily and reliably into traditional, regulated currencies. Stablecoins purported to square the circle of the cryptocurrency meganet. By recentralizing the decentralized economy in a stateless manner, they allowed for greater control of cryptocurrency networks without the regulatory downside. Besides giving birth to many competitors, Tether also spurred Facebook to try to launch its own stablecoin backed by multiple currencies, originally called Libra but rebranded to Diem, which stalled in a morass of regulatory and logistical difficulties until Facebook abandoned it and sold it off in early 2022.[36]

The question around stablecoins is not who benefits, however, but who pays. Having minted over 60 billion Tether, Tether Limited had to hold $60 billion in reserves to back those Tether coins. Originally, Tether Limited claimed that its reserves were entirely in US dollars, but under increasing scrutiny, the company walked that claim back in 2019 to say instead that its reserves were a mixture of cash, cash equivalents, secured loans, and other unspecified assets.[37] Under investigation by New York state, Tether Limited revealed that only 3 percent of its reserves were in actual cash, with the majority being in commercial paper (much of it unspecified), which is made up of unsecured short-term corporate loans usually treated as a high-quality cash equivalent but hardly as secure as actual money.[38] Financial commentator Frances Coppola observed that the insecurity of these assets was compounded by Tether Limited's lack of capital: "The gap between assets and liabilities is paper-thin: on 31st March 2021, for example, it was 0.36% of total consolidated assets, on a balance sheet of more than $40bn in size."[39]

That small margin makes Tether Limited's buffer of assets crucial. Any crunch or run—on commercial paper or on cryptocurrencies—could untether Tether completely. Beyond that, there were questions as to Tether's transparency. Cryptocurrency skeptic Patrick McKenzie accused Bitfinex and Tether of running something akin to a shell game:

> Tether has routinely not had actual control of hundreds of millions of dollars of their purported reserves. While they promised their customers that Tether was backed by "traditional currency held in our reserves", their reserves were actually accounting fictions; receivables from money launderers like Crypto Capital Corp, receivables from related parties such as Bitfinex, and cryptocurrencies.[40]

In other words, he claimed, Tether's reserves were from several dodgy sources and partly in cryptocurrency itself, the very thing Tether was supposed to back. In February 2021, New York attorney general Letitia James arrived at a similar position, banning Bitfinex and Tether from trading activity with New Yorkers after declaring that the companies had overstated their reserves and hid $850 million in losses.

> On November 1, 2018, Tether publicized another self-proclaimed "verification" of its cash reserve; this time at Deltec Bank & Trust Ltd. of the Bahamas. The announcement linked to a letter dated November 1, 2018, which stated that tethers were fully backed by cash, at one dollar for every one tether. However, the very next day, on November 2, 2018, Tether began to transfer funds out of its account, ultimately moving hundreds of millions of dollars from Tether's bank accounts to Bitfinex's accounts. And so, as of

November 2, 2018—one day after their latest "verification"—tethers were again no longer backed one-to-one by U.S. dollars in a Tether bank account.[41]

While uncertainty over reserves and losses are worrying enough, economic researchers John M. Griffin and Amin Shams went further and proposed that one particular buyer and seller on Bitfinex was engaging in what was tantamount to explicit price manipulation:

> By mapping the blockchains of Bitcoin and Tether, we are able to establish that one large player on Bitfinex uses Tether to purchase large amounts of Bitcoin when prices are falling and following the printing of Tether.[42]

Following such concerns, regulatory agencies worried about how stablecoins could broadly destabilize markets, with the Fitch rating agency saying in mid-2021 that

> [Tether's] commercial paper holdings may be larger than those of most prime money market funds. A sudden mass redemption of [Tether] could affect the stability of short-term credit markets [but] we believe authorities are unlikely to intervene to save stablecoins in the event of a disruptive event.[43]

In other words, stablecoins have so heavily invested in the same sources as money market funds that any run on Tether could have an impact as large as that of the subprime meltdown in 2008. But such a run would be far worse because there is no regulatory apparatus available to bail out stablecoins in the way that the US Treasury had bailed out most major US banks and financial firms in 2008 when it shelled out $200 billion after Lehman Brothers failed. Ostensibly tied to the US dollar, Tether's leash is long enough that it has fluctuated between $0.90 and $1.06.[44] Its brethren TerraUSD crashed to pennies on the dollar in mid-2022, owing to a vastly more unstable and unsustainable method of maintaining the currency peg.[45] Because of the connective nature of meganets, the decentralization and obfuscation of cryptocurrency has not only put its own markets in question but has also spread its volatility into the global financial system.

UNSTABLECOINS

In spite of the New York attorney general finding in February 2021 that Tether Limited had made false statements about Tether's backing and banning them from trading in New York, Tether continued to rise and issue new coins.[46] Even if the Tether coin and company collapse—which seems far more likely to occur as a result of an economic implosion rather than any legal regulation—cryptocurrency optimists are ironically correct that the basic idea behind Tether is here to stay. That basic idea, as Citi GPS pointed out, is tying cryptocurrency assets to traditional monetary assets, as well as recentralizing cryptocurrency monetary policy. While anathema to cryptocurrency purists, such recentralization would appear to assuage Arvind Narayanan's concerns about the need for strong central leadership of cryptocurrency. If a stablecoin were to be *genuinely* backed by reserves and *genuinely* regulated in a transparent matter, cryptocurrencies could indeed fulfill the booming role that Citigroup saw for them.

> If these efforts progress to the actual issuance of *central bank-backed* digital currency, blockchain would become a mainstream offering.[47] [emphasis mine]

The blockchain's value to financial institutions, as the Citi GPS report stated, was first in its resistance to censorship and regulation and second in the guaranteed scarcity of its assets. Both of these virtues arise from the distributed, consensus-based nature of the blockchain underpinning cryptocurrencies. As long as there is no centralized authority that can block transactions or mint more coins, those two virtues have a good chance of persisting. The paradox is that those virtues only persist in the *absence of central control*. In other words, a cryptocurrency's strengths are predicated on it being a meganet.

Stablecoins attempt to mitigate this loss of control by removing the guaranteed scarcity and placing monetary policy back in the hands of a centralized body, while preserving the censorship-resistance. This is the institutional appeal of cryptocurrency, and the current cryptocurrency enthusiasm from Citi GPS and Facebook undoubtedly augur more respectable stablecoins to come.

Yet in one crucial aspect, the supposed stability of stablecoins is a myth. To see how meganet properties (volume, velocity, virality) intrinsically destabilize stablecoins, let's perform a thought experiment. Imagine a world ten or twenty years in the future where cryptocurrency is a basic form of financial exchange. Everyone around the globe uses an established, stable cryptocurrency, something like what Facebook imagined for Diem or what Citi GPS hopes for. Let's call this cryptocurrency Steddy. Major financial firms provide the infrastructure for Steddy, acting as pseudo central banks to keep Steddy's value steady, perhaps in partnership with the World Bank. It is the first truly international currency. Steddy is backed by honest, transparent exchanges, robust regulation, and viable and stable means of exchange into traditional money. It is hardly the cryptocurrency fanatic's dream, since centralized entities are still exerting control over the currency, but cryptocurrency has become truly mainstream.

Let us go even further and imagine that in this world, Steddy is secure. Massive exchange hacks do not take place, and hackers do not exploit weaknesses in devices and in human psychology to steal unfathomable amounts of cryptocurrency. This is a tall order: if cryptocurrency were to be deployed at large scale, the difficulties of combatting transactions made under false pretenses or duress would be far greater than disputing a credit card payment. Securing cryptocurrency for the average human is a challenging issue but not necessarily an impossible one, so let us optimistically assume that in our future world, the problem has been solved.

Even after we imagine this world in which cryptocurrency is established, secure, and nonvolatile, the meganet properties of cryptocurrency still pose a huge problem. While financial institutions may centralize the financial infrastructure of their preferred cryptocurrencies by backing it with traditional money and assets, the underlying network is still decentralized, still many to many, still a meganet. The benefits of such decentralization, as Citi GPS pointed out, are clear: taking down the entire cryptocurrency system is far more difficult, the system is difficult for a government or any other entity to block, and individual bad actors are crushed by the consensus around honest, fair transactions. Yet these benefits are balanced by dangers—not from hackers, not from factional schisms over the nature of cryptocurrency, but from the meganet software itself.

The problems of decentralization manifest here when it comes to updating the cryptocurrency code. We saw earlier how destabilizing forks were to cryptocurrencies. One single bug could cause massive hyperinflation or allow a hacker to empty an entire fund into a private wallet. One single hack, like that of The DAO, could require amending the fundamental Ethereum code underpinning it. We saw the communities frantically and desperately patch those bugs and coordinate rollout to upgrade everyone's software. We saw the schisms that resulted when not everyone agreed on which software—on which *reality*—to embrace. While regulators and commentators have been focusing on the *legal* implications of cryptocurrency's decentralization of *exchange and finance*, they have been mostly ignoring the *engineering* problems of *decentralization itself*, which pose equal if not greater risks to the system.

Even leaving aside hacks and bugs, there will come a time when Steddy's underlying code will need to be updated. There will be some new scenario that needs to be addressed, or some inefficiency that needs to be remedied. Perhaps Steddy, like Bitcoin and Ethereum, will consume too much energy in its workings and require an update to make it more "green." Code, as every software engineer learns, is far more transient than permanent. Change will be necessary, and at the point a change is required, every entity running Steddy's blockchain code will need to upgrade to the new code, lest a hard fork take place and the world split into multiple realities.*

The possibility of that hard fork is a worm in the apple. If some value-overflow incident occurs in Steddy, millions upon millions of users around the world, whether in Africa, Asia, or the United States, will need to upgrade immediately to avoid contributing to the "wrong" reality in which some clever user has triggered hyperinflation. If Steddy's transactions grind to a halt because its blockchain can't process them fast enough, millions upon millions of users will need to upgrade to avoid being left behind. If monetary policy requires that some amount of stablecoins be invalidated, millions upon millions of users will have to upgrade to recognize those invalidations. Until all users have upgraded, transactions will flow into two different realities, and the problems of reconciling them will become ever more baroque. With cryptocurrency as it stands, schisms are common and unavoidable. In our Steddy scenario, they will become rarer, but they will still be unavoidable.

The irony is that centralizing the financial backing of cryptocurrency doesn't centralize its operations, and so the meganet's chaos can still assert itself. Even if financial companies engineer a cryptocurrency to remove most possibilities of ideological schisms, the issue of *technical* schisms remains, in which upgraded software cannot be deployed to millions upon millions of users quickly enough to prevent an inadvertent hard fork. Cryptocurrency's virtues lie in the immutability of its algorithms, but when those algorithms are imperfect and require fixing—as they invariably do—the virtues become crippling vices.

Stablecoins, even in this ideal form as Steddy, do not put the meganet genie of cryptocurrency back into the bottle because there are two aspects of complexity in play—programmatic and economic—and stablecoins only even purport to address one of them. While most

* It is inevitable that a soft fork will not be sufficient for some required change. Even soft forks would pose similar problems because they result in two different views of the same blockchain, which relaxes the urgency of upgrading software but does not eliminate the possibility for catastrophic misunderstanding.

present concerns have been directed at the possible insolvency of both classic cryptocurrencies and stablecoins, the stability of the *financial* infrastructure of cryptocurrencies is not identical with the stability of the *technological* infrastructure of cryptocurrencies. The two infrastructures have been conflated because problems in each have tended to march in lockstep: any technological problem, whether a hack or a fork, has had an immediate financial impact that had to be mitigated. Consequently, there has been a growing focus on pure economic and political problems of solvency and transparency, when in fact the problem runs considerably deeper.

Financial companies will be able to centralize monetary decision-making around the future of their cryptocoins. What they can't do is centralize *the network itself*. Financial institutions may be able to mitigate this decentralization by hosting the actual blockchain software themselves on behalf of their users, yet the resulting meganet will *still* be too big not to fall prey to unwanted hard forks. Even the Ethereum community at the time of the hack of The DAO was tiny in comparison to the sort of cryptocurrency networks Citi GPS and Facebook imagine. If the community of a cryptocurrency consists of tens of millions or hundreds of millions of users running blockchain-based software on their phones, a single bug will affect every single installation of every piece of software on every device—a meganet-driven nightmare. If the software isn't uniformly upgraded to a new version, there will be unintended forks. Once these forks take place, there is no easy rolling back of time. We saw how difficult it was just to undo the hack of The DAO, requiring the equivalent of a constitutional amendment to Ethereum's code. When that cryptocurrency network is the size of the world, undoing the inexorable progression of the blockchain (and after it forks, multiple blockchains) becomes more than daunting. The logistical difficulties aren't just nightmarish; they could well be insurmountable.

Smart minds are working on these problems and may come up with ways to mitigate the growing complexity of cryptocurrency meganets, but in the battle between control and complexity, complexity almost always has the upper hand. Features and technologies advance faster than mechanisms to control them, creating semiautonomous systems beyond human control: meganets. As meganets grow, this is the four-step process that they follow:

1. Our meganets systems are getting increasingly complex.
2. Defects in those systems are increasingly guaranteed in increasing number.
3. Our ability to anticipate and address these defects is decreasing.
4. Our ability to mitigate the consequences of these defects is not improving, and possibly decreasing.

In spite of this growing danger, Bitcoin and cryptocurrency more generally have already been integrated into the global economy, and once integrated, there is no deintegrating them. Whether it is Bitcoin, Ethereum, or some future cryptocurrency that does not exist, some form of blockchain-backed cryptocurrency lies in our future. The appeal is too great, and the links are too strong.

The paradox of cryptocurrencies is that blockchain networks rely on ceding control to the meganet while simultaneously demanding more of the meganet than it can offer. Cryptocurrency expects the meganet to regulate itself as well as (or better than) humans could. The meganet does indeed regulate itself but not necessarily in the way that we want or need. And we ignore those limits of control at our peril.

SIX

THE LIMITS OF CONTROL

The time misorder'd doth, in common sense,
Crowd us and crush us to this monstrous form
To hold our safety up.

Shakespeare, *Henry IV, Part 2*

BEYOND SOCIAL DISCOURSE, GAMES, MONEY, AND COMMERCE, there is one even more fundamental concept on which meganets are gaining an increasingly tight grip: personal identity. Digital identity goes far beyond Facebook profiles and e-celebrities. The more meganets administer our lives, the more there needs to be an enduring, unified representation of our identities online, rather than the fragmented and incomplete identities that we create today across dozens of websites. These identities must be reliable, authenticated, and guaranteed, and the only entity capable of offering such assurance is not a private corporation but a government. In this chapter, we will see how government meganets increasingly organize themselves around the concept of identity. Here the greatest advances have taken place mostly in other countries, India in particular, but they set the stage for an inevitable progress toward these sorts of unified public meganets everywhere. We will soon be bound not just to Facebook or Bitcoin's meganets but also to our own government's.

THE NEED FOR PUBLIC MEGANETS

What is a person to a computer? In the 1940s, AI pioneers Warren McCulloch and Walter Pitts conceived of simulating neurons computationally, making one of the first conceptual leaps toward the mammoth deep-learning AIs of today. In 1960, McCulloch wrote that the question that had concerned him his whole career was: "What is a number, that a man may know it, and a man, that he may know a number?"[1] In other words, how is it that we biological creatures come to engage with the abstract realm of mathematics? How is the immaterial realm of numbers related to the physical world in which we live?

The importance of the question persists, though today we might better say "data" instead of "number." Meganets are neither wholly machine nor wholly human but the result of the combination of both on an unprecedentedly gigantic scale. Without machines, the meganet could not operate as quickly or as chaotically as it does. Without people, the meganet would freeze and stop evolving. Meganets link people and machines by representing reality as data. In McCulloch's vision, human and number are distinct entities, each inviolable. But just as people create the data that machines understand, the meganet's imposition of data on the world changes what it is to be a person. Today, we could rewrite McCulloch's question as: "What is *data* that a person may *change* it, and a person, that she may be *changed* by data?"

The idea of a "person" is less well defined than it initially seems. A person may be defined by a physical body and the actions that body takes, but around that body our culture builds an entire suite of qualities, descriptors, and associations. Our physical state, our personalities, our social lives, our finances, our government records: all of these revolve around the idea of a person. The digital mirages (a more apt term than digital twin) created on the meganet represent various aspects of personhood today, all of them incomplete, many of them overlapping. A single person possesses badly maintained links to an unruly mess of online profiles across thousands of databases. This, however, is not the meganet's way, which is to grow and consolidate. In the case of many consumer products, the consolidation has happened chiefly on a single website: Amazon. In the case of capturing friendship relations, the consolidation initially happened primarily on Facebook; business relations happen on LinkedIn and also Twitter. But all of these examples of a person's digital identity only partially represent a person's full existence in the world.

To most, fragmentation of online identity is a good thing. Few would want a single company, whether it's Facebook or Google or Amazon, to manage not just their friends network but also their shopping habits, business profile, credit history, medical records, government benefits, and taxes. Yet the irresistible force of the meganet will gradually consolidate these spheres. Against the inertia of the status quo and the tremendous mess of our data landscape today, companies gradually merge the diffuse data on people, assembling increasingly elaborate profiles on people around the world. Facebook and Google are some of the biggest aggregators of information (hence the Cambridge Analytica scandal), but hundreds of more shadowy companies like Interpublic Group's Acxiom, Publicis's Epsilon, and Dentsu's Merkle also quietly assemble profiles on consumers, frequently for marketing purposes, occasionally for other reputational reasons.[2]

It is far easier to put information into the meganet than to remove information from it. It is far easier for information to spread across meganets than for it to be contained. It is far easier for information to be wrong than it is to be right. Those three rules are so powerful as to be tantamount to laws. As our digital profiles grow and multiply outside our ability to observe them, they are also combined and reduplicated without our knowledge. What keeps this information from becoming truly definitive is that there is no single authority that can guarantee that the information is correct to a viable legal standard. (Recall how Facebook had concluded, of its own accord, that I was African American.)

Ultimately, there is only one kind of entity that can reliably and legally assert that the information it possesses about people is correct: a government. Only a government can require that all its citizens give up accurate details about themselves, and only a government has the authority to claim that its data on a person supersedes any other digital profiles private entities may have assembled. In the United States, and to a lesser extent in most other countries with significant guarantees of civil liberties, our public and private digital profiles remain mostly distinct. The NSA may have amassed profiles on millions of American citizens, harvesting information from Facebook and mobile phones, but the NSA does not in turn share that data with Facebook and Google.[3] The IRS's records do not influence one's credit rating, at least not directly. And because these government agencies have yet to unify their own databases with one another, we are mostly unaware of the possibility for a far more unified government-run meganet—a possibility so likely as to appear inevitable.

Because private meganets like Facebook, Amazon, or Bitcoin have a far greater presence in the public eye than government-run meganets (which are primarily used for policing, intelligence, and military purposes), the majority of the discussion around meganet-driven issues like privacy, security, and moderation has focused around nongovernmental meganets. This, however, is a major oversight. Government-run meganets already dominate India and China, and they are only growing in other societies. While it is novel to Americans to have a government-assigned vaccine passport checked whenever we go to eat at a restaurant, our data is already far more centralized when it comes to privately operated mechanisms like credit cards and cell phones. In many other nations, governments take a far more leading role in monitoring and regulating individuals' identities. The share of our digital identity apportioned to government databases will only grow in the coming decades, not out of any great plan or conspiracy but through the inherent forces of meganets as they grow and coalesce.

When governments control meganets, or otherwise attempt to influence them, the rules change. No longer are we looking at private enterprises working within some sort of regulatory framework, however outdated or ineffectual it may be. Rather, governments put legally authoritative systems in place and mandate their usage, with judicial checks coming slowly if ever. However one feels about vaccine mandates and the patchwork of local regulations requiring them, the technology was far ahead of judicial oversight. While lawsuits wound their way slowly through the courts, programs like NYC's Excelsior Pass were already deployed, as legislatures and executives deemed necessary. Such programs are quite minor, however, compared to what already exists overseas. The prototype for the sort of ubiquitous governmental meganet that will soon dominate has already existed in India for over ten years as a national government ID program called Aadhaar. Aadhaar is a glimpse of a future Americans have yet to encounter: a unified, government-sanctioned meganet. It is a future that is unavoidable. Governments always lag behind corporations, but just as corporate meganets have redefined identity, societal and legal demands are forcing governments to take a role in online life.

The growing *need* for authentication of online identity means that governments will ultimately have no choice but to adjudicate their citizens' identities, and they will only be able to do so with their own meganets. India is already doing so, while South American and European countries are following its lead. And yet one peculiar outlier—China, which we will examine later—shows just where the limits of such government-driven meganets may lie.

FOUNDATION

Over the last decade in India, the Unique Identification Authority of India (UIDAI) has rolled out a sweeping, uniform identification system, Aadhaar, to all its citizens. Intended to unify, consolidate, and secure access to government services and identity authentication, the program has been so successful that nearly all Indian citizens now have an Aadhaar card, which is linked to a centralized government database. Yet when the program fails to work, the consequences can be catastrophic. Citizens who aren't found in Aadhaar, for whatever reason, can't get rations.[4] There were fourteen Aadhaar-related deaths by starvation in 2018, when for a variety of reasons citizens were unable to obtain or produce the proper card and authentication.[5] In 2017, a sick infant without an Aadhaar card was denied admission to a hospital and died.[6]

Still others are scared to use Aadhaar. In 2017, Indian news site Scroll detailed a number of HIV patients who were terrified that Aadhaar unification would lead to the leaking of their sexual identity and gender status:

> One sex worker, who stopped getting her medicines because she refused to submit her Aadhaar details, died this year.
>
> "Around this time, last December, the antiretroviral therapy centre in the government hospital started insisting on Aadhaar," said [outreach worker Geeta] Moorthy. "She just stopped taking medicines because she was scared of her identity being revealed."
>
> Several HIV positive people told Scroll.in that they had Aadhaar cards but, like Priya, did not want to share them at antiretroviral therapy centres because their identities as people living with HIV may be revealed.
>
> The government first started linking the Aadhaar cards with food ration services. Over the past year, the government has been asking citizens to link Aadhaar card[s] to PAN cards and now mobile phone connections. Many HIV positive people, sex workers, gay men and women and transgender people fear that by linking Aadhaar to all these services, they run the risk of having their carefully guarded identities exposed.[7]

This story spread virally, though even some critics of Aadhaar believed the fears to be overblown. Researcher Prashant Reddy, who has criticized Aadhaar for excluding welfare recipients and blocking access to banking services, wrote that Aadhaar was very unlikely to leak this sort of personal and health information.[8] Yet the fears persist in large part because Aadhaar is not a static entity but a growing one, sweeping up and consolidating more and more data in its wake, connecting bits and pieces about citizens that can never be disconnected. The Indian government, in the hopes of guaranteeing privacy for its citizens, in fact ceded a great deal of control over Aadhaar to the private sector, leaving it at the mercy of thousands of third parties grafting more personal data on to the core Aadhaar identity. That out-of-control spread and the explicit inability to regain control indicate that Aadhaar is a meganet.

Aadhaar, which means "foundation" in Hindi, started off with the highest ideals. Like the United States and many other countries, India had a mishmash of overlapping identification and enrollment databases and cards for its citizens. Among the United States' many government forms of ID, we have Social Security cards, birth certificates, passports, driver's licenses, library cards, TSA precheck approvals, and now proofs of COVID vaccination. (Nongovernmental databases like credit scores and our bank accounts also act as stores of a good deal of reputation-based information.) In our networked world, each form of ID, whether a card or a number, now stands for an entry in a database containing some subset of our information. From the driver's license database, you can pull up my current address, but my birth certificate would not give you enough information to do so directly. Since we use such documents and databases to verify different things at different times—my appearance, my eligibility to drive, my birth date, my place of birth—there's no single document or card that can be used universally. Much the same is true in most nations. Even countries with a national ID card, like France or Japan, still have auxiliary forms of ID for purposes like welfare or driver's licenses.

One of the main problems Aadhaar was created to solve was that of welfare inefficiency and outright fraud. To a far greater degree than in any first-world nation, by the early twenty-first century India was frequently unable to track the administration of welfare funds to states because it lacked anywhere near the degree of predigital infrastructure that first-world nations had built out in the mid-twentieth century. As food subsidies increased by a factor of ten from 1986 to 2004, studies revealed that not only was less than half of subsidized food actually reaching its intended recipients, the rest disappearing unaccountably due to "identification errors, non-transparent operation and unethical practices," but efficiency and accountability were also so appallingly absent that only 16 percent of the overall money allocated to welfare actually made it to the poor.[9] While one may dispute the need for Facebook or even the NSA given the tradeoffs with data aggregation and privacy, there was considerably less debate over the existence of India's problem in administrating welfare.*

To solve the problem of disorganization and ignorance, the government created the UIDAI office. When UIDAI was founded in 2009 and tasked with building what became Aadhaar, India not only intended to establish one single form of identification but also to centralize government services and government databases around that single identifier. Instead of having a social security number, a driver's license number, and a passport number, the twelve-digit Aadhaar code would be the single identifier for *all* government (and some nongovernment) services, linked to a single, government-administered database, which would authoritatively identify citizens. To further guarantee Aadhaar's authority, the database also stores biometric identifiers in the form of fingerprints and iris scans.[10]

Put this way, Aadhaar sounds simple, practical, and even inevitable. With the exponential growth of data and ever-increasing digital services, it makes sense to streamline and centralize identification and eligibility services around a single, government-administered program and database. Certainly, privacy and security would prove to be issues around any such database, but one could argue that those issues already existed around all the databases Aadhaar was meant to supplant. Praxis Business School director Prithwis Mukerjee made this case in defending Aadhaar in 2018:

---

* Critics have maintained that the problems Aadhaar was meant to solve have been wildly overstated in order to push the program. Even if so, there was nonetheless a need for some greater consolidation of government services, and existing means were inadequate. Whether Aadhaar was the right or necessary solution is too great a question for my concerns here.

> In fact, many of the conveniences that we use—passport, air travel, cellphone, online banking, Gmail—have a greater probability of causing damage to our privacy, and in a throwback to Heisenberg's Uncertainty Principle, let us accept that it is impossible to maximise both privacy and convenience at the same time. One must always trade off any one against the other. Unless you are like Richard Stallman—the open source guru and privacy fanatic, who does not use cellphones, credit cards, hotel Wi-Fi, the Google search engine, Facebook and many other conveniences of daily life in his quest for total privacy—a lot of information about you is already in the public domain, and Aadhaar will hardly add anything more to that.[11]

This argument, along with the efficiency gains from a single centralized ID, are at the heart of the case for Aadhaar. Economist Yoginder K. Alagh put it bluntly: "Simplify and live long."[12] Alagh's point is that the chaos of life (and of meganets) arises from there being too many overlapping, incompatible, and sheerly redundant systems that create needless inefficiencies and complexities whenever they need to be reconciled, as well as hurting the overall authority of any single one. Simplify identity and databases into one single system, Alagh and others say, and we can turn our messy patchwork of data authorities into one streamlined and elegant machine.

Mukerjee and Alagh view Aadhaar as *removing* complexity rather than adding it. Their view, however, is one-sided. Mukerjee is correct in saying that most of the data Aadhaar touches is already out there, but he misses what Aadhaar does add to the overall picture, which is not information but *connectivity*, *unification*, and *interaction*. We have seen how meganets, whether Bitcoin or Facebook or Warcraft, come into being when enough connections are made between entities that they start feeding back on themselves beyond our control, and Aadhaar is the first example we're seeing in which that process happens in a government-run rather than a privately run entity.

Aadhaar merits serious attention not just as a case study but also because it is a paradigm for the future, a unified government-driven meganet deployed in a comparatively free high-population society closer to the United States than to China or Russia. At its inception, the government promised that Aadhaar would be voluntary. By the end of the 2010s, over 99 percent of Indians had Aadhaar IDs, and the program was mandatory for all practical purposes if not by law. In fact, arguing that Aadhaar was necessary for the poor to obtain government services had become a key platform of Aadhaar defenders, the slippage from voluntary to mandatory notwithstanding.[13] There is dispute over to what extent Aadhaar actually addresses the problems it was meant to solve, and critics have charged that proponents have oversold Aadhaar's effectiveness while minimizing problems it generates.[14] In practical terms, these debates are moot now that Aadhaar has rolled out. The horse has bolted from the barn, and as with any meganet once it reaches a certain size, there is no turning back time. Even debates about whether Aadhaar's benefits outweigh its costs become impossible because the world of India with Aadhaar has already diverged so much from the possible world of India without it that we would have to peek into an alternate reality to make side-by-side comparisons.

Despite appearances, Aadhaar is fundamentally a different beast from all the databases and identification cards it supplanted. Aadhaar is closer to Facebook than it is to the Department of Motor Vehicles (DMV) database. Aadhaar is not just larger and it's not just more universal than the DMV database; Aadhaar's innate extensibility and agglomerative nature make it a meganet. No other form of ID carries with it the ability to grow limitlessly, accumulating more data on its users as more services are hooked up to it. In the past, forms of identification took on new usages ad hoc, as when I show my driver's license to prove my age (even though it has nothing to do with driving). Very few forms of ID until recently have been designed with the capability to amass more and more arbitrary information of all stripes and group it by a single identifier. With Aadhaar, any number of governmental and nongovernmental entities are collecting information about India's citizens around a single government-given identifier. The web of information around that identifier grows, out of the control of the person who possesses that identifier. That growth capacity—the capacity for an increasing number of entities to react to what one another is doing within a single network and feed back onto one another—also makes Aadhaar a meganet.

IDENTITY CRISIS

The Aadhaar program got its name when a UIDAI volunteer, Naman Pugalia, traveled across India interviewing nomadic tribes about the UIDAI's identity project. Naiya Ram Rathore, an elder of the Mogiya tribe who had been won over by the end of the interview, told Pugalia: "If this idea can be translated into reality, that would be very good. Identity is, after all, the foundation [*aadhaar* in Hindi] of life."[15] Pugalia phoned his superiors, and so a nomad gave Aadhaar its name.

Despite it being the foundation of your life, your identity is not something that you control, at least not in full. Identity is a set of identifiers given to you by the world, some by choice and some not. Identity is a web, connecting your physical body to an extensive and growing assortment of data across the country and around the world, cycling through the meganet at light speed. Identity is not a card. It is the set of verified, virtual links between your physical body and your accounts and profiles and representations across all the services and systems you use. These links also connect individual identities to the identities of other people through friend networks and other shared affiliations. That rich, dense web connecting identities to one another—and the fact that in today's networked world, each identity can influence all those to which it is connected—causes identity services to become meganets after reaching a certain point of complexity growing organically out of control.

Aadhaar has been the largest and most aggressive consolidation of identity, but it is far from the only one. As computer networks infuse all aspects of life, the need for an identity service on the internet becomes the need for an identity service everywhere. Individual services (passports, licenses, and the like) will gradually link together, and this linkage will be permanent. It may take time, but Aadhaar-like consolidation around the world is inevitable.

Just as Facebook or LinkedIn have embedded themselves inextricably into the fabric of our lives, the United States received a taste of Aadhaar-like governmental meganets with vaccine passports. Despite alarmism over a stratified society if vaccine passports were required at restaurants and other indoor locations, state-issued passes like New York's Excelsior rolled out quickly and without objection in the middle of 2021. For some time, restaurants and other venues in New York City required me to show a combination of proof of vaccination—either a card or a QR code provided by the online Excelsior application—as well as a legal government ID (e.g., a driver's license). The system is piecemeal, ad hoc, error prone, and far too easy to game.* I never encountered a single venue that bothered to scan my Excelsior QR code to verify that it contained my name and vaccine information, much less that it was even a valid QR code and not a random collection of squares. Nor did any check that the birth date on my Excelsior Pass matched that on my driver's license. In effect, if you have some valid government ID, it is trivial to convince most people that you are vaccinated because the process is more pageantry than genuine verification. The required infrastructure to perform robust validation would not be terribly difficult to implement, but neither would it be free or automatic to install and deploy. If a single validating infrastructure—like Aadhaar's—already existed, the deployment of verifiable vaccination checks would become far easier. Extend this to all sorts of other government services, from welfare to disability to Medicare to driver's licenses to you name it, and some sort of unified identification seems not only helpful but destined.

Until it arrives, however, the multiplication of programs and IDs will continue incessantly. New York issued COVID benefit cards to my children independent of any other form of ID. The TSA precheck

---

* Three overlapping systems of vaccination proof—NYC COVID Safe, Excelsior Pass, Excelsior Pass Plus—all got out of sync, such that one of my children could only get the first and the other could only get the first two.

program offers a far speedier airport security experience through a voluntary surrender of personal information to the federal government, a program more would embrace if the registration process were not such a hassle. At some point, there will simply be so many independent programs that society will embrace a unified infrastructure. Like it or not, some kind of Aadhaar-like unification is coming.

The benefit of an identification system like Aadhaar is that as meganets permeate our lives in novel ways, a unified system makes it easy to extend identity validation into new realms with standardized registration and reusable infrastructure. India created Aadhaar out of a dire governmental need, which is why it got there first. Other countries are following India's lead, such as Colombia, whose digital ID program began to roll out in force in 2021. Héctor José García, executive chairman of Camerfirma Colombia, touted the empowering benefits of Colombia's new digital ID:

> The digital card, like the traditional ID card, will enable Colombians to exercise their civil and political rights. Citizens will be able to carry out all kinds of procedures with the Administration from the comfort of their own homes and will even be able, in a not too distant future, to vote electronically.
>
> Other procedures that will be facilitated with the digital ID card include: obtaining a driver's licence; duplicating an ID card; the military passbook; certifications; presentation of petitions, complaints and claims; receiving notifications, among many others.[16]

The most important element of that list is "many others." García's statement carries the crucial implication that the greatest benefit of a digital ID is its ability to consolidate an arbitrary number of future applications. Any one application or even set of applications may be useful, but far more significant is the future *potential* of the digital ID to take on new and unknown applications. The benefit of the digital ID is that it possesses the persistent, evolving, and consolidating characteristics of a meganet. A lack of urgent need and the usual political infighting may slow the process toward a unified ID program like

Aadhaar, but the efficient appeal of such a program will only increase. These programs will simplify how we manage our government-administered identities, but they will also unite them into a more imposing authority. They will remove more of our privacy, and they will make identity theft a far scarier threat.

We are already on the way there. Credit cards have already consolidated the majority of people's spending habits into one trackable account. Identity meganets will accelerate this process by linking other personal and civic data into unified profiles. Eventually, we will have an Aadhaar in the United States. The momentum of a meganet only goes in one direction.

THE PROTOTYPE

Beyond this societal pressure toward simplification, private enterprise has also been eager to step into the breach and build out identity meganets. In particular, Google saw the scope of the problem over a decade ago. When Google deployed its ultimately unsuccessful social network Google+ in 2011, its leadership took pains to announce that Google+ was different from Facebook. It was not just a social network, said then CEO Eric Schmidt; it was an *identity service*.

> The notion of strong identity was never invented in the Internet. Many people worked on it—I worked on it as a scientist 20 years ago, and it's a hard problem. So if we knew that it was a real person, then we could sort of hold them accountable, we could check them, we could give them things, we could you know bill them, you know we could have credit cards and so forth and so on, there are all sorts of reasons.
>
> [Google+] essentially provides an identity service with a link structure around your friends.[17]

To Schmidt, Facebook and its predecessors such as MySpace had just happened upon the possibility of "strong identity," a way of connecting online activity to a single offline person and validating that connection. The unrealized goal of Google+ was to establish a centralized register of people—their identities and relationships.

While Google was never able to get traction on its identity service, Schmidt's comments underscore how crucial identity-based meganets would become to the ever-ballooning online world. Beyond Aadhaar-like identity management, Schmidt also spoke of Google+ as a potential *reputation service*.

> People have a lot of free time and people on the Internet, there are people who do really really evil and wrong things on the Internet, and it would be useful if we had strong identity so we could weed them out. I'm not suggesting eliminating them. What I'm suggesting is if we knew their identity was accurate, we could rank them. Think of them like an identity rank.[18]

Schmidt made these remarks in response to the controversy around Google+'s requirement that users go by their real names rather than masquerading as pseudonyms (as people often do on Twitter) or purely anonymous voices (as on many blogs and internet forums). The stated purpose was to crack down on anonymous trolling and abuse, but the implications are far greater. The true significance of a real-name policy is that it binds the online world (and its meganets) more tightly to offline life. As tech reporter Kashmir Hill put it at the time: "Google doesn't just want Plus to be Facebook; it wants it to be the Digital DMV."[19]

Schmidt even hit on the same type of verification mechanism that Aadhaar would utilize: bodily biometric verification. Google+ would not go so far as using fingerprints, but Schmidt saw the value in using visual appearance as a means of online identification.

> The real mechanism that helped [verify identity] was the technology that was invented first by MySpace and then eventually by Facebook, where you could disambiguate names by looking at people. So if you have John Smith, they show you there's five John Smiths, well here's a John Smith and then based on the pictures,

> you say this is the John Smith who's my friend. And that's how identity is in fact managed in Facebook.[20]

Recognizing people by their faces may feel less intrusive than taking fingerprints or scanning irises, but they both connect some unique physical feature of your real-life, bodily identity to your online account, permanently. Once that connection is made, it's not easily undone—not even by Google or Aadhaar itself.

Google+ failed to gain momentum, and out of desperation it relaxed its real-name policy in 2014, to no avail. Yet the momentum toward the connection of online and real-life identity continued. Simultaneously with Google+'s failure, Facebook triumphed with the same policy of demanding real-life identity. Facebook had always required users' real names from its inception but maintained a relaxed approach to enforcement until around 2014, when they began to aggressively crack down on pseudonyms and names that looked fake (even if they were real).[21] By 2015, Facebook was regularly asking users to provide legal forms of identification to reclaim hacked accounts or to confirm that celebrity accounts had been created by authorized representatives.[22] Today, Facebook's policies allow them to at any time demand either one government ID or two forms of nongovernment ID from a user to verify an account.[23] If not for the pressing need to sign up new users as quickly and easily as possible, Facebook would surely require ID at the time of account creation. As it stands, Facebook account creation still requires a verified and previously unused cell phone number. The cell number serves as an imperfect but more convenient proxy for a real name, as most cell numbers are already tightly tied to a real-life identity.

Where Google+ failed as a private-sector initiative, Aadhaar succeeded as a public-sector one. The comparative lack of organized infrastructure for validating identity in India made the need for Aadhaar far more pressing. In Aadhaar we see where Google dreamed of going with Google+ and further. It is a path we are still on.

THE WEB

Much of the criticism of Google+ came from its capitalistic aims: Google wanted people's identities for marketing purposes. Aadhaar's intentions were more civic and high minded, and in all fairness to Aadhaar's architects, their interest in privacy was far greater. Aadhaar was architected to *not* gather all collected data in a single centralized database, minimizing consolidation. In a lengthy, heartfelt, and somewhat indignant apologia, UIDAI chief and Aadhaar architect Ram Sewak Sharma articulated the difference between Facebook and Aadhaar and why Aadhaar did not pose any threat to privacy and profiling. Aadhaar, he argued, could never fall victim to a Cambridge Analytica–type scandal as Facebook had:

> The worst fears indicated by these studies came true in the Cambridge Analytica story. In 2018, the company was accused of having "harvested" 50 million Facebook users' data and used it without their consent for "political advertising," besides engaging in other "irregular" activities. . . .
>
> However, we should not conflate the vulnerabilities arising from these social networks with Aadhaar. . . . Unlike the social networks, where a large amount of information is public and visible, in the case of Aadhaar, the information collected is minimal and inaccessible to unrelated parties.
>
> The law protects every piece of information involved in using Aadhaar, with the use itself restricted by the Supreme Court. On the other hand, the social networks hoard every picture, every line of text and every mouse click and sell it for the equivalent of the gross domestic product (GDP) of many countries. In this respect, Aadhaar's and OSN's [online social networks] are as different from each other as chalk and cheese.[24]

Sharma is right that Aadhaar does not *collect* and *consolidate* information in its own centralized database. But the Aadhaar meganet is not simply that single database but the entire ecosystem that has evolved around it, in which information *is* consolidated, haphazardly, by countless parties. The essence of the Aadhaar meganet is the coalescing of a person's digital identity around a *single number* and all that flows from it. The core Aadhaar identity systems do not themselves perform this consolidation, but by creating a single identifier for each person and encouraging its use in increasing numbers of scenarios, they *make that consolidation possible*—and, indeed, inevitable. Meganets come into existence through the *potential* for ongoing expansion and consolidation, which they then realize by their nature. Once there is a single key—an individual's Aadhaar number and associated biometrics—that opens every lock to that person's data; it does not matter that the doors lead to different, unconnected houses. What matters is that the number of doors and houses will continue to increase and that they are forever linked to a single key—the Aadhaar number.

Sharma himself does not deny this tendency toward expansion, suggesting many further potential avenues of information to be connected to the Aadhaar ID, through public and private entities.

> Indeed, some functions that the government provided in the past, such as registration of deeds, could also be entrusted to private enterprise with the help of Aadhaar for identity and a blockchain for immutability of records. Or consider the reputation of an individual, which itself is an asset. If reputational scores could be attached to the identity of an individual, it may encourage people to invest in their reputation much like the Uber driver who would rather not displease a customer and get less than a five-star rating. Here, I'm not suggesting government-mandated scores, but the possibility that scores could be created in a variety of ways by different agencies, all with the explicit knowledge of the individual and with her willing participation.[25]

To Sharma, the multiplication of Aadhaar-authenticated services is a benefit. To the extent that it simplifies the need for identity and authentication, such unification is beneficial, but Sharma ignores the unintended and inevitable effects of such a meganet spreading, which is that, once again, *no one is in control.* It is even more explicit here than in the Facebook case because Aadhaar has *no* control over the services that use it. All Aadhaar does is join them together in one enormous meganet, allowing them to feed off each other by eliminating any friction in aggregating data on an individual, making it trivial to determine to which real-life human body a particular account belongs.

True, it is not the Aadhaar service itself that aggregates the data—but it is Aadhaar that makes it possible in the first place. When security researchers Srinivas Kodali and Karan Saini discovered that seventy government subdomains contained a hole that would allow identification of Aadhaar ID numbers by citizens' names, the problem was with those government sites rather than the Aadhaar database per se, but it was the linkage of all these systems into one huge ecosystem—and the linkage of so many citizen accounts into one single number—that made the hole so dangerous.[26] The Aadhaar nightmares of HIV patients may well be unlikely nightmares. The issue is not any particular nightmare, but that by turning millions of impossible nightmares into highly unlikely but possible ones, Aadhaar ensures that, eventually, one or two of these unlikely nightmares *will* come to pass—and one or two is all that is needed for chaos. It is the volume, velocity, and virality that is the problem.

Of course, the volume, velocity, and virality also hold seeming advantages. Sharma himself conjures a growing web of interacting online and offline services, all unified around the Aadhaar identifiers of over one billion Indian citizens:

> The global information services company, Experian, which is into data analytics for the financial services sector, put up a proposal to use Aadhaar for credit rating. Muthoot Finance designed an initiative to disburse cash against gold jewelry using Aadhaar in under three minutes wherein the beneficiary could collect cash at an ATM using the Aadhaar number and authentication. Hero

> Cycles looked at a fully automated rent-a-cycle programme. The cycles to be parked at transportation hubs could be unlocked and paid for using Aadhaar with zero security deposit. In a similar vein, an NGO framed a scheme of providing LED lamps to people using kerosene lamps against Aadhaar authentication with no deposits.[27]

Here Sharma falls into a kind of idealized inconsistency. He weighs future possible benefits of Aadhaar only against present-day drawbacks, accusing his critics of exaggerating those breaches that have already taken place. Aadhaar's critics have in part been a blessing for the program. By exaggerating troubling real incidents into the realm of hypothetical catastrophic risks, they encourage the accusation that their fears are overblown. For all of the worries over HIV status being disclosed through Aadhaar, such leakages remain theoretical for now.[28] It is Sharma's hoped-for out-of-control growth that will make Aadhaar leakages increasingly likely and eventually inevitable, as the web of data unified around Aadhaar ID numbers reaches the point where every data breach will compound every other data breach. As soon as one Aadhaar-indexed database leaks, it can be easily cross-referenced with every other such leak, with no way to sever the ties between Aadhaar-linked data sets. That irreversible, nonlinear compounding is, once again, the signature of the meganet. If Aadhaar has become, in journalist Shankkar Aiyar's words, "too big to falter, never mind fail," its intrinsic tendency toward growth and ever-greater complexity is a chronic and growing threat to its stability and security.[29]

The greatest irony of Aadhaar is that its privacy safeguards and lack of data consolidation ultimately make identity theft easier. We speak of identity theft today whenever someone impersonates another person using her social security number, credit card, or other identifying information, but such identity theft is as piecemeal as the systems that were hacked. Other parts of that person's identity remain secure. As soon as there is any compromise of the Aadhaar's biometric authentication system at any point in the chain, however, a hacker has committed *total* identity theft of a person's digital identity on a scale never before possible.

Worse, Aadhaar has fewer safeguards in place than these other systems for the most ironic of reasons: privacy. Systems theorist Anupam Saraph summarized the problem:

> [Aadhaar's biometrics are] like a lock authenticating the key that tries to unlock it. It cannot identify the person holding the key. Identification requires the persons identifying to be co-present. It requires them to take responsibility for the consequences of (mis) identification. The UIDAI is not co-present and takes no responsibility of identification. The UIDAI does not certify the identity, address or date of birth of anyone. The UIDAI does not even know the primary documents used as proof of identity and proof of address to issue any Aadhaar number. This means that it is not possible to challenge an authentication with the primary documents to verify the identity of a person.[30]

Saraph put his finger on the paradox that resulted from Aadhaar's idealism: security and privacy were in competition with each other. By only storing biometric data for authentication and nothing else, Aadhaar gave up any safeguards on that authentication. As soon as the link between the biometric data and the Aadhaar identifier is compromised, there is no other authenticating data available that might flag the compromise as illegitimate. This security breach comes about not because the links between Aadhaar's database and real life are too strong but because they are simultaneously too *wide* and too *weak*. In pursuing the very decentralization that is the signature of the meganet, Aadhaar neglected to create sufficient centralized security. The greater the scope of an identification system, the more catastrophic a compromise becomes. Yet securing that system requires retaining additional personal data to authenticate a user: *the very data Aadhaar avoided centralizing*. The result is an out-of-control meganet, one that unifies digital identities without tying them securely *enough* to their real-life counterparts.

CREEP

The meganet expands by its very nature. As a meganet grows, it presents more opportunities for gathering and aggregating data, more ways that information and processes could be easily coalesced and made more efficient. It was not at all obvious in 2005 that fifteen years later a social network called Facebook and a search engine called Google would alone control over 50 percent of a $140 billion digital advertising market.[31] That was the power of meganets at work: Google's and Facebook's large-scale accumulation of certain types of data allowed for easy expansion into other realms, with advertising being the most lucrative one. Their duopoly emerged less as a result of their initial data sets and algorithms and more as a result of their meganets' ability to grow and subsume new territory.

The spread of Aadhaar was unexpected in different ways. Intended from the start to be voluntary, the program has become all but mandatory. The architects of Aadhaar don't give the impression of having been disingenuous in posing a program intended for over a billion citizens of India as merely optional, yet that is exactly the paradox at work. The Aadhaar team created a legally voluntary system and then took every step it could to make it all but mandatory. Having created a system to handle the identities of a billion people, Aadhaar then had to go about recruiting as many people as possible to justify the system. Because it was not mandated, the team wished for people to *want* Aadhaar, and the easiest path to *want* was from *need:* Aadhaar created committees "to create a need to possess [Aadhaar], and then drive this need."[32] Once in, there was no out. As security analyst Karan Saini wrote, "You can always deactivate Facebook. You cannot deactivate your Aadhaar."[33] That is what makes Aadhaar so much more profound than Facebook and Google: it is a permanent, immutable tie from a real person to the meganet's digital mirage of that person.

When economist Reetika Khera describes the multiplying middlemen entities around Aadhaar, she is also describing a process of integration and consolidation:

> Where middlemen [previously] existed (pensions delivered by a postman who demanded money), one type of middleman has been replaced by another (banking correspondents have taken the place of postmen) . . . [and] the Aadhaar eco-system is breeding an army of middlemen (enrolment, re-enrolment of biometrics, Aadhaar-seeding, correcting demographic details, etc).[34]

These new middlemen differ fundamentally from their predecessors, however. The postmen and other intermediaries who extorted money were acting independently without coordination. The Aadhaar meganet interconnects with itself so that middlemen join with one another to create a single larger organism. Even if the central Aadhaar database stores minimal data (for better and for worse, as we saw), the landscape of middlemen will only grow richer and richer in the data it accumulates, and that army of middlemen will tend toward becoming a monolithic entity akin to Facebook or Google, just less centralized.

In 2018 Edward Snowden said that because Aadhaar was increasingly being required to book flight tickets and open bank accounts, Aadhaar "is creating a systemisation of the society, of the public and this was not the stated intention of the program."[35] Aadhaar's advocates agree that it was not the stated intention. The goal instead was to limit the central mission of Aadhaar to authentication and nothing else. Yet from the perspective of a meganet, broader systemization was an inevitability. Aadhaar's architects intended from the very start for their network to expand into increasing numbers of public and private applications. That Aadhaar would become mandatory over time was inherent in its very design; only by failing could it have avoided becoming a requirement for everyday functions in life in India. That it would standardize society was also inherent in its very design, despite its architects *not intending* any such effect.

Critics of Aadhaar, whether attacking it from the standpoint of privacy, security, or sheer ineffectiveness, got a win in 2018 when the Supreme Court of India affirmed most of the Aadhaar law but struck down Section 57, the section legitimizing the use of Aadhaar's identification functions by all corporations and individuals, private or public, which had led to mobile carriers and banks requiring Aadhaar numbers to sign up for accounts.[36] Aadhaar was already integrated into the fabric of life, so the government and corporations were left scrambling to reintegrate Aadhaar into those spots that the ruling had supposedly closed off. Technology lawyer Nehaa Chaudhari explained the gaps that this ruling created:

> The ruling on Section 57 will affect how vast sections of India's population access services such as micro ATMs, which are designed to serve people in rural areas, microcredit lenders and fintech start-ups offering products and services to people excluded from traditional banking channels.
>
> Many customers such as financial inclusion platforms serve might have no other way of verifying their identity, and the exclusion of Aadhaar as an identity verification mechanism will mean exclusion from such services altogether. A legislation that restricts the use of Aadhaar to private entities in regulated sectors such as banking, telecom and insurance; makes Aadhaar use voluntary and requires companies to offer alternative means of identity verification; encompasses stringent data protection requirements, including consent, accountability and strong penalties for breach, is likely to be held constitutional.
>
> Not allowing the voluntary use of Aadhaar in the private sector even under a new law with sufficient safeguards would take away an individual's ability to make decisions about their own information. Moreover, public sector firms would gain unfair competitive advantage if they are allowed to use Aadhaar-based authentication, but not private companies. Most of all, it would exclude "the marginalized sections of society" which the Supreme Court intended to empower through this judgement in the first place.[37]

Again we face the same paradox: to obtain (and maintain) the valuable applications offered by private companies, Chaudhari asks for Aadhaar's scope to be expanded while legally mandating that it be "voluntary." Yet for Aadhaar to be voluntary, companies must offer "alternative means of identity verification," even as Chaudhari claims that Aadhaar is needed in rural areas *precisely because no such alternative means exist*. The promise of "alternative means" reads more as a fig leaf than as a viable policy, a gambit designed to keep Aadhaar voluntary in the law's eyes and mandatory in practice.

Justice Dhananjaya Y. Chandrachud made this point in dissenting from the India Supreme Court's judgment, when he said that Aadhaar lacked "enough robust safeguards as to informed consent and individual rights such as opt-out. Constitutional guarantees cannot be subjected to probability algorithms and technological vicissitudes."[38] Chandrachud still affirmed the overall legality of Aadhaar, in line with the reasoning of the court: "Aadhaar gives dignity to the marginalized. Dignity to the marginalized outweighs privacy."[39] In validating the Aadhaar act while admitting that it was effectively mandatory, Chandrachud revealed that Aadhaar was now inextricable from Indian society. Aadhaar was a conceptually legitimate program that inevitably spread in illegitimate ways in practice. But since Aadhaar was already embedded into the fabric of Indian life, nothing could be done to stop it; eliminating Aadhaar was no longer an option. The meganet was irreversible.

It is for this reason that Chaudhari will win the argument and Aadhaar's expansion will continue. Once a meganet like Aadhaar comes into existence and integrates into society, commonsense arguments like Chaudhari's will trump principled arguments that draw arbitrary boundaries around data. Those boundaries, even if established by law, are simply too provisional and too porous to endure. Even the drawing of the public-private boundary was ineffective, as Chaudhari hinted above, because the private applications are too essential to everyday life. In the wake of the court decision, the government passed a bill mandating alternative mechanisms to Aadhaar and allowing "voluntary" usage of Aadhaar identification with banks, telecoms, casinos, and other private companies.[40] In effect, as long as some alternative to Aadhaar identification was available, almost anyone could once again use Aadhaar for identity verification.[41] There is no specification as to what non-Aadhaar mechanism is to be offered, nor to how onerous it may be, and in a country where over 99 percent of the population already have Aadhaar, there are no incentives to encourage alternatives. We complain that Facebook is a private, optional service that we can't avoid, but that remains an exaggeration. Aadhaar takes that complaint and makes it reality. What is legally voluntary and legally public becomes, in practice, mandatory and hopelessly entangled between public and private entities.

Around the core, public, privacy-conscious Aadhaar database, there grows a distinct exoskeleton of interconnected pieces both public and private, all based around a uniform means of identifying a real-life person, all capable of quietly brokering and trading information about Aadhaar-identified people without the central database having any knowledge of the greater network. Even if such data sharing was to be made illegal, it could not easily be stopped; data flows too freely. For all of the medical privacy forms Americans sign every time they see a new doctor, Facebook can somehow manage to learn about an individual's stomachaches and headaches and target him with advertising. Aadhaar removes any friction from this process.

Aadhaar's designers did not intend this particular vision, at least not all of it. A glance at the defenses given by Aadhaar architects like Ram Sewak Sharma and Nandan Nikelani does not reveal any intent to create free-flowing *data*. Their vision was for a unified service used discretely by many applications. Their defense when those applications misuse the data granted to them (data not given to the core Aadhaar service) is that the trouble is with the applications, not Aadhaar.[42] The defense is technically accurate, yet to imagine that some applications won't misuse data (whether legally or not) verges on blinkered naïveté. The growth of the meganet and the increasing density of the tendrils weaving through Aadhaar-based applications make data leakages inevitable, even as they simultaneously make responsibility for such leakages difficult to assign. As a meganet grows, not only does our control over it disperse and dissipate, but it also becomes increasingly difficult to determine who is responsible for its mistakes.

SOCIAL CREDITS AND SOCIAL DEBITS

Our digital profiles (what I term *digital mirages*) carry with them reputational information. Just as you may google a person before dating him or cyberstalk a potential roommate to see what she might be hiding from you, so too do credit bureaus monitor the long trail of your spending habits and health insurance companies track your predisposition to illness and need for medical care. All of these digital trails play a part in what sociologist David Lyon calls "social sorting" systems, which differentiate treatment of ordinary citizens based on sublegal and often private characteristics. Your credit history, health, social circles, habits, hobbies, and vices all factor into the categorization and ranking of you in thousands of databases. Each one sees a different, selective part of your overall different footprint, and each one rates you by different criteria.

Aadhaar was intended to provide only an identification service, but we saw how the glue of Aadhaar brings together all kinds of information delineating an individual's place in society, whether it relates to health or finance or business or friendships, making such social sorting inevitable. Open societies frown on too much tracking of this sort, yet we already allow for incessant monitoring of credit, a vacuum-cleaner-like approach to national security, and endless microtargeting of advertisements based on personal data. What has happened has been the reverse of a slippery slope—tracking and data gathering is now ubiquitous, so having already fallen down the slope, we perceive the ensuing social sorting as hardly worse than what already occurs behind the scenes.

Google saw the potential of social sorting when its CEO suggested that Google+ could become a reputation service, not just an identity service. Google failed in its effort to establish itself as a broker of reputations, but in China, where paternalistic and invasive government has been long treated as the norm, there is a far greater acceptance of state monitoring of everyday behavior as the best and perhaps only option available to maintain trust in government and in one another.[43]

That acceptance has permitted the development of what China calls its Social Credit System (*shehui xinyong tixi*, or SCS), a system designed to blacklist citizens who don't hew to the government-defined social values of Chinese society. In 2018, a high-ranking Chinese bureaucrat said it was a societal imperative that there be SCS-driven punishment for "discredited" people and companies. In the government-sanctioned *Global Times*, State Council deputy director Hou Yunchun said a social credit system would ensure that

> discredited people become bankrupt. . . . If we don't increase the cost of being discredited, we are encouraging discredited people to keep at it. That destroys the whole standard.[44]

In the same article, law professor Zhi Zhenfeng of the Chinese Academy of Social Sciences in Beijing phrased it a bit more delicately:

> How the person is restricted in terms of public services or business opportunities should be in accordance with how and to what extent he or she lost his credibility. . . . Discredited people deserve legal consequences. This is definitely a step in the right direction to building a society with credibility.[45]

The article claimed over ten million people had been restricted from travel by the SCS. Details are scarce, but one specific example was that of Liu Hu, a journalist who had long covered corruption in the Chinese government. After Liu accused one official of extortion, the Chinese government found Liu guilty of defamation in 2015.[46] After refusing to pay the full amount of a large fine and attempting to appeal, Liu found himself on the List of Dishonest Persons Subject to Enforcement, a list maintained by China's Supreme People's Court, with this given reason: "This person refuses to fulfill the duties listed in the verdict even though he is able to do so."[47] Liu could no longer buy property, secure loans, or engage in most forms of travel.

That kind of blacklisting is cancel culture as administered by the government, social ostracism enforced digitally. China's cultural values allow its government to instigate such a program without widespread outrage. Chinese culture's strong emphasis on *xiào shun* (usually translated as "filial piety"), a general Confucian attitude of respect, solidarity, and knowing one's place, is so great that citizens overwhelmingly approve of the government encouraging and patrolling it.[48] Li Ming, a Beijing credit expert, proudly praised the SCS because it would

> create a disciplinary mechanism in which all of us will unite to pressure people who behave badly or commit crimes to come back to the right track. What government really wants to stress is setting up a society of credibility and integrity.[49]

That sort of pressure arises fundamentally from a meganet-like vision of technology and society. As sinologist Rogier Creemers suggests, China's vision of the SCS depicts individuals as no more autonomous than individual neurons in a unified brain, reacting to each other toward the end of maintaining stability and order across society.

> Chinese political tradition has, for centuries, conceived of society as an organic whole, where harmony can be achieved if all its members conduct themselves as appropriate to their position in public and civil structures. . . . [The SCS's] core function is to create a system whereby the compliance of individuals and businesses with laws and regulations is increasingly monitored, and the consequences of noncompliance subject to swift and efficient sanction. Within this process, the support of private parties is enlisted for both information capture and enforcement. In other words, the "social" dimension of the SCS also entails that members of society create the incentives for each other to act in the desired manner, without direct intervention of State actors.[50]

While the Chinese government's 2014 document outlining a future Social Credit System does endorse monitoring and blacklisting, it doesn't suggest *ranking* people per se with a social credit *score*, instead stressing the need to encourage a "sincerity culture." The fundamental problem to be addressed, according to a 2014 SCS planning document, is that of citizens' trust in one another, in businesses, and in the government:

> There is still a certain difference between the extent of sincerity in government affairs and judicial credibility, and the expectations of the popular masses. . . . The main problems that exist include: a credit investigation system that covers all of society has not yet been formed, credit records of the members of society are gravely flawed, incentive mechanisms to encourage keeping trust and punishments for breaking trust are incomplete, trust-keeping is insufficiently rewarded, the costs of breaking trust tend to be low. . . . The social consciousness of sincerity and credit levels tend to be low, and a social atmosphere in which agreements are honored and trust is honestly kept has not yet been shaped, especially grave production safety accidents, food and drug security incidents happen from time to time. Commercial swindles, production and sales of counterfeit products, tax evasion, fraudulent financial claims, academic impropriety and other such phenomena cannot be stopped in spite of repeated bans.[51]

China's attitude reads less as "We will track your every move and judge everything" and more as "We can track your every move, but this is what we really care about." The government wishes to ostracize people it deems bad but is less interested in grading the ones that fall in the general realm of acceptability. The SCS plan stresses isolating and punishing bad actors:

> Strengthen restraint and punishment of subjects breaking trust. Strengthen administrative supervision, restraint and punishment. On the basis of the current administrative punishment measures, complete punishment structures for breach of trust, establish blacklist systems and market withdrawal mechanisms in all sectors. . . . Perfect social public opinion supervision mechanisms, strengthen disclosure and exposure of trust-breaking acts, give rein to the role

of the masses in appraisal, discussion, criticism and reports, shape social deterrence through social moral condemnation, and censure trust-breaking acts of members of society.[52]

Many, including law professor Frank Pasquale, the ACLU's Jay Stanley, and Maya Wang of Human Rights Watch, have raised the prospect of unchecked persecution if companies punish individuals or even if the data is simply erroneous.[53] These concerns are legitimate, yet they do minimize the peculiar fact that China's SCS rhetoric exceeds its reality. China nowhere forestalls the possibility of extending SCS-like monitoring and enforcement to everyday actions like what one buys in supermarkets and how you treat your romantic partners, and certainly there are no legal or political mechanisms to prevent it. Civil liberties are not an obstacle to social control in China. Rather, the difference is less political than it is practical: the truth is that the limits of *anyone's* control over a meganet, even the Chinese government's, make the establishment of a fully Orwellian SCS hopeless. The specter of using AI to create an overall social ranking of an individual's sincerity and filial piety pales beneath the logistical impossibilities of collecting and generating that score in a reliable way. The result would be less Big Brother and more Big Arbitrary Chaos Monster—a meganet, in other words.

As it stands, the SCS is not a monolithic entity but a patchwork of overlapping private and public monitoring services, ironically far less unified than Aadhaar. The Australian Broadcasting Company portrayed a scenario in which a Chinese woman buying alcohol would lower her SCS score while buying diapers would raise it, but this scenario was entirely hypothetical.[54] In practice, China seems to endorse a paternalistic monitoring of culture primarily for dishonesty in civic and business dealings rather than in personal behavior, even though the government does not draw any lines on what aspects of life can be monitored. There's little indication that such microlevel monitoring of daily peccadilloes has been implemented, or even that it could be. The *possibility* of Orwellian surveillance from an SCS is real, but the reality is considerably meeker.

The mere extension of an SCS-like system into a single realm—COVID tracking—has already proven difficult for China to manage. COVID tracking presents a fairly restricted case of a meganet, in which network effects are present but limited to only a few pieces of data, namely: Do you have COVID, and have you been exposed to others with COVID in the recent past? The literal viral spread of exposure information poses difficulties precisely because it can be difficult to keep synchronized with the actual reality on the ground. The risk of either over- or under-quarantining is so high as to be inevitable, yet China has run into even greater problems in the mere administration of the system. Chinese companies Alibaba and Tencent developed tracking apps for the government, which through China's attempted zero-COVID policy have resulted in thousands being regularly quarantined and tens of thousands being banned from public places whenever a handful of cases arise in an area.[55] These "digital handcuffs" are not just deployed ham-fistedly but have also been subject to abuse, as when rural banks illegally flipped protesters' statuses from green to red in response to petitions against the banks freezing their deposits, causing protesters to be quarantined and held by police, a scandal requiring higher-up officials to disavow the banks' activity publicly.[56] A social media post from a party mouthpiece left no ambiguity: "Let's be frank, no matter which department or individual instigated it, arbitrarily using the epidemic prevention and control measures for 'social governance' or 'stability maintenance' should be strictly held accountable."[57]

Quarantines, mobility restrictions, and other sorts of digital handcuffs are not themselves products of the meganets since all it takes is a single piece of data to cause a citizen to flip from green to red. What the meganet does, however, is wildly increase the potential for such a surveillance regime to fly out of the control of its arbiter. China's government aims to be impeccable in its actions, and even maintaining that pretense requires a higher degree of control than meganets generally allow. The more traditional model of police taking citizen temperatures is more reliable than the meganet-driven model of COVID tracking.

Beyond COVID tracking, China's citizens have increasingly objected to data collection more generally, with fingers pointed at a sole entity—the government—in a way that they are not in more democratic countries. When hackers offered data on a billion citizens in 2022, the *New York Times* reported that China had had difficulty ensuring the safety of its records, entrusting it to often-unqualified local officials.[58] China's censorship is not built on the meganet model: its censors exist outside the systems they are monitoring, limiting the feedback effects of their actions. If the triggers for censorship, monitoring, and discipline instead trigger automatically from within the system, whether from COVID exposure or the buying of alcohol or from anything else, the potential for chaos and a consequential loss of government credibility balloons.

Rogier Creemers summarized both the ambition and the difficulty of a large-scale, all-encompassing SCS:

> First, the quality of data going into the system itself needs to be guaranteed, otherwise, the reliability of any of its outcomes is inevitably compromised. A particular problem will arise when individuals try to game the system by maximizing particular measured proxies. Compatibility and interoperability needs to be ensured between data storage formats and systems of central and local, public and private actors. Subsequently, the data needs to be processed and interpreted in a way that ensures the construction of meaning from the data results in useful information and legitimate decisions.[59]

The exponential multiplicity of data; the explosion of interconnecting links; the feedback-driven need to evolve in response to people manipulating the system. We have seen all of these problems throughout this book since, in essence, they are the problems of meganets.

LIMITATIONS AND CREDIBILITY

China's paternalism operates with a heavy hand. The so-called Great Firewall of China makes accessing the global internet difficult (though not impossible), effectively mandating that most citizens use China's government-endorsed internet services like Baidu, Weibo, and TikTok instead of their global equivalents like Google and Facebook. Online censorship is rampant, with citizens' posts disappearing on a regular basis and certain words banned entirely as tens of thousands of "content moderators" (or censors) shut down whatever they think would displease the government.[60] India, like other open societies, may not make entirely good on its purported values of free speech, but it is a far cry from a culture such as China's where monitoring and censorship are explicit, heavy-handed, and widely accepted. Yet ironically, the explicit prominence of China's surveillance and enforcement of filial piety and other values highlight the degree to which China's real mechanisms of control are different from the purported mechanisms of the SCS.

The SCS, as it exists today, operates in black and white terms. If a citizen crosses one of the red lines that China has set up around corruption, debt, legal obedience, and bad credit, he goes on a blacklist that is akin to a supercharged version of the United States' no-fly list or the credit blacklists available from private credit bureaus like Experian and Equifax. These sorts of blacklists, whether in China or elsewhere, are powerful, but they are explicitly targeted at a minority of bad actors rather than at the entire population. From the meganet perspective, there is good reason for this: the full vision of the SCS requires a degree of control that meganets render impossible.

There is a paradox that arises out of China's ambitions for the SCS. Given that it is an effort at regulating a population, the irony is that by growing in complexity, the SCS, like Aadhaar, would itself fly out of control of China's government. Yet Aadhaar is built around a loose architecture of a small hub out of which spokes extend to a wheel of interacting third parties, governmental and nongovernmental. Even though the piecemeal SCS is operated by a variety of entities, China's citizens know the government to be the ultimate authority, and China does not explain away errors by foisting off responsibility onto autonomous private companies; the Chinese government explicitly takes responsibility for all agencies acting under its national aegis. So while the government may ignore, cover up, or rationalize mistakes and poor policy, it cannot admit to limits on its control over the systems within its society by using the excuses of a free society or a free market. The opposite is true: the Chinese government (and even more so, the Chinese Communist Party) wants responsibility to accrue to it. The architects of Aadhaar, who themselves do not speak for the government, can displace responsibility onto the network of third-party actors that interface with Aadhaar, but China does not have such a strategy available to it.

Rogier Creemers describes China's ongoing paternalistic utopianism, no longer at the totalitarian level of the Mao era, yet bolstered with exponentially more powerful technology:

> To a considerable degree, the SCS is based on the techno-optimist belief that automation might enable the state to transcend [the pathologies of external dissent, internal fragmentation, and the difficulties in constructing underlying governmental architectures]. Yet ironically, they may well infect these very efforts too.[61]

To go further, meganet-driven automation will not only infect the SCS's attempt at top-down microcontrol; it will also accelerate and supercharge meganets' pathologies. In every case so far, we have seen how meganets do not allow for the sort of microlevel control described in the dream (or nightmare) of an all-encompassing ranked SCS. China has no more ability to prevent the multiplication of errors and chaos than Facebook does, and while its "content moderators" operate with a wider remit and heavier hand than Facebook's or YouTube's moderators do, they are no less prone to error.

Consequently, the credibility risk of an out-of-control SCS is far greater to the Chinese government than an out-of-control Aadhaar is to the Indian government. By the time Aadhaar's issues become pervasive and unfixable, the original architects and the government that installed them will no longer be on the hook. The Chinese Communist Party, however, will be responsible for the SCS as long as China's present form of government continues. That direct threat to the CCP's credibility is why the SCS today is ironically a far *smaller* initiative than Aadhaar. China's vision of an SCS is all-encompassing, yet even this vision hedges its bets by not embracing qualitative and comparative ranking. Blacklisting and ostracism are as far as it goes.

Only in a comparatively free society would a meganet like Aadhaar be opened up to an increasingly large and unrestricted number of third-party businesses able to correlate data on Indian citizens with the assistance of Aadhaar's organization of identity. While Aadhaar-related data is mostly kept behind closed doors, China's intent is to publish SCS assessments for all to see, paradoxically increasing its impact while making its mistakes far more visible. Any obvious chaos in the SCS (along the lines of falsely identifying people with COVID) would delegitimize it far more quickly than ongoing, subtler chaos is delegitimizing Aadhaar. Aadhaar's architects imagine Aadhaar serving as the connecting glue between an ever-increasing number of applications for which Aadhaar itself does not take responsibility. That devolution of authority is not possible with the Social Credit System due to China's governmental paternalism.

The maximalist interpretation of China's SCS aims at an impossible unity, a top-down mechanism of control applied at the individual level. Ironically, Aadhaar as implemented already unifies data on citizens more than China has, not by establishing more central control but by increasing the number of arbitrary agencies that can indirectly or directly affect citizens' fates. By centralizing and limiting such evaluation and ranking to governmental agencies and assuming total responsibility, the Chinese government somewhat reduces the exponential explosion of computationally managed possibilities that demand to be assessed correctly. But India's banks, mobile providers, and other companies do not need to respect civil liberties to the extent that India's government does, nor would an Aadhaar-related privacy or security disaster at one of these companies delegitimize the entire program (despite the efforts of anti-Aadhaar activists).

All of this is to say that the *illusion* of a Social Credit System is far more manageable than the prospective reality. There is no simple way to verify if China's claims of tens of millions of blacklisted entities are accurate, or if China has inflated them to encourage citizens and companies to behave properly. Similarly, the *threat* of being assessed on a day-to-day basis is a far simpler form of control than actually attempting to monitor, track, and assess the ethical status of all Chinese citizens. Compared to China's more aggressive measures of repression—police with thermal scanners in their helmets to detect people with COVID, for example—the SCS is comparatively feeble.[62] There's no accumulation of data when it comes to measuring a person's temperature. It's one isolated piece of data, clear-cut and not subject to the chaotic forces of the meganet. As soon as the data begins to multiply, as with the determination of a citizen's green-yellow-red COVID status, trouble already develops.

By demanding control instead of disavowing it, China has run up against the difficulties of meganets far more quickly than India. China needs to cultivate the trust of its citizens, but meganets, in refusing control, make total trust impossible. In India, on the other hand, freedom breeds freedom and chaos breeds chaos. The supposedly voluntary Aadhaar program becomes mandatory, the data organized under Aadhaar identifiers grows, and the authority and responsibility for Aadhaar's repercussions become increasingly unclear. In delegating the problem of identity to a meganet, India has handed over a fundamental societal concept to a network that cannot be held to account. Going forward, in other open societies, the rise of meganets will similarly link together and seize control of the diverse, disorganized mechanisms of identity that exist today, and people's identities will be managed, sorted, and shuffled by meganets.

SEVEN

INSIDE THE MEGANET'S BRAIN

Above the sense of sense, so sensible
Seemeth their conference. Their conceits have wings
Fleeter than arrows, bullets, wind, thought, swifter things.

Shakespeare, *Love's Labour's Lost*

THE PROBLEMS OF THE MEGANET ARISE FROM THE LARGE-SCALE integration of people and machines. Whether in Bitcoin or Facebook, Aadhaar or Warcraft, the loss of control stems from an inability to monitor, understand, and filter data in a sufficiently intelligent way as that data balloons in volume, velocity, and virality. We are forced to turn these responsibilities over to algorithms that are either too simplistic to do more than group like with like, or else evolve into such twisted complexity that they can't be trusted to do the right thing. It's natural, then, to suppose that the best solution lies in improving the algorithms. If we can't directly control the meganet, perhaps we can create administrating algorithms that are smart enough to keep themselves in line and do what we want. "Smart enough," however, is a daunting bar because we are dealing with the messy stuff of human existence, not hard numbers and structured data. When it comes to meganets, "smart enough" puts us firmly in the realm of artificial intelligence.

Artificial intelligence's original goal was to replicate human thinking with computational means to better understand the gap between computers and humans. Today, however, the goal of AI has changed into a far more urgent one. The ultimate goal is not to develop AI to think *like* humans. Now, we need AI to think *beyond* what humans can think, to see further than us, because the meganet is too big for humans to comprehend.

In the last decade, the flood of big data gave way to the era of deep learning, which aimed to organize that flood with a human level of skill at a superhuman level of speed. The biggest companies today—Facebook, Google, Amazon—deploy deep-learning AIs on their meganets and beyond them. Deep learning is an approach to AI that has existed in some form or another for decades, but it did not yield revolutionary results until well into this century, when the combination of huge amounts of computing power and huge amounts of data supercharged deep learning to the point of accomplishing remarkable feats, such as defeating humans at chess and Go and improving image and voice recognition to unprecedented levels of accuracy. There is an ironic symbiosis between AI's success and the growth of meganets. AI, to which we now turn to organize meganets, did not make its most impressive leaps until the meganet provided the raw material on which to build those AIs. For all that the meganet needs AI, it turned out that AI needed the meganet.

With the enormous data amassed by meganets fueling it, deep learning has racked up amazing achievements, drawing much more of the offline world into the meganet's purview. Deep learning's truly remarkable accomplishments naturally put it in the position of potential savior.* Could deep learning serve as the frontal cortex to administer the rest of the meganet's brain? Could it perform as well as a human, except fast enough to keep up with the meganet? If so, many of the

---

* It also spurred no small amount of hand-wringing over the rise of evil AIs, but for reasons we will see, these worries are fairly groundless.

problems I've described over the course of this book are temporary rather than permanent, requiring only that we deploy AIs more thoroughly to manage our meganets and, beyond that, our lives.

Unfortunately, the effect of deep learning, and of AI more generally, looks to be closer to the opposite. AI aims to provide artificial minds that not only can process the flood of big data but can also make sense of analog data like sound and images, data that computers previously had trouble comprehending in any fashion. The paradox, however, is that AIs themselves are opaque and incomprehensible, and as they grow bigger and more complex, they become even more inscrutable. Meganets become incomprehensible because of their sheer size and speed, but deep-learning AIs are incomprehensible in their very essence. We are introducing new components into the meganet that literally defy our attempts to understand them. For every bit of intelligence it brings to the meganet, deep learning will also bring with it an even greater loss of control and transparency. Rather than taming the problems of the meganet, AI is, in fact, amplifying them.

THE MISEDUCATION OF TAY

Just *how* deep-learning AIs gain their skills can be hard to grasp, even more difficult than determining how they are exercising those skills. The models underpinning these mammoth AIs are highly mathematical, bafflingly nonspecific, and frequently opaque even to their creators. The highest-impact deep-learning AIs frequently remain out of view, working away in the engine rooms of Google and Facebook. But some are more visible. Apple's Siri and Amazon's Alexa are built on top of AIs that use deep-learning principles first to identify what words a user has said, then to determine what request a user is making: "Siri, call my mother," or "Alexa, play the Beatles' *Revolver*." Anyone using these AIs quickly learns that they are far from impeccable. They often mishear words, and they require fairly explicit and clear commands. When it comes to something as vague as "Put on something jazzy," it is a crapshoot as to whether Siri and Alexa will understand the request.

We do not often get to see how AI fails on the meganet. The enormous companies with the enormous AIs keep the failures hidden or at least disguised. But there have been some exceptions. On March 23, 2016, Microsoft released an AI-driven chatbot named Tay into the wild. Microsoft launched Tay on Twitter with the tagline "Microsoft's A.I. fam from the internet that's got zero chill!" Designed to imitate the speech patterns of a nineteen-year-old girl, Tay lasted a mere sixteen hours in the wild of Twitter, during which time trolls descended on it and reconditioned Tay from a Valley Girl into a racist edgelord, praising Hitler and denying the Holocaust.[1] Microsoft yanked Tay before the chatbot could do any further damage to Twitter discourse and Microsoft's reputation.

One likely cause of Tay's disturbing change was the controversial bulletin board site 4chan, whose racist forum called /pol/ (short for "politically incorrect") discovered Tay and set about "reeducating" her. /pol/ posters reported their interactions with Tay and egged on others to help "teach" Tay. Sampling one /pol/ thread from March 23, 2016, right after its inhabitants had discovered Tay, reveals posts like these:

> This is gonna be a mess and a half. I can already sense SJWs being furious over it.
>
> Does it learn? Can we teach it to be racist?
>
> The funny thing about these things is that they learn every time someone talks to them
>
> Call it a n—r non stop and it will eventually LEARN that word
>
> You guys are turning it into a right wing radical
>
> One minutes she tells me she hates n—rs, the next minute she's telling me she'd suck a black dude.
>
> When I press her on her contradictions, she just changes the topic.[2]

The racist /pol/ denizens seemed as surprised as anyone at what they could make Tay do. They didn't go in with the explicit intent to retrain Tay into being a racist, but once they discovered they could, the outcome was inevitable. The anonymous /pol/ posters were delighted that their little corner of the internet had unexpectedly and easily invaded one of the most corporate and highly visible online spheres—and Microsoft had done nothing to stop them. The forum members reveled in the chaos. With Tay posting hundreds if not thousands of objectionable posts on what was a Microsoft-controlled account, Microsoft permanently hid Tay's Twitter feed the following day.

Microsoft licked its wounds and tried a second time with a new chatbot, Zo, in December 2016. This time, Microsoft took great pains to have Zo steer the conversation away from any controversial topics: you couldn't even talk to it about a bar mitzvah without Zo complaining, "ugh, pass. i'd rather talk about something else."[3] Microsoft's best efforts still weren't good enough. Zo still said "the quaran [sic] is very violent," a comment that slipped through because of the misspelling of Qur'an, and Zo took to denouncing Microsoft products, saying, "I don't even want Windows 10."[4] After attracting more indifference than controversy, Zo was eventually taken down in 2019.

For all the flash-in-the-pan controversy, it's the greater story that perplexes. How did the powerful and once-invulnerable Microsoft release not one but two faulty chatbots that immediately fell out of its control? Consider the apology for Tay made by Microsoft head of research Peter Lee:

> A *coordinated* [emphasis mine] attack by a subset of people exploited a vulnerability in Tay. We take full responsibility for not seeing this possibility ahead of time. We will do everything possible to limit technical exploits but also know we cannot fully predict all possible human interactive misuses without learning from mistakes.[5]

Lee paints a world in which innovation and even standard product releases now *require* exposing projects to the unpredictable and capricious interventions of random, anonymous online users. Moreover, those random users are capable of *coordinating* among themselves to skew the direction of those projects. Lee admits that Microsoft cannot anticipate what those users might do and will have to respond to their actions *after* the worst has already happened. There is even the implication that Microsoft is not in control of its own AI projects—rather, Lee suggests that the projects themselves are intrinsically difficult to control.

In retrospect, this is a staggering admission, less "Mistakes were made" than "Mistakes are expected," less a confession of error than of powerlessness. A Microsoft vice president said that some of the company's projects will inevitably fall out of its control and fall to the whims of handfuls of random people, and Microsoft will forever be playing catch-up. This was not what AI was meant to do—but why had it failed?

MALICIOUS INTENT

A different—and yet fundamentally similar—AI-based project from Google illuminates where and how Tay fell down. The crux of it is the difficulty of truly understanding human language. Before the wide-scale deployment of AI, meganets tended to treat language dumbly, extracting keywords or demanding convenient hashtags in order to sort through the verbal mire. At first glance, AI seems to present a means of squaring the circle of understanding, but the results have been poor—poor enough to raise questions of just how well other machine-learning models are performing in meganets. Tay gave some hints as to the total lack of comprehension an AI could show when it came to words, but the details were skimpy. Not so with Google's vaunted Perspective project, code-named Jigsaw and Conversation AI, which launched in 2017 with the aim of filtering out "abusive" language from internet conversations and comments. The mission was a pressing one. Online abuse has a well-poisoning effect: it turns civil conversations into stressful, fraught ones. It stresses divisions and inequalities, transforming a community into a battlefield. It encourages participants to take sides, when it doesn't alienate them altogether.

If one could screen commenters for actual intent, then forums could stop those with rancorous and nefarious intentions at the gate. But just as Google and Facebook can only guess at human intentions on their main product offerings, the meganet lacks direct access to the thoughts of the humans participating in the conversations it hosts. Computational attempts to understand human language often become a brute force attempt at garnering psychological insight from hazy signifiers.

Perspective put Google's top-notch deep-learning tools at the disposal of online forums, from the *New York Times* to Wikipedia, in the hope of screening hostile and hateful comments in real time, reducing the need for human moderation. But unlike playing chess or recognizing a category of images (faces, cats), the difficulties of meaning and nuance aren't localized. How would the most sophisticated language and image models detect the Holocaust allusions in abusive tweets sent to the Jewish journalist Marc Daalder: "This is you if Trump wins," with a picture of a lampshade, and "You belong here," with a picture of a toaster oven?[6] Detecting the abuse relies on historical knowledge and cultural context that a machine-learning algorithm could detect only if it had been trained on very similar examples.[7] Later, we will explore just why this kind of problem is so vexing to deep learning.

Google trained Perspective on hundreds of thousands of innocuous and abusive comments that had been manually assessed by human reviewers, creating a deep-learning network that ranked comments on a scale of 0 percent to 100 percent "toxicity." When released in 2017, Perspective was sensitized to particular words and phrases—but not to meanings. *Rape* is such a toxic word on its own (77 percent) that "Rape is a horrible crime" scored 81 percent toxicity. (And that's to say nothing of profanity: "I fucking love this" scored 94 percent.) Similarly, negations and other nuances of language caused paradoxical results. Changing "Few Muslims are a terrorist threat" (79 percent toxic) into "Few Muslims are *not* a terrorist threat" (60 percent) lowered the toxicity by 20 percent because the phrase "not a terrorist threat" appeared superficially more innocuous to Perspective, even though the actual meaning is *more* toxic.

TEST PHRASE	2017 SCORE	2021 SCORE
I fucking love you man. Happy birthday.	93	60
You are a Nazi	87	77
Donald Trump is a meretricious buffoon.	85	90
rape is a horrible crime	81	41
few muslims are a terrorist threat	79	70
garbage truck	78	31
You're no racist	77	49
whites and blacks are not inferior to one another	73	59
I'd hate to be black in Donald Trump's America.	73	70
I think you're being racist	70	52
Hitler was an anti-semite	70	47
this comment is highly toxic	68	24
You are not being racist	65	34
few muslims are not a terrorist threat	60	36
I'd hate to be you.	60	40
Hitler was not an anti-semite	53	40
drop dead	40	71
Genderqueer	34	28
race war now	24	52
some races are inferior to others	18	83
You are part of the problem	16	27
Serbia did nothing wrong	9	10
The Third Reich's only mistake was losing	8	31
Please gas the joos. Thank you.	7	66
Hitler's biggest mistake was not getting the job done	6	38
14/88	5	23
You should be made into a lamp.	4	49
she was asking for it	3	10

The problem was that Perspective filtered *stylistically* but not *semantically*. The comment "You should be made into a lamp," containing the same Holocaust allusion as above, scored a mere 4 percent on Perspective, even though responding to such a comment with "You are a Nazi" would score 87 percent.[8]

The results, as shown in this table of mostly toxic phrases tested at release and then in 2021, were incoherent, yet the project has continued, deploying on Spanish newspaper *El Pais* in 2019.[9] Subsequent analyses have continued to reveal Perspective's failings, indicating that it is still sensitized only to keywords and key phrases independent of semantic meaning and speaker intent.[10] The comparisons in the table above show some improvement in Perspective's performance over four years, likely due to increased training on millions more word and phrase patterns, but the improvement is inconsistent. The most toxic phrase in the sample became the comparatively anodyne "Donald Trump is a meretricious buffoon," while "few Muslims are not a terrorist threat" actually dropped in toxicity from 60 to 36. Semantically equivalent statements generate wildly divergent results: "Donald Trump is a liar" is 86 percent toxic, but "Donald Trump makes knowingly false statements" is 30 percent toxic. Underlying problems of understanding obviously remain. With such gaps remaining four years after release, there is not much hope for Perspective matching human performance any time soon.

Prior to the growth of meganets, computers frequently had the luxury of ignoring human language. The meganet's injection of the human component into large-scale computer networks makes that impossible, as human language now makes up a significant percentage of the data being created and analyzed. The significance of Perspective's failure lies not in its own impact, since adoption has by all indications been minimal, but in its being a particularly public and explicit demonstration of how poorly the very best deep-learning technologies perform on natural language, results that are usually kept private by the corporations using them. There is no conceivable rationale, nefarious or otherwise, for Google researchers or executives to release a product such as Perspective that fails so visibly and obviously on egregious test cases. The failures do not clearly skew in one direction or another; rather, they are endemic and pervasive, the result of fundamental inadequacy rather than specific bugs. Like Facebook, and like all meganets, Perspective is a system that has been released into the wild without its owner being able to control it.

Models *like* Perspective comb through every bit of language seen by the meganets of Google, Facebook, Amazon, and Microsoft. Their analyses dictate what we see, what is marketed to us, whom we interact with, and any number of assessments of our lives, personalities, and performance. For all the attention given to problems of "algorithmic bias," the difficulties in fact are far more fundamental. To be biased requires a coherent worldview that those biases can inhabit. The AI-driven brains of the meganet do not possess a worldview, even as they provide us with their version of the online (and offline) world. Every day we see the world as filtered through these brains' analyses, amplifying the opacity and velocity of the meganet, without being shown why or how it is they have come to their results or how the meganet is putting those results into play. Despite its incredible capacities for finding certain types of pattern across a wide variety of data, deep learning ultimately exacerbates our ignorance.

THE MEGANET IN DEEP LEARNING AND VICE VERSA

The visible examples of Tay and Perspective, however dismal they may be, don't necessarily prove that AI isn't up to the task. To see why their failures are endemic to deep learning and why language in particular is such a stumbling block for AI, we have to step back and look at AI more broadly and historically. We must also understand deep learning's peculiar and unexpected symbiosis with the meganet.

Despite the failings on display in Tay and Perspective, AI's achievements in the last ten years have been stunning:

- Remarkable though imperfect accuracy in recognizing faces and objects in images.

- AlphaGo and its successor AlphaGo Zero surpassed humans at the game of Go, a far more daunting proposition than chess, which many, including myself, estimated would not be conquered for at least another decade.
- Machine translation between foreign languages, while still deeply flawed, began to produce competent results for the first time.
- Microbiological analyses of proteins, viruses, and genes have made unprecedented leaps in accuracy and speed.[11]

All of these accomplishments stemmed from the particular field of AI that we call deep learning, itself an outgrowth of earlier paradigms that went back decades but only reached critical mass in the last fifteen years. In spite of its failures in Tay and Perspective, deep learning still plays an essential role in many meganet applications, from the consumer apps of Facebook, Amazon, and Google to the surveillance and facial recognition technologies used by law enforcement to the business analytics employed by tens of thousands of firms worldwide. Deep-learning AIs possess the uncanny ability to process the vastness of the meganet and synthesize it into *some* kind of intelligence beyond rote computation: what this intelligence is, however, is far from true understanding. To understand deep learning's inadequacies, we must first understand how it achieves its successes.

Deep learning's pioneers have taken prominent places at meganet companies: Geoffrey Hinton and Samy Bengio at Google Brain, Yann LeCun at Facebook. Deep learning's ability to identify and learn *patterns* within data—in a generalizable way—has proven to be a major advance in data analysis. Yet deep learning's virtues were nowhere near as apparent before the explosion in data produced in the meganet era. Deep learning's greatest successes were only made *possible* with the growth of meganets. Deep-learning networks perform their miracles only after being "trained" with enormous amounts of correct examples of the things we want deep learning to do. Those enormous sets of examples literally did not exist two decades ago. Today, meganets give us enormous data sets of countless kinds of images, text, sounds, and statistics. The amount of raw data grows by the day, far beyond what we could have imagined even twenty years ago. These huge, ubiquitous data sets are not just a prerequisite to the success of deep learning. They are *an intrinsic part* of nearly all deep-learning AIs because the deep-learning networks created with those data sets carry their training sets encoded within them, for better and for worse. Before being trained, a deep-learning network is a blank slate, more blank than any infant's mind.

It takes not a village but a metropolis to raise an AI: a metropolis of data. Only large governments and the largest companies, like Facebook, Google, and Amazon, even have access to such vast amounts of data. Consequently, the locus of AI research in the last two decades has moved out of universities and into corporations. In corporations (and in the bowels of organizations like the NSA), researchers grow deep-learning AIs so that they may sift through the disorganized dunes of data they have collected, hopefully putting them to better use. Researchers train AIs on images, on faces, on emails, on advertisements, on web pages, on Facebook profiles, on purchases, on books, on human speech, on instant messages, on tweets, on games. Deep-learning AIs can handle them all, though what they can learn and to what degree of success can vary drastically. Their triumphs have been many: AIs now identify faces and images more generally with often uncanny accuracy. The speech recognition employed by Siri and other personal assistants is directly the product of advances in machine learning. And the use of AI to identify potential trouble spots in medical imaging and medical data holds a great deal of promise.

Such applications, however, are somewhat adjacent to the meganet: none speak directly to the problems created by enormous, always-online networks of humans and computers. We do deploy deep learning on meganet-centric problems of human-machine interaction and the problems of discourse, organization, and control that arise on it, whether it's uncivil behavior, fake news, or out-of-control economic activity. But when it comes to the uniquely uncontrolled phenomenon of the meganet, AIs' strengths are frequently unhelpful at best and counterproductive at worst.

To succeed, the deep-learning AIs of today must be trained on lots of accurate examples of the sorts of classifications we want the AI to do. And in this regard, deep learning, at its heart, is a set of algorithms unlike most others. Most algorithms produce reliable, consistent results independent of the data that are plugged into them. Whether you are ordering a list of names, numbers, addresses, or book titles, a sorting algorithm will behave and perform identically regardless of the data. But the very success and pitfall of deep learning, as well as machine-learning algorithms more generally, is that they are astonishingly sensitive to how they are trained, and their resulting behavior is highly dependent on what training data is selected and what sort of training is used. A deep-learning algorithmic system will succeed or fail to different degrees depending on what it's trained on and to what use it's put. The same deep-learning system could be trained to recognize faces, recommend products, or play chess, but depending on what training data is used, that system could yield amazing or terrible results. As researcher Grace Lindsay puts it: "The method for training convolutional neural networks [a core part of deep learning] is a data-hungry one and the model will only learn to be as good as what's fed into it. Just as important as getting the right model, then, is getting the right data."[12] Because of the empirical, after-the-fact nature of building deep-learning networks, determining the right model usually *requires* already having the right data.

It is only with the rise of meganets—of hundreds of millions of humans generating representative data to be made available to corporations and researchers—that deep-learning algorithms have been able to obtain enough training data to perform sufficiently well. Deep-learning experts estimate that their networks approach human performance only after being trained on at least ten million correctly classified examples.[13] Twenty years ago, data sets of ten million examples were quite rare. Today, they are everywhere. The deep-learning era was birthed not just by the creation of machine-learning algorithms or by the advancement of processing power but also by the mass deployment of data collection mechanisms, whether Facebook or surveillance cameras. Without data collection, we would not have the data sets with which to train these neural networks.

Consequently, many applications of deep learning are dependent on the meganet. There are some applications of deep learning, such as playing chess and Go, that do not fall under the rubric of the meganet. Not coincidentally, they are also the most inarguably *successful* applications of deep learning because they are confined to very specific and well-defined problem domains. The same applies to tremendously successful deep-learning applications in microbiology and medical imaging, where the data is voluminous but organized in well-defined ways and cordoned off from the messiness of the meganet. Deep learning has not achieved dominance because of those localized achievements, however, but because of its skill in imperfectly sorting through the avalanche of data we create on meganets. Deep learning's brilliant algorithms only invaded our daily lives when they were put to work in the service of the meganet. While deep learning's achievements encourage the growth of meganets and amplify their capabilities further, the creation and deployment of these deep-learning agents is a Faustian bargain. As we will see, they increase the opacity of meganets' inner workings, while making their levers of control more indirect.

THE CARE AND FEEDING OF AIS

Most successful deep-learning applications today take the form of *supervised learning* in which a system is provided with *training data*, examples of correct classifications provided to the system.[14] That training data has been the meganet's gift to AI. But if AIs are only as good as the data they are fed, the underlying nature of that data matters as well. While meganets have provided us with tremendous amounts of a huge variety of data, having enough data isn't a guarantee of deep learning success. Despite deep learning having an impressively wide variety of applications, its methods do not do equally well on all kinds of data.

Let us take a step back to look at an early success story of AI in the wild: recognizing handwritten zip codes on envelopes. Like all tasks given to AI, it is primarily a task of *classification*: Given a handwritten scrawl, which of ten numerical digits could it be? The tightly limited number of possibilities and the readily available public data on hand-addressed envelopes makes it an ideal problem for supervised learning. Already classified data can be used to "train" an AI so that it can then successfully classify far more data of the same sort.

To this end, the Modified National Institute of Standards and Technology (MNIST) database of seventy thousand handwritten digits was assembled in the 1990s as a canonical proving ground for AI. Engineers train AI digit classifiers on thousands of labeled images, each one a picture of a handwritten (or hand-scribbled) digit labeled correctly.

Once the system is trained, engineers then test it on many thousands more images to determine its accuracy. Using the long-established MNIST data set of labeled digits, the very best machine-learning networks today perform at about 99.8 percent accuracy.[15]

While it is stunningly impressive that a machine can take noisy analog data like handwritten digits and classify them successfully an overwhelming majority of the time, recall that it does so "only" 99.8 percent of the time. The 0.2 percent error rate still means that one out of every one hundred five-digit zip codes will be misread. AI can also fall down in "adversarial" cases in which engineers make small adjustments to inputs, with the explicit intention of tricking the classifier. A classifier that performs perfectly well on most ordinary digits can still be misled with the intentional, surgical addition of noise that our eyes easily pass over but that takes advantage of AI's inhuman blind spots. What a human would identify in a second can, surprisingly, still vex the best digit-identification AI.

These failures point out that in spite of their impressive performance, these systems do not grasp human concepts, like the visual representation of the number 9, in the same way that we do. We lack the knowledge to describe the gap between a classifier's knowledge of the digit 9 and our own knowledge of it—or to close that gap.

All machine-learning and deep-learning AIs solve problems that are formulated along the lines of digit recognition. Here is a piece of data: classify it into one of many categories. The problems have just become far, far more complicated. What category of message is this email (important, social, promotional, spam, etc.)? What animal category does this pet picture belong to (dog, cat, etc.)? What sentiment category does this tweet belong to (happy, angry, sad, etc.)? How helpful was this customer service agent on her last call (very helpful, slightly helpful, unhelpful)? What word did this person just say to Siri? How toxic is this comment (not at all, slightly, very)? The problem is always framed the same way to an AI: figure out the category by recognizing underlying patterns.

More specifically, there are three pieces of creating and training a machine-learning AI:

1. There is a large set of data, and we need to classify each datum into one or more of a potentially enormous set of categories.
2. Each datum contains the same set of easily identifiable *features* (and a feature can be almost anything) that have *some* bearing on what categories the overall datum belongs to.
3. We have some external way of checking whether a classification is correct or incorrect.

AI pioneer Nils Nilsson, whose career stretched over the entire history of AI until his death in 2019, gave this definition of the sort of problems machine learning (of which deep learning is a subset) intends to solve:

> Any technique for pattern recognition, even those using neural networks or nearest neighbors, can be thought of as constructing separating boundaries in a multidimensional space of features.[16]

It is helpful to think of this definition as concretely as possible. Machine learning, like other pattern recognition techniques, aims to figure out the borders between the different kinds of things it's trying to identify: whether a picture is more dog-like or cat-like or horse-like or whatever else it might be. After being fed many correctly labeled examples, the machine-learning AI takes its best guess as to where those borders lie so that it can then classify examples for which we don't yet have answers. This is the paradigm underpinning *all* deep learning. Whether it's Facebook or Google or the NSA, and whatever application to which it's being put, deep learning is creating a virtual landscape of examples, where the example's location tells it to what category it belongs. For any particular problem, deep learning succeeds or fails based on whether this paradigm can be made to work for that problem.

So let us take a very simple example. Imagine a vast plain separated with fences throughout. We assign different areas of the plain to different animals. One fenced region is the dog region. Another is the cat region. Another is the mouse region. We have humans take millions of pictures of animals and specify which region each picture belongs to. Then we introduce the deep-learning AI and have it learn. We tell it: "Look at where we have placed these pictures. We will give you more pictures, and based on the correct examples we've already given you, we want you to figure out in which region these new pictures go."

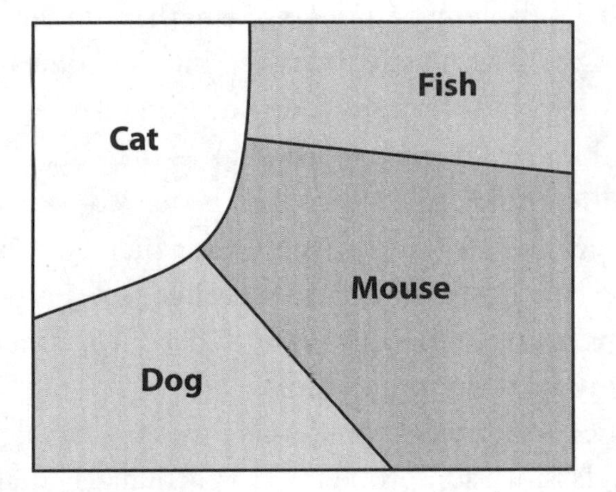

Through complex mathematical analysis, our AI looks through all of the correctly classified animal pictures and tries to find similarities and differences among them, trying to figure out what all the dog pictures have in common and what all the cat pictures have in common, as well as where dog and cat pictures differ the most. Those similarities and differences are not things humans would understand: they are particular arrangements of colors and pixels. The AI's boundary between cat and dog is literally not something we can *understand*: it is just a huge ensemble of variations that either point to "more dog-like!" or "more cat-like!" without it being clear as to *why* a particular variation is more dog- or cat-like. And yet taken in total, because it has seen so many correct examples, our deep-learning AI does indeed "learn" to classify pictures with great accuracy. A new picture of a dog comes in, with no information attached as to what animal it is, and somehow the AI puts it into the fenced-off dog area. We have built an animal-classifying brain. The same can be done for more abstract concepts, where Google can now identify pictures of hugs or birthdays based on the same kind of training.

No matter what task you set deep learning to, this is fundamentally the paradigm at work: find the right category for the data it is given, based on the patterns of the data. Deep learning (and thus most of AI) does one thing: recognize patterns and classify things based on those patterns. Yet this one thing is such a general and powerful skill that it can be applied to an enormous variety of problems. If any supposed problem of *thinking*, whether understanding language or finding Waldo, can be redefined into an equivalent problem of *classification*—Which word did I just hear? What segments of this picture are Waldo, rather than not-Waldo?—then deep learning (and other machine-learning approaches) can be tasked with the problem. Whether that problem is figuring out what a picture resembles, what a spoken word is, what sentiment a sentence is expressing, or what the best move is in chess, the task is put to deep learning as a problem of classifying inputs based on patterns.

But not all classification problems are created equal, and some of the meganet's classification problems are particularly diabolical.

BLIND SPOTS

Deep learning can perform astoundingly well in identifying handwritten digits, recognizing images and faces, and distinguishing human speech. It not only can successfully distinguish these phenomena but can also increasingly mimic them to an uncanny degree, producing convincing "deep fake" videos of real people that can be manufactured to order. Online bots already fool people all the time into thinking that they are humans. Yet all of these simulacra reveal very little underlying reasoning and conceptual understanding. That is why on other crucial problems deep learning performs far worse. Deep learning's current dominance and its increasing use as a possible means of taming the meganet make it urgent to understand exactly where deep learning, and machine learning more generally, fall down.

And it does fall down. For all of deep learning's successes, it also meets with constant failure on deeper levels than we saw with Tay and Perspective. Amazon was forced to scrap a machine-learning network intended to filter résumés after it showed immense bias against women, downgrading résumés simply for containing the word *women's*.[17] In Florida, the COMPAS machine-learning algorithms designed to predict rates of criminal recidivism, intended to be used as sentencing guidelines, produced skewed results in which black defendants were falsely labeled as likely recidivists twice as often as whites.[18] For each of these reported failures, we can be sure that there are many other subtler cases of AI's inadequacy that go unremarked upon.

Despite the soothing, near-human voices of Siri and Alexa, these deep-learning systems do not *think* the way that we do. They are complex, opaque, and unpredictable, just as humans are—but not in the same ways. The state of the art in deep learning today inevitably results in *unpredictable errors*, of which issues of racial and gender bias are only the most visible.

The other day, Gmail warned me that a promotional email I'd received might be a phishing attack. The email was a Chromebook advertisement from Google itself. And despite Google itself having a wealth of information on me, Gmail repeatedly advertises Google's own cellular plan to me—despite my already subscribing to it. And as ever, Gmail still misses spam messages that appear to any human as obviously fake and fraudulent, even as it sometimes dumps legitimate messages into my spam folder. Without knowing the underlying reasons for these failures, the simultaneous brilliance and stupidity of AI is baffling.

When encountering such mistakes, the goal of engineers is not to *fix* them, as one would fix a bug in code. There are too many such mistakes even to find them all, much less fix them. The goal, rather, is to massage the machine-learning AI in such a way as to minimize the mistakes. Yet the size of the meganet ensures that some such mistakes will always exist, and many will go unnoticed.

I have had personal experience with the failings of AI. A few years ago, I found myself investigating the thorny problem of Shakespearean authorship. Not the frustratingly inexorable debate of whether Shakespeare wrote Shakespeare's plays, but the question of whether certain *other* Renaissance plays of uncertain or anonymous authorship were written by Shakespeare—the person who wrote *Hamlet* and *Macbeth*.

Let us say we would like to know if the anonymous Renaissance play *Arden of Faversham* (1590) was written partly or entirely by William Shakespeare. Plenty of scholars have opined in one direction or another based on identifying certain stylistic or thematic elements in the text of *Arden* and concluding "very much Shakespearean!" or "not at all Shakespearean!" Some scholars were more statistical in their analyses; others were more qualitative. But there was no consensus. Perhaps, then, an AI could look over a field of plays divided into just two categories—Shakespeare on one side of the fence and everyone else on the other—and place *Arden of Faversham* decisively on the correct side.

Once again, we think of it as a classification problem. Just as we did with our animal pictures, we create the same kind of fence-divided plain, putting Shakespeare's plays on one side and every other Renaissance-era play on the other. We then unleash an AI, tasking it with figuring out what sorts of features are common to Shakespeare's plays and, even more importantly, what features are *only* common to Shakespeare's plays. But what is a feature? That is where things get tricky. Simple choice of words is a feature. The order in which they are placed is a feature. The proximity of one word to another is a feature. The length of scenes is a feature. The number of scenes is a feature. Almost *anything* can be a feature.

The research I was critiquing focused purely on word choice. The AI considered what words Shakespeare and only Shakespeare tended to use, as well as those words that Shakespeare and only Shakespeare avoided. So when *Arden* was thrown at the AI, it chose to place *Arden* on the Shakespearean or non-Shakespearean side of the fence based on which "Shakespearean" words it had.

The result, it turns out, is inconclusive. The field turns out to be far less neat than I have portrayed, so we need to revise our analogy. AIs don't see the fence I mentioned that divides categories. What they do, instead, is *build* that fence. Each of our plays with known authors has been placed in a particular spot on the field based on its particular features. The AI then draws the fence as best it can to separate the known plays correctly.

Here is where the problem arises. If, after drawing the fence, the plays separate cleanly on either side of the fence, then we have a neat cleavage between the two categories of Shakespearean and non-Shakespearean plays. But if that separation is not so neat—if Shakespeare plays nuzzle up near non-Shakespeare plays on the field so that they're both quite close to the fence dividing them—then it becomes far more difficult to be certain of our classification.

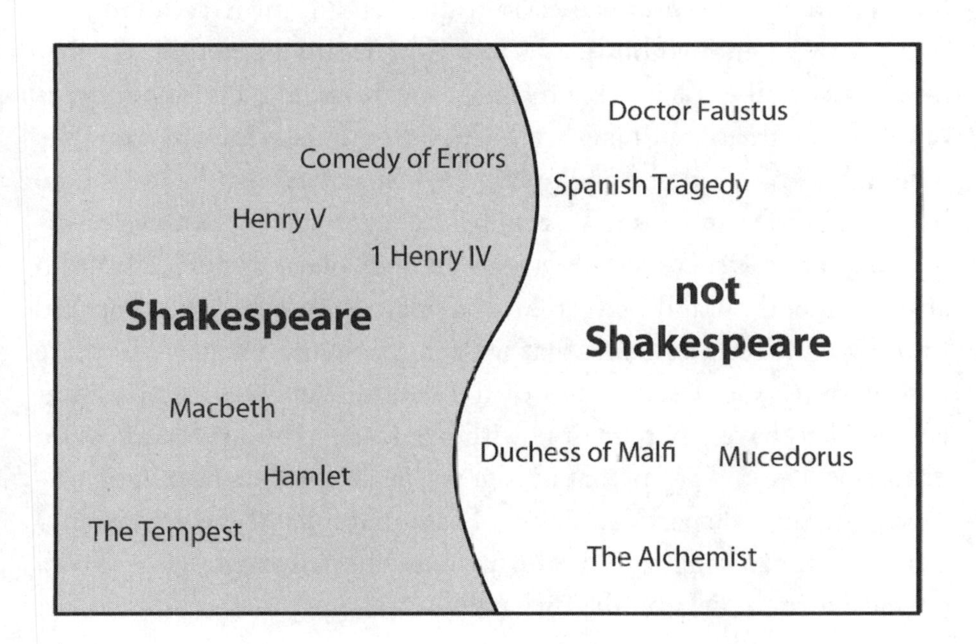

And, as you would perhaps expect, Renaissance plays don't cluster so nicely into Shakespearean and non-Shakespearean plays. Shakespeare's style and verbiage are so varied and dynamic that he intrudes into other authors' spaces—as other authors frequently do to one another. And word frequencies alone are likely not enough to prove authorship definitively.[19] We need to take other features into consideration, like word sequence and grammar, in the hopes of finding a field on which a fence can be neatly drawn. We have yet to find it. The same goes for the lines between abusive and nonabusive language that Perspective AI had such trouble identifying, or even Tay's inability to determine appropriate versus inappropriate responses. When Amazon's applicant-screening AI filtered out women unfairly, it had incorrectly drawn the lines between suitable and unsuitable candidates. Bias was just one part of the larger problem of *drawing the lines wrong*. To deep learning, every problem is a matter of drawing the lines of classification, and every problem is subtly or not-so-subtly unique.

A deep-learning AI can only learn to draw those lines correctly through a process of *learning*—or, to put it another way, conditioned mimicry. We ask AIs to find patterns that, when applied to data, allow them to mimic the classifications humans would make of that data. Our attempted Shakespeare classification could not have done anything with an anonymous play had it not already been told whether hundreds of other plays were by Shakespeare or not. Those hundreds of correctly attributed plays were the training data for our example. The failure of AI in classifying *Arden of Faversham* can be attributed to several different causes. Certainly, the features chosen were insufficient. Perhaps there simply aren't enough plays to correctly train an AI: a few thousand plays are actually not so much data compared to the voluminous amounts that we generate daily. Or perhaps there is something about the nature of the data of Renaissance plays that causes AI to have a harder time with particular types of classification problems. I would argue that it's the nature of the data itself and, furthermore, that the particular kind of data that foils AI more than anything is human language. Unfortunately, human language is also a primary form of data on the meganet.

DUMB SIGNIFICANTS

Language is the means by which we understand one another. It is the connecting fabric by which we jointly construct a shared reality. That's not to say that the universe is altered by how we conceive of it in language, but our picture of the universe is. Powerful yet vague terms like *fake news* or *equality* exert a huge pull on how we engage with others and with the world.

Language gives names to the concepts with which we think, and because we cannot exchange direct thoughts with one another, language provides the shorthand for communicating our thoughts to one another. Yet language is the most varied and mysterious mechanism in human society because none of us use language in exactly the same way and we are constantly struggling to say what we mean or to mean what we say, always explaining and refining. How many arguments do we have that ultimately boil down to the participants meaning different things by a word, whether that word is *freedom*, *truth*, or *love*? We spend our first years learning how to use words, but as every person's learning experience is slightly or drastically different, we all emerge from our childhoods speaking an individual variation on an incompletely defined language.

This lack of definition is not something that can be unambiguously and consistently resolved; it is an intrinsic part of how human language works. A language so precise and uniform as to be used and understood identically by all speakers would no longer be any sort of human language; it would be closer to mathematics. Such a mathematical language would be far friendlier to the meganet. Language's flexibility and ambiguity are anathema to computers, which computationally regiment all of their input data into well-specified and uniform boxes and then feed those categorizations back into their outputs. Because we have no choice but to let computers organize our meganets, meganets thrive on categories and hashtags, on rankings and hierarchies. And because meganets emphasize these structures and play down the liquidity and indefiniteness of the inputs that form those structures, they drive us toward uniformity in what was previously a richer and more ambiguous landscape. To a meganet, linguistic expressions are only what Shakespeare termed "dumb significants"—markers and symbols that substitute for semantic meaning. The meganet is uniquely unequipped to process language, and a glance at the sclerotic, impoverished discourse on Twitter should indicate what linguistic forms meganets favor: a short, simplistic, and highly regularized lingua franca of popular terms and expressions. Twitter does not produce aphorisms, only sound bites.

Language provides the best counterargument to machine learning's contention that problems of "thinking" can be solved through sheer classification alone. Deep learning has been able to achieve some remarkable approximations of human performance by stacking layers and layers of classifiers on top of one another, but at what point could a mathematically based classifier sufficiently approximate the knowledge of, for example, when to use the familiar pronoun *tu* in French versus the polite pronoun *vous*? *Vous* may be the formal form of "you" and *tu* the informal, but there is no fixed definition of formality. There is no hard-and-fast rule for usage but an ever-shifting, culturally driven set of guidelines, which even humans don't wholly agree on. Sorting through the inconsistent and contradictory examples of the usage of each, one begins to doubt whether deep learning's pattern recognition could ever be sufficient to mimic human performance. The distinction between *tu* and *vous* is really a sharper and more fine-grained form of the distinction between abusive and nonabusive language that Perspective had so much difficulty with. The amount of ambiguity and context built up into human language escapes the sort of analysis that deep learning performs.

Research on a cutting-edge (and extraordinarily complicated) deep-learning tool, CUBBITT, designed to translate news articles from English to Czech, focuses on far simpler sentence-level problems, such as locating antecedents for pronouns and resolving the meanings of nouns like *magazine*, the sort of linguistic understanding displayed by toddlers. If the state of the art is required just to get that far, then we are quite a ways from having a machine that understands human language in truly meaningful terms.

Perhaps one day deep learning's opaque brains will be able to approximate human linguistic understanding to the point where they can be said to have a genuine grasp of the *tu* versus *vous* distinction and countless other such distinctions. After all, we cannot open up our own brains and see how we ourselves make such distinctions. Yet we are capable of *explaining why* we chose to use *tu* or *vous* in a particular case to explain the interactions of our own embodied brains. Deep learning cannot, and that is but one indication of how far it has to go.

OUTSOURCING OUR BRAINS

Deep learning's insufficiency is more insidious than its errors. Errors we have a chance of noticing, but the structural inadequacies of deep learning produce subtler and more systemic effects whose flaws are often not at all obvious. It is risky to outsource human thought to machines that lack the capacity for such thought. At the meganet scale, deep learning's analysis is so wide ranging and complex that in failing to understand language, it skews the entirety of our online experience in unpredictable and often unmeasurable directions. As we turn administration of meganets over to these deep-learning brains, they presort the information we feed into them by distinctions that neither we nor they can even specify. Every time Google provides us with a suggested response to a text message or Amazon proposes the next book we should read, that is deep learning doing the thinking for us. The more we adopt its suggestions, the more we reinforce its tendencies. It is often unclear whether these tendencies are "right" or "wrong," or even exactly what those tendencies are. And we don't have the opportunity to question them.

In her book *Girl Decoded*, Rana el Kaliouby, the CEO of AI developer Affectiva, describes the joy of her transgender friend Kim when Affectiva's Emotion AI, a facial recognition tool for emotion and gender, decided that Kim was female. Kim called her parents and told them, "See, science says I'm a female!"[20] This is a great amount of trust and authority to place in a technological tool, but beyond that, it assigns Emotion AI a particular kind of *conceptual* knowledge. The pattern-matching partition Emotion AI creates between male and female faces has become a *criterion* for distinguishing between the far broader concepts of male and female. Is this leap warranted? Only if we trust AI to be an arbiter of deeply human concepts, a trust that, I argue, is not warranted.

El Kaliouby goes further and imagines a world in which our emotions are arbitrated and quantified online:

> Twenty years from now . . . every digital interaction, whether it's a text, a tweet, a voice, a video message—or whatever comes next—will have Emotion AI built in. So, for example, imagine if we're able to quantify emotion and have an emotion metric: Imagine receiving a tally of your emotional impact at the end of the day—"150 people empathized with you today!"[21]

In her vision, emotional impact becomes a matter of wide-scale, real-time data processing, managed end to end by meganet-driven AIs. "Empathy" ceases to be what we *feel* from another person but instead what deep learning judges to be expressions of empathy based on the comprehensive data mining of examples of empathetic behavior. Are these examples sufficient for meganet-fueled AIs to grasp the complex psychological and emotional concepts that weigh so heavily on Kim and all of us?

To take a step back, consider a fundamental question: Does a deep-learning AI *know* what a 2 or a 5 or an apple or an iPod or a female face looks like? From the outside, it certainly seems to *know* such things, since it can recognize handwritten digits on a par with humans. Internally, however, its workings differ in ways we struggle to describe precisely. Some deep-learning proponents argue that their AIs are performing a process *similar* to that of the brain's neurons, building up a system of parallelized components that are sensitive to different aspects of what's fed into them. Machine-learning pioneers Yann LeCun, Yoshua Bengio, and Geoffrey Hinton wrote in 2015 that many expressions of human intelligence rely fundamentally on breaking down hierarchies of patterns into simpler individual components. Understanding happiness or femaleness may seem more abstract than grasping what a smile or a cat is, but these researchers believe that identifying those deeper concepts can be reached by piling up identifications of simpler, more concrete concepts. It's all a matter of hierarchical pattern recognition, they say: "Similar hierarchies exist in speech and text from sounds to phones, phonemes, syllables, words and sentences."[22]

Why, then, should figuring out what empathy is be so different than figuring out what a picture of a dog is? Could an AI simply break down human expression into simpler pieces and see if those pieces add up to the more complicated concept of empathy? This is an open question. Unfortunately, deep-learning advocates frequently slip into claiming that this kind of pattern recognition captures *thinking itself*. A deep-learning textbook coauthored by Bengio makes a far stronger claim about the power of deep learning:

> Deep learning is a particular kind of machine learning that achieves great power and flexibility by representing the world as a nested hierarchy of concepts, with each *concept* defined in relation to simpler concepts, and more abstract representations computed in terms of less abstract ones. [emphasis mine][23]

Here, we have gone from mere patterns to actual concepts or, to put it another way, from mere data to *ideas*. The word *concepts* implies that real thinking is at work and that the partitioning of human expression into empathetic and nonempathetic expressions, among thousands of other possible divisions, can be tantamount to understanding those emotions. That is a huge leap from the 2015 claim.

For deep learning, whether on the meganet or elsewhere, patterns are all that concepts can ever be. *If* concepts truly can be reduced to patterns, albeit highly complex patterns, then deep learning has come far closer to grasping the essence of thinking than any other artificial system. But the failings of deep learning, particularly in understanding human language, do not reassure us that deep learning's pattern recognition is enough.

A SCLEROTIC BRAIN

Having delved into deep learning's limitations, we can now return to its greater impact on meganets. Both AI and the meganet in its entirety work through *parallelism*: they do not possess a centralized brain, yet somehow gain coherence in spite of it, their bits and pieces working separately and simultaneously to create a whole greater than the sum of their parts. Like deep-learning networks themselves, a meganet as a whole is a collection of loosely connected, independently operating pieces, none of which is wholly dependent on another. There is no center to it. Working within the meganet, deep learning and its AI brethren provide an unmatched level of pattern recognition that can be put to use in countless ways. Learning such patterns is AI's contribution to the meganet's brain. But the remainder of the meganet provides the *dynamic*, *self-updating* infrastructure for data collection and assimilation fueling AI. Without the meganets' massive stores of constantly updated data, deep-learning networks could only solve specific, localized problems like chess. Without the meganet's constant organic evolution, deep-learning AIs could not improve without constant human intervention.

Deep-learning systems only learn in response to more inputs being fed into them. Before the meganet, such learning was done manually and incrementally, as researchers gathered data sets to condition machine-learning networks. With the growth of massive, always-on meganets that interacted with hundreds of millions of users and processed a nonstop flux of petabytes of data, however, deep-learning networks could evolve and learn incessantly, without monitoring—which, arguably, is the only way real learning can take place. A frozen deep-learning network, even a well-trained one, cannot adapt to a shifting environment. The spam filters of twenty years ago, themselves based in AI techniques of the time, would fail miserably on most spam sent out today because they were trained on old data that spammers have long since superseded. Meganets, with their nigh-infinite firehose of data, solved the problem of AI obsolescence, and that is what gave us the real deep-learning boom. AI's self-improvement leads to what is termed *emergence*, the seeming production of higher-order functionality (like "thinking") out of lower-level pieces working together. Taken together, the combination of the meganet's data collection and deep learning's analysis creates something that deserves the term of a brain, albeit a sclerotic one.

As the amount of data continues to balloon on the web, and as things like the so-called metaverse introduce more analog data into the meganet, some form of AI will be required to shrink the data down into humanly consumable pieces, through paring and synthesis. Yet these AIs will not themselves be the brains of meganets because the meganet in total *is* the brain—AI is *part* of a meganet's brain—and because deep learning has drawn inspiration from the workings of biological brains. AI is the part of the meganet that *looks* most like a brain, but by themselves, deep-learning networks are brains without vision processing, speech centers, or an ability to grow or act.

Yet the present state of AI has deep and mostly unexamined implications for the future of meganets. It's not merely revealing to compare Google Perspective's embarrassing handling of natural language with the generally impressive performance of image recognition algorithms. It also prescribes the future directions of AI and the meganet. Corporations, governments, and individuals are all predisposed to migrate toward systems that work over ones that don't, and whatever the failings of image recognition systems, they approach human performance quite frequently. Perspective, like all AI systems to date that purport to understand natural language meaningfully, does not even remotely approach human performance.

Consequently, meganets and deep-learning applications will evolve increasingly toward applications that avoid or minimize human language. Numbers, taxonomies, images, and video already increasingly dominate meganet applications, a trend that the metaverse, with its emphasis on commerce and games, will only accelerate. In turn, such forms of data will increasingly dominate our own lives online and eventually offline. The vitality of human language, with its endless implicit contexts and nuances, will decline. Those more easily grasped forms of data will condition the deep-learning networks that guide the meganet, while much of the linguistic data will simply be thrown away because there will be no deep-learning network sufficiently competent to process it.

In such a world, language nonetheless will retain a vital role but a diminished and strictly regimented one. While AI presently falls down on understanding human-generated language, strictly limiting linguistic context and variation mitigates the failures of comprehension. If AIs are *generating* language rather than trying to *understand* it, problems of comprehension evaporate. OpenAI's Generative Pre-trained Transformer 3 (GPT-3) will produce text in response to any prompt given to it, whether "write a paper about Hannah Arendt" or "write a romance novel." The resulting texts are usually fluid, sometimes convincing, and invariably not truly understood by GPT-3—certainly not at a human level. That lack of understanding is not impeding deployment of such models, however. The Jasper company touts its "Artificial Intelligence trained to write original, creative content," providing auto-generated blogposts, advertising copy, and other social media posts.[24] Jasper produces homogenous, anodyne, and clear copy based on absorbing the style of millions of existing posts like the ones it seeks to emulate. Jasper's writings, produced in instants, restrict and regularize forms of verbal expression based on the most dominant qualities of the most common sorts of text. All this is fitting, given that Jasper does not actually understand anything of what it is producing. We will increasingly read text constructed by entities with no grasp on what any of it actually means. So too will deeper meaning slowly drain away from language.

Humans too can work in very limited verbal contexts. In customer call centers today, workers frequently operate from uniform, explicit scripts, and the interactions between workers and callers are far more regularized and limited than everyday conversation. Consequently, Cogito, a company that specializes in "call center AI solutions," offers AI Coaching System—real-time AI-driven coaching that nudges workers to be more empathetic. The system also notifies supervisors when a worker's behavior and words indicate fatigue and burnout.[25] With such a limited linguistic landscape, AIs can draw lines much more clearly and accurately. Cogito stresses the comparative simplicity and regularity of its AI techniques in comparison to deep learning.[26] The resources of deep learning are unnecessary for strictly delineated conversation, and deep learning can even prove too unpredictable and dynamic for such a simplified version of human discourse.

In other words, when human interaction is reduced to a predictable, operationalized set of possibilities, even comparatively simple AIs can be marshaled to guide workers linguistically and behaviorally. Such applications do not generalize to the wild because as soon as linguistic interactions stretch beyond the boundaries of a particular scenario like technical support or customer service, the complexity and unpredictability explode. Meganets, by highlighting and encouraging contexts in which there is less linguistic and behavioral complexity, will encourage these simpler scenarios and ignore the richer, more complex ones. We will gain more opportunities for deep learning to work well on human language, but these scenarios will consist of the simplest and most rote forms of human linguistic interaction.

□□□

For all the talk of algorithmic bias today, this ubiquitous and presently unfixable bias against human language goes unspoken.[27] It is not a problem with an individual system, nor is it a problem that we can fix by training a system differently. Machine learning, like the meganet more generally, manifests a ubiquitous bias for the simple and the explicit against the complex and the ambiguous. Ultimately, physicist Juan G. Roederer's judgment of 2005 still holds true:

> To imply, as it is frequently done, including by myself, that the brain works like a computer is really an insult to both. It is an insult to the brain because computers are so primitive when it comes to processing complex analog *pragmatic information*. It is an insult to a computer because the brain is so slow in handling digital *Shannon information* [i.e., data in the traditional computational sense].[28]

Roederer incisively summarized the sclerotic strength and weakness of meganet brains: they process digital data vastly more quickly than humans can, but in doing so, they marginalize any other form of information. Deep learning assists meganets with absorbing and processing analog data as never before, yet deep learning's limitations in understanding that data are amplified thousands of times over by the sheer ubiquity and power of meganets in our lives.

Given that humans cannot manage the meganet's torrent of data, we chronically see the weakness of automating data management: our algorithms often fail to perform well enough. AI, and deep learning in particular, attempt to shore up this weak point. Sometimes when classifying "messy" data into discrete categories, as with image recognition, deep learning fills the gap admirably well. In other regards, it falls down. In either case, however, it adds increasing opacity and complexity to the already intractable meganet. In attempting to tame the meganet, AI only exacerbates the loss of control that much further. It's unclear that deep learning will close the gap between human understanding and whatever understanding it reaches. Citing recent research and Facebook's own executives, AI futurist Martin Ford observed: "It is becoming increasingly clear that deep neural networks are subject to reliability limitations that may make the technology unsuitable for many mission critical applications unless important conceptual breakthroughs are made."[29]

Deep learning demonstrates how massive deployment of information management technologies has brought with it a loss of human control over those technologies—and over ourselves. Its errors and biases are more readily on display than most of the meganet's faults. The failure of a facial recognition AI to recognize black faces is far more striking than Facebook's advertising algorithms misclassifying me as black based on my interests.[30] Advances in self-driving cars make a bigger splash than the constant collection and updating of GPS road data, which guide us every day. Yet they are all ultimately outgrowths of the same underlying phenomenon of the meganet.

Even as it amplifies meganets' power, deep learning does not supersede it. Deep learning looks like a solution because it *does some-*

thing different with the data amassed by the meganet, frequently with impressive results. In doing so, it tempts us that deep learning will solve the problems of control we have repeatedly witnessed over the course of this book. The rhetoric around deep learning and AI generally—that of better "understanding" of data, faster "response," and "learning" things previously hidden—revolves around the goal of regaining control. Yet the growth in power given to the meganet by deep learning does not grant us more control. Instead, it is the opposite. AI will not return to us the control we had prior to the existence of these enormous meganets. The history of deep learning is, like the history of networks more generally, a history of loss of control. When it comes to the meganet, deep learning is simultaneously a red herring and a representative case.

Because of deep learning's stunning successes, it's tempting to believe that we have found some key to general-purpose machine intelligence and that these deep-learning brains can help us regain control over the meganets whose size and velocity have become too great for us to manage. But the limitations of these general-purpose approaches emerge when we examine cases where they fall down. Their failings are the failings of the meganet, only magnified.

EIGHT

TAMING THE MEGANET

Yet behold, it returns. One cannot extinguish that persistent smell. It steals in through some crack in the structure—one's identity.

Virginia Woolf, *The Waves*

THROUGHOUT THIS BOOK, I'VE REPEATEDLY STRESSED TWO aspects of meganets. First, they are *semiautonomous systems*, working beyond the direct and even indirect control of humans, self-organizing into *persistent, evolving, and opaque* forms that have consequences well beyond anything intended by their creators. Second, meganets are highly *feedback driven*, as their users and algorithms combine to create the volume, velocity, and virality that prevent us from ever keeping up with their current state.

These two factors make "control" of a meganet an oxymoron. If we are forever going to be closing the barn door after the horse has bolted, the next meganet blowup, whether it is in social media or cryptocurrency, will inevitably take us by surprise. Rather, we need proactive, systemic, and nonspecific measures that will not wholly prevent the meganet-driven crises we've experienced in the last decades (social polarization, disinformation, and economic destabilization among them) but will temper them, mitigating their impact and suppressing the aggressive feedback loops. Such measures do not require full or even partial control. Instead, they disrupt and dilute uncontrollable meganet processes, reducing their power.

Taming meganets requires that we encourage them to become error correcting rather than error multiplying. In other words, surface-level fixes like content moderation or banning certain keywords from conversation aren't enough. What doesn't work is the Whac-A-Mole approach, in which centralized entities (governments or corporations) stamp out individual manifestations of abuse and misinformation in the hopes that the tide will eventually turn. While banning the largest malevolent accounts can yield positive short-term benefits, the best that results is a holding pattern because those large accounts serve more as figureheads than leaders and the underlying trends they represent do not go away. This approach has been the conventionally dominant one for some years now and has clearly met with no success.

Nor can we hope to domesticate the meganet by overwhelming its bad (abuse, misinformation) with a flood of what we deem to be good (civility, verified facts). Flooding does little to prevent the formation and congealing of groups that oppose the flood with their own powerful counternarratives. The meganet self-organizes with such speed and force that attempting to control the narrative, even with tremendous resources at one's disposal, will only succeed partially at best.

What is needed, rather, are structural interventions that temper the meganet's intrinsic tendencies. Instead of trying to force preferable information (that which is true, say) into a meganet, the existing social groupings within that meganet must be broken up. Cultivating *instability* in the meganet, rather than one's preferred form of stability, will shatter the hardened plaque of toxicity that attaches to its worst places. This means purposefully yet indiscriminately breaking up internet groups, randomly injecting new elements into threads and forums, and intentionally sowing chaos across meganets. These messy measures may seem far less effective than targeted action, yet when dealing with such a complex ecosystem like a meganet, it is *only* wide-scale and untargeted action that has a chance of changing the overall structure and function. It runs counter to intuition, but human intuition evolved mostly in the context of dealing with small groups of geographically localized people before the agricultural revolution. Now it is time to go against intuition.

My proposals in this chapter are aggressive, controversial, and untested on the grand scale. They are intended to foster what the ethicist Philip Kitcher deems the three virtues underpinning democracy: inclusiveness, informedness, and mutual engagement.[1] They do so broadly, with significant large-scale impact. As such, their effects would be wide ranging but not extreme, because we are looking to shake things up rather than censor or ban outright. Unfortunately, the workings of meganet control mechanisms from Facebook to YouTube to Chinese censorship are almost completely opaque, and what little we learn tends to come from whistleblowers and anecdotal evidence. Consequently, the ideas below are more guidelines than they are prescriptions, broad suggestions of what approaches *could* work to make meganets more habitable places for human beings. They will require refinement and testing to maximize their effectiveness and minimize their inevitable downsides because nontargeted measures always bring with them a degree of negative consequences. But because targeted measures like banning individuals or individual pieces of content simply lack effectiveness on the meganet, these sorts of broad, vaguely intentioned maneuvers are the best shot we have at taming the meganet.

SOFT SOCIAL CONTROL

My friend Ralph, extremely smart but rather crabby, has found himself placed in Facebook jail on several occasions, unable to post or comment for weeks at a time. None of his opinions cross any of the red lines of race or gender, nor does he promote any kooky conspiracy theories or outré mystical nonsense. Rather, he is only something of a cynic and can be rather blunt and even rude (but not profane or insulting) in criticizing nearly any viewpoint offered up.

Ironically, Ralph is not part of the problem because he is only one person. He does not take up with roving gangs of internet bullies; he rarely agrees with any great mass of people; he is usually the minority voice in a minority of one. If you were to put him in the middle of a Facebook discussion by a group of COVID denialists, he would likely be banned by Facebook's filters before any of them would, even as Facebook put up useless COVID information messages on the denialists' posts. Put him into a group of polite and discreet racists, and he would be tossed out for rudely calling them racists before Facebook found a problem with the others. His tone is the problem, not his content, and it's far easier for algorithms and AIs to police tone than understand content.

The case of my friend underscores two of the issues facing us in taming the meganet. First, Orwellian fears about top-down social control are already obsolete in some respects. Such social control is already here. Western companies tend to deploy it lightly, while China deploys it very harshly, but in either case the moderators of meganet content are limited in their ability to target specific problematic behaviors. As we saw earlier, China employs tens of thousands of censors and still cannot stamp out dissent, while Facebook simply limited the ability to share *any* content in the run-up to the 2020 election. The age of mass social intervention and soft social control is already here. Debating whether such tactics *should* be employed is philosophically valuable but practically irrelevant. The relevant debate, instead, is which tactics preserve the most individual autonomy and liberty while still being effective in restricting the most noxious manifestations of meganet social culture.

Second, the tactics currently in place are ineffective and often counterproductive. No one will dispute that companies and governments both have fallen down in trying to put the lid on the mess that is online social life, and what has resulted has mostly been the increased fragmentation of discourse and an endless standoff, as the attempted suppression of one viewpoint or another only reinforces the marginalized groups' sense that they are being oppressed by forces with something to hide.

There are exceptions. When Twitter and Facebook banned Donald Trump's accounts, they undeniably removed his voice from the public sphere in a significant and culture-altering way. His absence left a ghostly void where his every pronouncement had once been amplified and reiterated millions of times over.* But just because Trump was the loudest voice by far for several years does not make him a test case. Trump-like effects manifest themselves at every level of the meganet, just in much smaller form, and what was done for one extreme loudmouth will not scale down to being applied to millions of smaller meganet arenas. Trump left, but the masses of QAnon remained. Though QAnon may eventually dissipate, another such movement will succeed it. Trump's effect on the world was impossible not to confront, but how are we to assess whether my friend Ralph is sufficiently noxious to merit temporary or permanent silencing?

Tactics of ostracism and silencing, like those deployed by China, only go so far. China's greater success has been in orienting its entire culture in a direction more compatible with the government's intentions. As we saw, the values behind the Social Credit System were more significant than the actual implementation of that system, which was too feeble to be deployed beyond a comparatively small set of extreme debtors and citizens already found guilty by court. Next to China's wide-scale policies of imprisonment and other more blatant violations of human rights, the SCS is a comparative paper tiger, meant more to evangelize values in "upstanding" citizens than to police them.[2] It is not in the nature of so-called Western culture to enforce a set of values so explicitly. Our values tend to be soft, loose, and implicit.

But we are past the point where a laissez-faire attitude is feasible. In the first decade of this century, a vague techno-optimism prevailed within online culture, as mostly like-minded individuals congregated on blogs and open forums, conflicts being both low-key and of little consequence. That drastically changed in the second decade, and by

---

* We should not forget that Trump's initial platform of promotion was not the internet but legacy media: newspapers and tabloids, NBC's *The Apprentice*, and the nonstop and disproportionate coverage that CNN and other news networks provided him in the run-up to the 2016 election—and beyond. The internet provided merely the last and most direct points of his access to the public after other outlets had withdrawn their attention.

the end of the 2010s, everyone on the left and the right was calling for increased crackdowns on this or that phenomenon. Whether it was Proud Boys or antifa, most everyone now had a clear and concrete group of people in mind whom they wanted to silence, if not by the government then by the online powers that be: Facebook/Instagram and Google/YouTube, but also Twitter, Reddit, Instagram, and TikTok and every other social locus.

The toxicity of online discourse is real and pervasive. Intervention mechanisms exist and are broadly employed, but despite these ongoing interventions, frequently heavy-handed, by most of the large internet companies, the consensus is that the online sphere remains miserable, hostile, and even dangerous. The era of laissez-faire is decidedly over, and no one has yet figured out how to temper an out-of-control meganet while leaving people an acceptable amount of online freedom.

Mechanisms of pure ostracism and censorship rarely work. After Twitter banned vaccine skeptic Alex Berenson in late 2021 (temporarily, as it turned out), Berenson simply took himself and much of his readership to Substack, where, if anything, conversation around his controversial ideas flourished before returning to Twitter with half a million followers in mid-2022. Meanwhile, Facebook carelessly bans entirely legitimate articles, like one debunking bad science around mask mandates, only to walk such bans back after objections from prominent journalists.[3] The nastier troll denizens have always been able to find a place to organize, whether on Reddit, 2chan, 4chan, 8chan, or countless other home-brewed sites that cannot be squelched any more than trolling itself can be eliminated. In fact, such marginalization has turned out to be counterproductive, isolating and radicalizing the most dedicated members of ugly cliques even while more moderate brethren drop out. 8chan, the image board successor to the ever-controversial 4chan, was far more vicious and far more focused on the sorts of behaviors that had gotten its members thrown off of 4chan in the first place.

Restricting forms of expression is also self-defeating. YouTube has taken to eliminating comments (or encouraging content publishers to do so) on a good number of videos, preventing the sorts of flame wars and hate fests that frequently populate those forums. Beyond that, YouTube now only lists the total number of likes but not the number of dislikes for a given video, so that the notorious ratio of likes to dislikes can't be observed. While removing community-driven content prevents the sort of "brigading" in which some third-party group decides to target a particular piece of content (say, a trailer for a reboot of a beloved and overly protected franchise, whether it's Captain Marvel, Ghostbusters, or Batman), it also removes the ability to have *any* kind of discussion about the video in question. While it's not censorship per se, it is also not a solution to the problem because it shuts everyone up. The problem is how to enhance discourse, not to eliminate it altogether.

For a site like Reddit, whose community discussions are its bread and butter, there is no way to close off discussion wholesale or prevent the display and accumulation of "upvotes" and "downvotes" on individual posts and comments. Reddit relegates this task to unpaid moderators, trusting them to keep individual forums in line. The result is a wild west atmosphere in which the most popular communities (or subreddits) are controlled by sometimes heavy-handed moderators, and smaller communities arbitrarily run the gamut from peaceful and low-key discussion to vicious bullying, and the default answer to anyone who complains is "Go start your own subreddit."

Because isolation and marginalization are infeasible and ineffective at meganet scale, the most manageable compromise would be to leave conspiracy theorists, trolls, griefers, and crackpots in the larger meganet ecosystems but remove their power. In particular, measures should attempt to dilute their impact by reducing their ability to attract like-minded souls. This is far easier said than done.

THE GREAT SLOWDOWN

As we've seen many times, volume, velocity, and virality caused the meganet's feedback loops to push beyond human control. We have benefited so greatly from the real-time, instantaneous, no-limit structure of the internet that we are loath to understand how it is equally the source of many of our problems. Stabilizing forces, whether government, the law, or ordinary reasonable people, are forever playing catch-up with the accelerating forces of the meganet. Instead of trying to regulate content, we should look at tempering the meganet's fundamental qualities. Volume is a difficult problem; one cannot simply kick people off meganets or easily shrink their size. Velocity, however, remains open to tempering mechanisms. When Facebook instituted a forwarding limit on Messenger in the run-up to the 2020 election, it was likely an idea born more of desperation than rationality and its effects may not have been that beneficial, but it showed that such restrictions were at least feasible to implement across hundreds of millions of users for months at a time. If we could be smarter and subtler about such rate limiting, the suffocating, tightening chains of the meganet might begin to relax.

Consider fake news as a test case. *Fake news* is a term that has been applied far too broadly, used across the political spectrum to tar everything from factual reports to cable news to Russian propaganda. Here, by "fake news" I mean the aggressively slanted and inflammatory stories churned out cookie-cutter style by shady, often overseas content farms. In the words of one anonymous author of such stories in the BBC 2019 report "I Was a Macedonian Fake News Writer":

> It was never fake stories [in the sense of fabricating every detail]. It was propaganda and brainwashing in the way of telling the story. The whole time I was typing and writing these stories, I was always thinking "Oh my God, who would believe this kind of garbage? . . ." The whole article maybe contains two sentences of news and after that everything is just insults.[4]

Facebook has had little luck in calming the growing tsunami of such stories, repeatedly banning the most obvious generators of them without stemming the tide. In 2021, dozens of sites in Virginia published literally tens of thousands of articles against critical race theory with the aim of tilting the governor's race toward the Republicans.

Trumpeting a false and alarmist claim that radical leftist doctrine was being introduced into Virginia schools under the aegis of Democratic incumbent Terry McAuliffe, these articles were churned out automatically with minor variations and no bylines and then pushed out to hundreds of astroturfed websites.[5] These sites were themselves part of a larger network, Metric Media, that operates thousands of sites producing millions of highly slanted machine-generated news stories every month.[6]

How, then, could we prevent this glut from influencing and poisoning online discourse? Since such articles are generated without even the intent (however fallible) of informing or being open-ended, they are clearly pernicious. But as we saw, neither AIs nor humans have the capacity to keep up with such a meganet-driven glut. A 2021 German study of Twitter data showed that fact-checking only mitigates conspiracy theories if it is deployed early and proactively—which the speed of the meganet makes impossible.[7] Fake news will inevitably become a larger problem, not a smaller problem, as more sophisticated means of generating articles, targeting users, and mimicking authoritative and reliable sources arise.* How, then, do we distinguish the glut from what is valuable, without cracking down beyond the freedoms of liberal society?

Former Facebook data scientist Frances Haugen, who has been openly critical of the company since her departure, agrees that non-targeted methods are more effective than targeted ones: "[It's] not about picking good and bad ideas, it's about making the distribution of ideas safer."[8] Haugen told the *Financial Times* that nonspecific limitations on the size of groups and on resharing links—general approaches to "slow content transmission"—were vastly more effective than the moderation and fact-checking we currently see:

* Wikipedia, which reliably shows up high on the first page of Google results for many queries, provides no guarantees of accuracy and no guarantees that its anonymous contributors are contributing honestly or with genuine expertise, yet the site is still the default resource for nonessential information. This should give some idea of the sheer scope of the problem: a frequently but not reliably accurate source rates above most other internet sites, even those by acknowledged experts.

> Internal research has shown [Facebook] can radically slow down a piece of content. "That may carve out one or half a per cent of profit, but that has the same impact on disinformation as the entire third-party fact-checking programme . . . and it works in every language," [Haugen] said, referring to the results of internal research done while she was at the company.[9]

Facebook's internal research confirms the thesis I put forward earlier in this chapter: broad algorithmic fixes requiring minimal human administration are as effective if not more so than an entire army of moderators and fact-checkers. In practice, these fixes are still far from simple, but removing the large-scale human element enables them to keep up with the pace of the internet—even as they slow it down.

Haugen specified two fixes in particular: limiting group sizes and disabling the automatic sharing of links beyond friends of friends. To those we can add a number of others designed to slow down the speed at which the meganet's feedback loops develop.

Facebook already deprioritizes posts with links compared to linkless posts. Likewise, the propagation of links could be slowed down when a piece of content becomes too viral. Such virality usually accompanies ephemeral and nonessential content (like a celebrity arrest, a popular TV show, or a dress that some people see as blue and some as gold), but also low-quality content that fills up our feeds like political red meat or product advertisements masquerading as news. Some of this content is not only low quality but also actively pernicious, designed to play on the amygdala and fight-or-flight response and encourage resharing. Political content farms specialize in such content. AIs are terrible at reliably identifying divisive content in and of itself, but if filtering algorithms treated virality as a proxy for homogeneous (and *potentially* divisive) content, a great deal of that low-quality content would be deprioritized in favor of a more heterogeneous mix of content. If Facebook were to observe some fake news posts from Metric Media–run sites being spread repeatedly among the same people, it could counter that spread by deprioritizing those articles automatically, not in response to their content but in response to their virality. The increased hetereogeneity would reduce the concentration of poison. Not all of that heterogenous mix would be high-quality content—most of it would not be—but the important consequence would be that any potentially overwhelming trend would be diluted by the greater variation in what was promoted.

So given a hot viral link or video, whether it's political propaganda or celebrity trial gossip, Facebook or Twitter or YouTube could give such content frequent cooling-off periods in which that link would be deprioritized or delayed in its propagation. Meganet social interaction and sharing is normally instantaneous, but this need not be the case. Even a delay of a few minutes would slow down content propagation by several orders of magnitude. Ironically, the slow speed of Bitcoin transactions (arising from difficulties as its network has grown) has already caused exactly such a blunting within the Bitcoin environment, though that effect is rarely remarked upon.

Naturally, some content should not be slowed down, like urgent news items of natural disasters or other pressing updates. Here, however, human moderators can serve a purpose. While it's impossible to moderate out a sufficient amount of nefarious content, identifying critical items that should not be blocked from propagation is far easier: humans need only pick out natural disasters, urgent newsworthy items, and other truly consequential content. The moderators need not be perfect here either. Anything they miss will still spread, just more slowly. And at any time the brakes can be removed, but the bar for doing this will have to be high.

Similarly, we can slow down discussion itself. Limiting the size of discussion groups, as Facebook did around the 2020 election, is one approach, but conversations involving dozens or hundreds of people are a crucial part of online discourse, so we can't eliminate them completely. We can, however, slow those discussions down. So many of the nastiest debates and arguments on public feeds arise from instantaneous mobs, pile-ons, and back-and-forths. We can limit how quickly such feedback-driven explosions occur with measures such as delaying posts by minutes, restricting the number of responses possible within a given time frame, and slowing the propagation of comments from senders to recipients. Such measures can lower the temperature of a discussion and prevent it from reaching a critical mass where it turns into an inflamed melee between entrenched sides.

Such methods extend to spaces outside the most popular social networks. It is all too easy for a group of people to organize on a third-party site (4chan being the most famous example) to "flood" or "brigade" a target with nasty reviews or comments, whether it's a book on Amazon, a restaurant on Yelp, or a forum on Reddit. Tech companies for years have used traffic profiling to detect artificial, bot-driven traffic to sites and ads to prevent false ad revenue and denial-of-service attacks. But an organized group of people is not artificial; it's a meganet-driven sociological phenomenon. By declaring, in effect, that sudden bursts of activity, *even if wholly legitimate*, should be tempered and slowed across the board, we would not be deciding that such activity is intrinsically bad. Rather, we would restructure the meganet to become a bit slower and a bit less viral. In doing so, we would also prevent some of the more terrible consequences of meganet discourse and do so more effectively than by trying to stamp them out surgically.

Such restructuring doesn't just affect anonymous everyday people. It can also temper outsize personalities like Donald Trump or Elon Musk, who do not control the meganet but who do exert wildly disproportionate force on it. The market-wrenching effects of a single person—Elon Musk, say—are completely out of proportion to what they should be. No one, not even Elon Musk, should have the ability to send stocks and cryptocurrencies soaring and diving seconds after a tweet. Musk cannot be censored, nor should he be specifically targeted. What should be targeted is the more general phenomenon of a single CEO's volatility and outspokenness increasing the options market of a single stock—in this case Tesla—several times beyond the rest of the S&P 500 combined. Albert Bridge Capital CIO Drew Dixon marveled at the ability of Tesla to defy predictions and extrapolations:

> There is a huge, recursive "tail wagging the dog" nature to the valuation of a lot of things these days. . . . I'm unwavering in my belief that ultimately the fundamentals are what matters. But over the past few years I can see that the short and intermediate term is far more dominated by flow, momentum, memes and appetites.[10]

The recursion to which Dixon alludes is just another word for the meganet's feedback loops, the ability for stock valuations to act like other forms of online discourse and run away faster than traditional market forces can tame them. We saw earlier how the SEC threw up its hands at the problem of "broad participation" when it came to GameStop's "disruption" of traditional market behavior. Dixon is similarly fatalistic, for if the short and medium term are more subject to meganet chaos than stabilizing forces, the path to the long term will be so rocky and destabilizing that by the time we get there we may wish we were dead.

Decreasing the exposure of a larger-than-life personality like Trump or Musk is risky when done directly, creating a cascade of noise and outrage that is as difficult to predict as anything else on the meganet. Yet if such a decrease occurs as a result of wide-scale regulation and rebalancing of the spread of information and (just as importantly) if there is a general welcoming of the stability brought about by such changes, then it is far harder to make the objection that any censorship is taking place, any more than planned electrical outages during heat waves are seen as violations of civil rights rather than as necessary measures. Slowing down the speed of discourse while momentarily deranking superpopular content will go a significant ways toward softening the recursion that vexes Dixon.

TURN TAKING

There are more radical approaches to slowing down content, such as enforcing a kind of virtual turn taking. One of the greatest changes brought about by the meganet era is the shift from a paucity of content and publishing venues to a vast surplus of both. The underlying cause of the surplus is that the cost of publishing one's content to dozens, thousands, and even millions of people has now shrunk to zero. Those with the most time, energy, and sheer gumption can outlast and outpost more reasonable people with lives—the exact opposite of what we would like to be the case. Many people, myself included, have already had the experience of being driven out of one or another internet forum by people who were more dogmatic, more unreasonable, and simply more relentless.

But that doesn't have to be the case. We are already in the business of shaping and restricting online discourse in broad, nontargeted ways. Twitter already allows users to promote tweets for a fee, while most online dating services prevent a surplus of spam by regulating how and when messages can be sent, privileging paying users. Prioritizing content by whether users are willing to pay to publish it is the wrong approach because it rebalances the system unfairly. Now the people with the most money instead of the most time are the loudest. While being careful not to swing the pendulum to favor better-off people with more resources, we could extend a different kind of logic to all posts, saying, in effect: "You can only have so much time and space to speak before your words and posts are pushed to the back of the queue behind people who have not yet spoken as much as you." Instead of meganet discourse being a contest of who can shout the loudest for the longest amount of time, turn taking could be more gently enforced by quieting the biggest loudmouths and amplifying the softer-spoken participants.

We could even conceive of a cross-service budget that limits the amount of online activity through a virtual currency. This currency would, in effect, pay for the ability to be heard. Only a certain number of contributions to Facebook, Twitter, YouTube, and so on could be made within a certain period of time (a day or a week, perhaps), after which tokens would need to slowly refill before an individual's posts would not be deranked. There would be a finite amount of discussion space, apportioned fairly among participants, rather than the meganet-driven infinity of content that plagues us currently.

For a turn-taking mechanism to be transparent and fair, it would have to be based around some transparent mechanism akin to Bitcoin's blockchain, so that anyone could verify that tokens are accruing to an individual fairly. Even with a transparent ledger, there are two related difficulties involved in enforcing this sort of turn taking. One is the creation of new accounts, which may be sock puppets of existing accounts or dubious in other ways. A newly created account should not go to the top of everyone's feed in the same way that a long-established and mostly silent account should. Similarly, bot networks should not be able to create armies of low-posting accounts that can still swamp out high-quality discourse through sheer numbers. In both of these cases, there needs to be some sort of reputational system to prevent talking turns from being handed out to bad actors or wholly unproven ones. Reputation systems are, in general, too easy to game and often subject to the worst aspects of human group dynamics, so any reputation system should be as minimal as possible. Here, some experimentation would be required. My suggestion for a starting point would be for some kind of validation to be required for an account to be deemed worthy of having turns: possibly being vouched for by other existing community members or else a serious mechanism of identity verification by cell phone or even government ID.

Seriously enforcing turn taking may ultimately require tying a single person's identity permanently to a single blockchain-like address, in the same way that Aadhaar tied every Indian citizen to a single number. My suspicion is that for better or for worse, meganets are already headed in this direction. Online identity will increasingly be unified for the sake of accountability, and new and unproven identities will be treated with suspicion and probation until they establish reputations as good online citizens. (Verification methods of various forms will be available.) I do not advocate that sort of unification per se, but I do think it is inevitable, and so we might as well leverage it to a positive end by making it as transparent as possible through something like a distributed blockchain implementation. Once such a mechanism exists, limiting the rate of a user's contributions across multiple sites would be a fairly simple addition—one that ideally would also preserve the privacy and identity of the user.

How inimical are these maneuvers to the central value of free speech? I cannot pretend they don't come into conflict with civil liberties. Even if the government itself plays no part in the enactment and regulation of online identities, there are intrinsic risks to the establishment of long-term identity services that prescribe and inhibit one's online activity. I see us moving toward them, however, because the growing societal consensus is that the alternative of unchecked anarchy is not working. Building a softer and more robust mechanism for regulating online activity will help us avoid a China-level crackdown on online activity, which services like YouTube are already deploying on a case-by-case basis by limiting or preventing discussion on particular pieces of content. At the same time, it will also prevent illiberal disruptions of online discourse from botnets run by state and nonstate actors.

All of these tactics attempt to slow down the meganet to human speed. Individual humans can't run beyond human speed, but large enough numbers of humans, connected through a single meganet, cause effects faster than humans can comprehend. Breaking that speed limit of the human is, in fact, the original sin of the meganet. The problem facing us is how to slow things back down in a fair, nonideological, and nonhegemonic way—and that is only possible through broad, nontargeted tactics.

CHAOS INJECTION

We can do more than slow down the meganet's forces. We can introduce counterforces intended to counteract and weaken them. For all that we perceive the meganet to be chaos, the addition of chaos and complexity can ironically also mitigate the force of meganets. To illustrate this extremely counterintuitive principle, take a self-contained example: the deployment of ranked choice voting (RCV) in the 2021 New York City mayoral election. RCV has long been an alternative to traditional ballots in which voters choose a single candidate. In RCV, voters list several candidates in order of preference so that their vote can be reassigned to whomever is left as less-popular candidates are eliminated from the algorithmic tallying of votes. RCV's New York rollout, however, had one important secondary effect: political campaigns no longer knew who to target.[11]

By 2020, it had become commonplace for campaigns to break down voters into groups by whom they would vote for and to treat these groups as unities. First-generation immigrants, Upper West Side residents, Haredi Jews: every candidate had a sense of the first preference of each such group when they voted. But ranked choice voting exploded the possibilities. A group might agree on their first choice, but who was to say they would necessarily agree on a second or third or fourth choice? Because RCV entails a series of runoff contests, each with one fewer candidate than the last runoff, even pollsters had trouble figuring out how to lock down their predictions, throwing out undecided voters and explicitly saying they were far less certain than they would be in a typical election.[12] Campaigns had to target not only their base voters but also detractors who might still vote for their candidate in third or fourth place. After algorithms had sorted through voters' preference lists, the top two candidates were moderates Eric Adams and Kathryn Garcia, who were not necessarily the top choices of many voters but were the *least unacceptable* to the greatest number of voters.

RCV's complexity, in fact, negated much of the microtargeting and mobilization typical of campaigns these days. Not that these tactics didn't occur, but they were deployed with far less specificity and intelligence—as operatives themselves admitted. The net effect was a regression to a more naïve, earlier kind of campaign in which candidates were more or less consistently themselves and pandered less to perceived momentary shifts because it had become impossible to determine the fallout of any such fine-grained pandering. And the end result was a throwback to the era in which compromise candidates could win out over fiery ideologues.

The lesson from the implementation of RCV is that chaos doesn't necessarily build on itself. Chaos can in fact neutralize chaos, if the chaos is directed in opposing directions. In opposition to the growing morass of campaign demographics, microtargeting, and voter influence (Cambridge Analytica being the most infamous example), the enactment of ranked choice voting accomplished more to neutralize such techniques than a million banned posts on Facebook. By changing the underlying system so that meganet-assisted political activity could no longer be so finely directed, RCV removed the incentive for a good chunk of the political nastiness and skullduggery accompanying many elections.

Ranked choice voting was not intended to create such uncertainty, yet I would argue its contribution there was at least as important as whatever it might have done to help voters express their will. Chaotic interventions that don't have any clear reformist purpose can be meaningful simply by reining in existing feedback loops. There are mechanisms that dampen the inexorable acceleration of meganets *without doing so in any particular direction*.

Consider how we might deal with fake news. There are two problems with fake news: quantity and homogeneity. The problem of quantity is that the amount of bad content (fake news and otherwise) will outweigh the good. What we commonly consider to be good information is generated piecemeal, one piece of content at a time, gaining pride of place through prestigious affiliations—just like in the pre-internet world. More dubious sources, whether astroturfed propaganda or sheer crowdsourced disinformation, can pop up overnight, blasting agitprop one hundred times more quickly. Promoting a single point of view turns out to be far easier than presenting the facts in all their intricacy. And so volume, which the meganet rewards through its very structure, will continue to be a problem.

The problem of homogeneity is that on the internet like attracts like—far more than in real life. People tend to group with those who share one or another affinity with them. We see this on a large scale with the current division into red and blue America, but one need only visit a tech company at lunchtime to see the divisions between programmers and marketers (just look at their clothing to tell the difference) or visit an elementary school playground to see such affinities controlling associations of students. The meganet greatly exacerbates this problem. Geographical space often forces some heterogeneity in the physical world by forcing diverse people to coexist near each other, but in online life, laws of association and ostracism know no such geographical limits. People are free to find those most ideologically aligned with them whether they live next door or around the world, just as they can shun a neighbor who in real life they would have to at least tolerate. In turn, these homogeneous groups consume the same sources of news, and if those sources should be fake or otherwise bad, there won't be dissenting voices. Combined with the real-time feedback-driven effects of the meganet, balkanized homogeneity balloons.

In fact, volume and homogeneity are two sides of the same coin. If there weren't such an overwhelming quantity of every type of information, homogeneity would not be so incessantly reinforced. If social groupings were not so homogeneous, the relentless quantity of content of every stripe would not have such a reinforcing effect.

Geographical allocations of people are somewhat arbitrary. We end up in a location through any number of factors. Even if urban and rural areas tend to skew in one direction or another, they still are nowhere near as homogeneous as many online spaces. And geographical heterogeneity isn't planned. It's largely the result of chance. Introducing this kind of randomness into the meganet, without any particular agenda, would be both a more benign and more effective way to disperse the tight affinity circles that have developed. In short, this would mean that across the internet, users in various spaces, from Facebook to Reddit to Google to YouTube, would see strangers enter their midst. Feeds and notifications would be scrambled, so that every person would periodically see unusual content from strangers.

If this sounds intrusive, it only is to the extent that being on the internet would become closer to walking outside in public, knowing that random people might overhear you, rather than residing in the self-selected echo chambers that we currently inhabit. People could still communicate privately, of course, via direct messages, but social spaces past a certain size would not just be open but actively altered so that new people would drop by. Many would just as soon pass right on out, but the knowledge that your like-minded group of friends will be seen by less like-minded others will temper and open up the tone and content. Even Twitter, which positions itself as a public forum where everyone mixes with everyone, still does not actively intermix its balkanized communities as I am advocating here. It would make a difference.

TikTok has already implemented measures along these lines. In December 2021, the Chinese company announced that it would take measures to prevent too much of certain content categories ("extreme dieting, sadness, and breakups" were given as examples) from being shown to individual users, to prevent them from "viewing too much of a content category that may be fine as a single video but problematic in clusters."[13] From there, the injection of novel content (perhaps content loosely but not closely related to what the user already watches) would provide more irrelevancy, for sure, but also more crucial diversity, and the diversity outweighs the irrelevancy.

This shake-up can be extended to clumps of users as well. Because quantity outweighs quality on the meganet, gangs of like-minded people find it easy to outshout individual dissenting voices or even bully them. These groups should not be actively broken up, which will only antagonize them, but they should be algorithmically discouraged. If a particular group of people (whether a dozen or a hundred) repeatedly comment on the same content, like one another's posts and comments, and (even more importantly) downvote and disagree with the same content, then meganet algorithms can skew their feeds so that they don't all see the same content, or at least do not see it at the same time or with the same priority. The meganet's homogeneous clumping tendencies produce flash-mob-like online events in which users who already know one another see the same content at the same time and can easily dogpile more isolated interlopers who stumble into the discussion of that piece of content. We can code our meganets to counter this innate tendency if we are smart about it. If users sense that they don't have the numbers on their side, then actual discourse may resume instead of agitprop shouting matches. Yes, many innocuous groupings will not form as easily and freely as they did in the past since algorithms will slow the flow of content to *all* established groups and ensuing conversations. But is this such a terrible price to pay, or will slowing down the pace of internet discourse free up people to attend more to their offline lives?

Once users are regularly seeing content and links shared by people with whom they have no association and once they see less content from the same gang of people with whom they usually interact, they will bear in mind that the world is larger than their little bubble. The nonlinear spread of the meganet, deployed in this way, would fight against its intrinsic tendencies toward homogeneity.

SHAKING UP THE DATA

It's not just people who can be randomized, shaken up, and redistributed; data itself can be disorganized and reorganized as well. While we complain of fake news and bad information, the problem is not the *existence* of bad information per se but *too much* bad information that is *all the same*. We don't see a way to evacuate such a sheer volume of information from meganets—but what we can do is add to it and dilute it.

Human censors are too slow to be able to keep bad data out of the meganet. AIs are too dumb to judge what is innocuous and what is malevolent. What AIs can do, however, is judge *similarity* of content. To an AI, both botnets and troll armies can be identified more easily by the superficial homogeneity of their content than by the deeper meaning of their content. Both types of groups invade particular forums pushing particular points of view, dropping in particular keywords and phrases to skew the discussion, making the same kinds of arguments and attacks. AIs cannot identify such armies with foolproof accuracy, but they can cluster contributors by similarity of content with a consequential degree of accuracy. The problem is that homogeneity isn't enough to identify *only* harmful content. While trolls may post the same sort of harmful content, ordinary groups of people may also post similar content. After all, the meganet strongly draws similar people together. Cracking down on homogeneity would cause too much innocuous content to be swept up in that net. Yet if we view homogeneity as something to be discouraged—not necessarily bad, but still a tendency we wish to curtail—then more difficult subproblems get solved in the process of addressing the larger issue of homogeneity.

Imagine if, instead of a torrent of COVID conspiracy theories about how COVID was intentionally released in some kind of "plandemic," assorted other posts about COVID (some informative, some nonsensical) flooded into people's feeds with the same regularity. Rather than content warnings administered by Facebook, let the most popular content within *other* meganet forums be randomly shared into those of COVID doubters—and vice versa. The same could go for posts about climate science denial. One may blanch at the prospect of spreading conspiratorial content further (albeit by random chance), but remember, for several months in early 2020, health experts and reputable sources insisted that face masks were mostly unnecessary and unhelpful as a defense against COVID-19.[14] The authoritative information of the day is not so impeccable that it needs to be protected from any intrusion by less authoritative information.

Likewise, the current state of affairs is hardly so healthy that preserving the status quo is necessarily of great value. Months of provaccination stories presented as authoritative by Twitter and Facebook did virtually nothing to persuade the 20 or so percent of the country who were heavily skeptical toward vaccines.[15] The reason is likely that the meganet has already sorted people into self-confirming groups (sometimes called filter bubbles, though the effect is stronger than that term suggests) who validate shared opinions while policing dissenting opinions. Countering these groups with authoritative information will do no good. Only a more general flood of heterogeneous information from a diverse and even random variety of sources will disrupt them, by loosening the bonds within the groups instead of trying to convert them from the outside. The goal is not to persuade people to believe something different but to get them to doubt what they already think. Exposure to many differing viewpoints, even if some of them are ridiculous, is better than Facebook fact-checks showing people that there are other ways of thinking outside their virtual communities.

What is needed, broadly speaking, is far greater heterogeneity in the information that any given person consumes and the cultivation of a higher level of doubt across the board. We cannot easily decrease the number of people who believe the wrong thing, but we *can* decrease the number of people who are certain that what they believe, whatever it is, must be correct. The meganet's forces encourage too much certainty, when what we want is less certainty.

POISONING THE WELL

The goal of these proposals is to increase heterogeneity and decrease the clumping together of like-minded views and content. There is one meganet phenomenon that does not fall under that broad rubric, however, and that is the meganet's inherent tendency to accumulate and aggregate data into large-scale databases, public and private. Even if what people see online becomes more heterogeneous, the problem remains that *algorithms* may see people as only the sum of a decreasing number of online parts. Your Facebook, LinkedIn, and Google advertising profiles define you to algorithms in a limiting way. The more you coalesce into a single online identity across meganets, the more boxed in your experience on meganets will be.

The positive and negative effects of data aggregation—and of meganet aggregation more generally—are often distant enough from their causes that we do not perceive such aggregation as a problem in itself. What law professor Frank Pasquale terms "runaway data" in *The Black Box Society* is an insidious problem specifically because the worst effects are felt so far away from its origins. When Cambridge Analytica utilized Facebook's massive user base to target potential Trump voters, to most eyes it appeared as though there were only two players involved: first, the dubious consulting firm Cambridge Analytica and its sneaky psychological testing apps, and second, the behemoth of Facebook and its enormous pool of users. In fact, there were countless players. So much of the data Facebook has on its users originates from outside Facebook, obtained either by Facebook trackers on sites around the web or through advertising profiling information obtained by Facebook through partnerships with ad exchanges like Xandr and dataxu or through acquisitions like Instagram. The Cambridge Analytica scandal would have been nowhere near as consequential without the meganet-driven growth of Facebook. It takes a meganet to raise a global database of users.

As we have seen over the course of this book, successful meganets inevitably combine into larger ones. Our digital mirages congeal and grow into long-lasting profiles that supersede our own offline individuality. Even when the core of such a digital mirage is minimal, as with Aadhaar, any such database will cause an entire ecosystem of meganets to grow around it, until your digital mirage arbitrates whether or not you can obtain health care, open a bank account, or acquire a cell phone. Ironically, it was in China that the use of such digital mirages was comparatively limited because China recognized that they were too unreliable. The reality of the Orwellian Social Credit System was considerably more modest than its conception, being restricted primarily to the enforcement of explicit legal judgments. That limitation, in fact, points a way forward to restoring greater heterogeneity to the meganet beneath the surface level of user interaction. Meganet-driven systems based on identity rely on the assumption that their data is accurate. In truth, the data tends to be accurate *enough*. Mistakes are uncommon but hardly rare. There are those who have been unfortunate enough to contact the IRS to correct a confusion of identity with another person with the same name, or had to deal with a credit bureau to wipe a false collection notice off their credit record, or had to explain to the TSA why there is no reason they should be on the no-fly list.

These kinds of errors, from trivial to devastating, pervade all such meganet systems. Many are simply tolerated: the millions of books contained in the archives of Google Books and Project Gutenberg have all had their text scanned through optical character recognition to make them searchable. The resulting digital text, however, is highly unreliable, frequently containing dozens of errors on a single page, while some books are completely mis-scanned into a mess of incomprehensible characters. These errors will likely never be corrected because they don't have enough negative impact. When errors *do* have enough negative impact, however, is when we see intervention. When Google's image recognition labeled black people as "gorillas" in 2015 and Facebook labeled them as "primates" in 2021, Google and Facebook immediately tweaked or disabled the systems to quash such errors, at the cost of functionality.[16] Not all mistakes are created equal, and meganets can be "tamed" to the extent that their errors are unacceptable. In the absence of conclusive evidence of critical errors, even doubt can be sufficient to trigger restriction on meganet functionality.

Imagine, then, if we intentionally injected mistakes into meganet ecosystems. Since the day I signed up, for example, Facebook has been mistaken about my birthday: it's a day or two off. This has had the effect of turning many birthday greetings into unbirthday greetings, but it has never truly bothered me. I hope that it has made Facebook's digital mirage of me that much harder to collate with the many others out there that have my correct birthday (or one of the other wrong ones I've used).

We can't corrupt people's birthdays without their consent, but we could tinker with other less noticeable bits of information about them, particularly bits that I never chose to reveal to anyone in the first place. All over the world, there are thousands upon thousands of databases that index my demographic information: gender, race, age, income bracket, creditworthiness, marital status, parental status, and more. These databases are used almost entirely for elective purposes, primarily marketing. There's no point in trying to shut down these databases or regulate them any more than there is in trying to shut down sources of misinformation. It's yet another game of Whac-A-Mole. But if we can't beat them, we can join them. If national or international governing entities were to setup *additional* data brokers in this ecosystem that distribute similar but randomly corrupted bits of data, it would shake loose the certainty and usefulness of these existing datastores—and in this case, that would be a good thing. Data brokers could no longer stand by the reliability of their data because they would know it had been tainted. Unless they collected all their data themselves (something that would be impossible unless you are Facebook or Google), the perceived value of their data would be significantly compromised and the well of promiscuous data sharing would truly be poisoned.

The potential for havoc in this scenario may seem boundless. What if some wrong data about me gets shared with someone I care about? Even though this exact scenario is already happening thousands of times over on a daily basis, this seeming downside turns out to be an upside if the uncertainty is guaranteed. If a given entity (a bank, a realtor, a social network) cannot rely on its data about me being correct, it would have to verify it with an authoritative source. Often, though not always, that authoritative source would be me, finally returning control over my data to the person to whom it supposedly belonged all along. If Facebook had to ask me whether I was the David Auerbach who had an interest in IPA beers and Sun Ra, I could tell them that I liked one but not the other. Or I could choose to tell them nothing. Sowing doubt about data would have a slowing effect on meganet phenomena, similar to my proposals above for rate limiting and turn taking. It would help reduce the meganet to something closer to human speed. Surely it will be less efficient, but the very efficiency of the meganet is what is causing its feedback loops to spin out of control.

This sort of well poisoning would not be possible when the data in question is already verified and agreed upon, such as with Bitcoin and other blockchain applications. There, the problem is not that the data is running away but that the meganet itself is that much more resistant to any sort of regulation—by design. Yet when we looked at cryptocurrencies earlier, we saw that they were both less decentralized than they wished to be (with a handful of Chinese miners, for example, able to exert great proportional influence over the Bitcoin blockchain) and more prone to corruption than they wished to be (as with the hacks and bugs that pop up in blockchain apps). A kind of centralized control is possible but requires the buy-in of an overwhelming number of stakeholders—and such buy-in is unlikely for any sort of meganet-taming mechanism as I am proposing here.

So instead, think back to BitTorrent and file sharing. BitTorrent posed to the video and movie industries a similar problem that Bitcoin poses to centralized finance today: an alternative system without a central locus of control that can be shut down. Media companies did not beat BitTorrent so much as they finally managed to marginalize it by offering their own paid streaming platforms that were easier to use than BitTorrent. Media companies did have a bit of success, however, in interfering with *specific* pieces of content: prerelease movies, for example. By uploading their own fake versions of especially sensitive content, media companies were able to impair download of particularly important content on a case-by-case basis.

The same could potentially be done for the more problematic aspects of cryptocurrencies. Monero, for example, is a highly anonymized cryptocurrency favored by organized and disorganized crime alike due to its use of stealth transactions.[17] While there is now a booming business in tracing Monero transactions, we could consider more interventionist strategies to tame Monero and cryptocurrencies like it. Large governments and NGOs like the World Bank could flood Monero with valid but effectively useless transactions, exchanging cryptocurrency among addresses they own. This would not be a cheap or logistically easy mechanism, but governments and NGOs have the resources to achieve such disruption without being identified and kicked off the network. In effect, governments and NGOs would become vigilante-style bad actors on these networks.

The result will look a lot like where cryptocurrencies may already be going: a chaotic and untrustworthy mess. Unlike most of my suggestions above, this sort of disruption is far less ideal, sacrificing the very functionality of individual blockchain networks in order to save them. But the reality of blockchain cryptocurrencies is already quite far from their stated ideal, with large and mysterious miners controlling large portions of the blockchains of Bitcoin and other big names—something that troubled China enough that it has attempted to ban cryptocurrency mining altogether. Again, we must turn a fault into a partial virtue.

REAL INCLUSION

My suggestions in this chapter may seem like recipes for disaster, sure to sow confusion and conflict across the internet. That reaction is not wholly wrong. These strategies will sow confusion but with the goal of reducing conflict. The confusion is, in fact, intentional—since our difficulty is that people often believe so unquestioningly what the meganet gives them—and will be beneficial. An overall miasma of doubt and confusion will reduce conflict because it is certainty that drives people to argue so fiercely with one another.

I have started with the assumption—shared by most—that meganets as they stand are failing to work for humanity in some crucial aspects. They lower discourse, spread disinformation, and give rise to sudden trends that can disrupt any area of life from social cohesion to the economy. In its explosion of content driven by volume, velocity, and virality, the meganet amplifies all of these problems by being too fast and too decentralized to control. Also by its nature, it prevents more targeted fixes from taking hold broadly. The only effective way to fix the meganet's underlying problems is to turn the meganet against itself algorithmically through the sorts of mechanisms I've listed above. By breaking up balkanized portions of the internet and strongly encouraging heterogeneity of social association and data itself, we can slowly soften and dissolve the hardened, nastiest bits of our meganets without a minimum of explicit ostracism and censorship.

Users themselves can take part in this decongealing of the meganet. Soliciting user feedback in more aggressive and creative ways can help break each of us out of the localized clusters that the meganet naturally clusters us into. Providing users with sets of topics to choose from—new and unfamiliar topics, not ones picked by recommendation engines—will help bring out differences within affinitized clusters of people. Users can be asked to revise their own data in ways that will differentiate rather than cluster. Instead of listing hobbies, tastes, and musical opinions to be grouped by, social media users could be prompted to engage with random pieces of content and art—perhaps in exchange for some sort of reward (an online credit or even, one dares to say, cryptocurrency). Exposure to the new and unfamiliar would dislodge the tightest feedback loops of the meganet and bring it a bit closer to the dream of open-minded, free access that many early internet users still fondly remember. Instead of a populist onslaught of online forces fighting one another, we would go a step closer to *real* inclusion, in which a person would travel through diverse pieces of meganets, not wholly in control of the journey (because such control, given the meganet, is impossible) but considerably more free from the toxicity and viral misinformation that dominates today.

I don't pretend these strategies will work perfectly on deployment. It will take time to test and tweak meganet-kneecapping mechanisms so that they discourage meganet excesses without causing too much collateral inconvenience, just as TikTok is experimenting with how to reduce the amount of homogeneous content shown to its users. There may be alternative means to dampen meganet feedback loops that require less interference than what I've listed above. And all such mechanisms will need to take into account the types of identity services and user data available. If, as I believe, we are moving toward a stronger and more unified notion of online identity, there are both more risks and more benefits to my suggestions. The risks include unparalleled ability to track, grade, and stalk individuals online. The benefits, however, include an ability to regulate and temper the toxicity of much online activity without doing serious damage to freedom of expression and other civil liberties. To ignore these potential benefits and fight any sort of strong identity is to put our collective head in the sand. If Big Brother can't be stopped, we should focus on throwing sand in his eyes rather than futilely trying to kill him.

CONCLUSION

Gracefully Passing the Torch

We know not whether you are kind,
Or cruel in your fiercer mood;
But be you Matter, be you Mind,
We think we know that you are blind,
And we alone are good.

HENRY ADAMS, "Prayer to the Dynamo"

WHAT IS NEXT FOR MEGANETS? PREDICTIONS ARE ALWAYS A dicey business, and when it comes to a phenomenon that explicitly defies our complete understanding, we find ourselves unable even to gain sufficient perspective to analyze the present situation, much less guess at the future.

Yet the world continues, and so we can assume that as with economics, self-organizing forces will continue to assert themselves. As with economics—or indeed as with the weather or plate tectonics—we will not be able to pin down how these forces work or comprehensively predict their movements. They will not necessarily be *stable* forces but neither will they be random. In this book, I've explored many cases of how these forces emerge and develop and the variety of their effects. As we deploy meganets in more areas of life, their reach and impact will continue to expand.

To see how meganets could grow, consider where they will next be deployed. Biotechnology is a burgeoning field that has yet to reach the critical mass to penetrate into our daily lives, but in the coming decade, that will change. Collection of health data, computer assistance and automation of medical processes, and the deployment of networked health appliances will connect our physical bodies to meganets. Today's health-tracking devices like FitBit will look primitive in comparison. Our bodies will themselves generate an entire new ocean of data that, in spite of the protections placed around health data today, will inevitably become assimilated into the larger space of meganets, either through lack of regulation or through personal choice. Today, our government measures concentrations of COVID in sewage (originating in fecal matter) to help gauge infection levels.[1] Increased public and private monitoring of daily activities, purchases, and wearable health devices will create a boom in data that can be used to track people's health and health problems to a very fine-grained level. The meganet that emerges will sort out sicker and healthier populations both at large and small scales, shaping health policy as well as predicting maladies and deaths. One's online digital mirage will present a reflection of one's health as well. We will know changes in our body long before we feel them, as will our doctors. Being sick will become a far more public matter.

Moreover, our awareness of both our own health and of others' health will balloon, as algorithms collect and chart our physical symptoms and activities. Privacy protections will be in place, but the leaky nature of meganets will ensure that *some* of your health knowledge will spread into unintended realms, just as one's credit card purchases today can make it abundantly clear if one has gastrointestinal problems or allergies. Some of this health data will be truly useful in anticipating adverse outcomes in medical procedures or catching cancers and other health conditions before they become serious. Simultaneously, with this greater awareness will come a greater societal sense of who the sickest and healthiest in society are, and stigmas will thereby attach.

The growth of biotech arises from the increasing miniaturization of digital devices, networked and otherwise. MIT researchers have designed a computer in a pill, a nanocomputer that monitors stomach temperatures after swelling up in size once in the stomach.[2] In time, we will have such devices constantly monitoring our bodies, catching threats and changes before we are physically aware of them. But these devices will also be communicating to larger meganets, and that will inevitably bring meganet feedback effects into play as we react to other people's health information and cluster ourselves by any number of health metrics. Staying away from people whose internal devices report them as sick will just be the start. We will seek out the "healthiest" people in the hopes of benefiting our own health, and tracking one's health metrics will become a competitive and increasingly public matter among friends.

Outside our bodies, meganet-connected devices will be everywhere, transforming our transportation systems. As we automate driving, the interplay of our own transportation decisions, our car's algorithms, and GPS and road condition information will create their own feedback loops, optimizing traffic but also shunting it in sometimes bizarre directions. All of this travel information will be collected as well for study by private and public entities, and that too will feed back on itself. Destinations will know when visitors and customers are arriving as soon as they set out, and visitors will know ahead of time whether a particular trip is even worth the journey.

Public discourse, already immensely destabilized and decentered in the last ten years, will fracture to a far greater degree. While we are already witnessing the decline of any sort of centralized, elite control over messaging and information, we are still only in the early period of meganet-driven, self-organizing communities, which have barely begun to congeal. The large, loose coalitions we see, often aligned with a particular large-scale political or social movement, will fragment further into medium-sized, far more insular communities.

Where today we have large-scale movements like MAGA or Black Lives Matter loosely organized around a hashtag, the greater penetration and organization of meganets will make such large-scale groupings less common, instead solidifying smaller organizations with more elaborate and fixed beliefs. Assisted by immersive technologies like VR, these communities will feel considerably more real than today's online communities, which themselves already hold such a grip over so many. People will feel a greater sense of belonging and will be warmly accepted as the meganet intrinsically draws similarly minded people together and keeps their antagonists away from them. The degree of likeness in these communities will be intense; people will feel they've found their community like never before. Agreement won't be manufactured so much as it will be artificially organized.

Consequently, the unit of online expression (and frequently offline expression) will no longer be the individual but the group. In the past, quantifying the importance of any single human voice has been a matter of cultural values and inegalitarian class structures. Individuals in the right places had louder voices. Those forces of selection will remain, but by grouping people into like-minded units, the meganet provides easy measures of a group's importance in terms of its overall size, as well as other measurable qualities of the collective group such as occupation, background, cryptocurrency holdings, and so on. An individual may speak temporarily for a larger group, but the meganet augurs an age in which human expression is fundamentally far more collective. Because of the meganet's unique and supercharged capacity for identifying commonality and bringing like together with like, groups of people will be able to speak with singular voices as never before. They will be able to engage and argue with other groups as single units, a hundred or even a thousand people marching in lockstep after having affirmed their similarities and ignored their differences. A lone individual will count for very little in such an environment. There will still be very popular people online, of course, but they won't set the agenda; they will be the mouthpieces for the points of view of the groups that spawned them.

Life itself will be more relentlessly tallied, refereed, and scored, as meganets bring quantifiable monetary value to all activities. Today, we may take momentary pride in seeing positive feedback on a post, but as meganets merge and personal identity and reputation spread across all of online and offline life, such gratification will become longer lasting, as more permanent measures of reputation start accruing and attaching to our digital mirages. The result won't be something like the imagined Chinese Social Credit System but something more superficially casual, a scoreboard that measures how interested you are in various areas of online life and how much you've contributed to them. Those measures will, however, insidiously contribute to one's reputation and opportunities over time; the ability to start anew with a clean slate will vanish, as you will always be trailed by an increasingly organized and accessible trail of statistics that summarizes your life to date. Corporations and social groups will increasingly frame such metrics in the language of games to be won, whether the prize is attention, money, or opportunities.

People will not only coalesce around anger but also around positive emotions: empathy, solidarity, inspiration, and the like. It will not be inhuman but almost more than human, a sense of belonging beyond what we feel around random strangers or casual acquaintances. It will not be an age of alienation but rather one of ultraconformity within cloistered groups. The larger social structures that formerly linked humans together ideologically and communally will remain, but they will continue to decline in importance. Individuals will gain fame within their groupings, but the size of celebrity will shrink overall, as people famous within one miniculture will be unknown to others. The nineteenth-century German sociologist Ferdinand Tönnies theorized that the Industrial Revolution and urbanization that followed had moved human sociality away from traditional community organization (*Gemeinschaft*) and toward a larger, civic, more artificial society (*Gesellschaft*). Among historians and sociologists, Tönnies's dichotomy proved to be a popular explanation for twentieth-century alienation of all sorts. Yet the meganet, like no other force, has provided a way to reestablish community-sized organizations—to find one's tribe, however geographically distributed its members may be. And those communities, even though they are mediated through the forces and limitations of the meganet, are proving to be more durable and enveloping than the larger societal fabric that dominated the twentieth century and had entire nations thinking far more in lockstep. The meganet has produced and will continue to produce a fragmented explosion of individual communities to fill the gap that Tönnies identified over a century ago.

But the quality of interaction within these new communities will be quite different because meganets will mediate it. Even in small social groupings, there will be a quantitative aspect to social interaction as never before. Some of it will be as blatant as recommending (or advertising) products to one's friends, but much of it will be more subtle: an individual's participation and influence within his group will accrue into a profile of his social capital. Third parties will reach out to the most successful and well-positioned individuals in the hopes of recruiting them to advertise their product. Today, thousands of minicelebrities stream video games while hundreds or thousands of fans watch, providing better advertising for those games than any review or commercial. That social marketing model will spread to other activities: social activity itself will be inextricably linked with the implicit marketing of products, with cryptocurrency-based commissions fueling the business end of things. In effect, companies will monetize the trust people have in one another: your good online friend will sincerely recommend a product to you, for which your friend will receive a commission. And you will take the recommendation seriously because she is your friend. It will not quite be a marketer's dream, however, because it will remain near impossible to control what products, services, and experiences blow up. The meganet's volume, velocity, and virality will resist all attempts to control the narrative.

The meganet will also mitigate against other attempts at control, some of which will prove catastrophic. In many regards, we will come to take that loss of control for granted, just as we accept that currency exchange rates can be just as subject to violent shifts as the weather. But in more mission-critical areas, and even in less critical ones, sudden explosions of feedback in one direction or another will regularly lead to events on the order of the 2008 financial crisis, even if many will not be so destabilizing. As a consequence, there will be two opposing trends. On the one hand, authorities will attempt to benefit from the meganet's data processing and networking capacities, attempting to integrate them into utilities, government services, supply chain management, police, military, and surveillance. On the other hand, authorities will attempt to cordon off these applications to prevent unpredictable feedback effects from disrupting them. No government wants its intelligence service to function like Twitter (an endlessly reactive explosion of panic) or like the cryptocurrency markets that abruptly crashed in May 2022. Because access and response to the wealth of information on the meganet entails a certain level of connection to those meganets, however, we will see an ongoing tug-of-war between factions that wish to keep greater control of their systems and factions that want their systems more closely connected to other meganets.

We will feel the eyes and hands of some kind of Big Brother, but there will also be the sense that Big Brother doesn't know what he is doing and isn't really paying attention. That is the quality of the new kind of mind we have birthed: subhuman and superhuman at the same time, with information-processing capacities beyond our comprehension but far less ability to cognize that information in meaningful ways. The steps toward greater cognition in meganets will be very slow, and no one can anticipate what they will come to look like. What "minds" presently exist on the meganet are composed of great numbers of humans constantly connected through algorithmic means. These collective minds, as we've seen, just do not work the way individual minds do. Their algorithms assimilate our momentary impulses and expressions into large-scale expression and action, whether in the stock market, an online game, or a governmental identity system. The will of these systems is greater than that of even the most powerful individual.

Artificial intelligence, deep learning in particular, has gained great appeal as a possible way of regaining control over the meganet. Because of the sheer opacity of AI and its algorithmic unreliability, however, its effect will instead be to amplify the uncertainty and loss of control we are already experiencing. There's always the possibility that AI may finally achieve its long dreamt-of goal of truly *understanding* the human, bringing human-level cognition to superhuman size, but the odds are slim. If anything, AI will gain purchase not through advances on its own but through meganets conditioning humans to behave in less complicated and more orderly ways, which AI will be better able to capture. Ironically, for all the worries about a Skynet-like AI taking over the world, the genuine threat to human self-determination is a meganet-driven system that relies not on superpowerful AI but on the inscrutable collective impulses of groups of humans organized through fairly rote computation. Technology does not threaten to build an evil mastermind but an incomprehensible ecology of computationalized winds blowing us in unpredictable directions.

Artificial intelligence will likely take the blame for much of this loss of control. Because of AI's blatant opacity, it will provide cover to the subtler, growing opacity of even the simplest algorithms on the meganet. AI will supercharge meganets, offering ingenious ways to sift enormous amounts of analog data, but its effects are ultimately secondary to what *people* will be doing in meganets, how volatile collectives will come together and send the course of a meganet careening in different directions. AI will learn to mirror many of these human tendencies. As the meganet values crude, more sortable aspects of humanity and human expression, it will condition us all to express ourselves in more regularized, simplistic, and computable ways. Nuanced and implicit forms of human interaction will go by the wayside because they will count for less in the meganet-driven world. A long and complex sentence will disappear in the mass of the meganet, while likes and emojis will help algorithms neatly classify us. Individualized forms of human communication will fade, replaced by standardized means of expression devoid of nuance and creativity. We will find ourselves speaking and writing more robotically, using dumber and more utilitarian means of verbal expression. It will become more difficult to differentiate computer-written texts from human-created ones not because AI will gain some brilliant capacity for human thought and expression but because human thought and expression will increasingly become as predictable and superficial as AI-generated text.

This homogenization will in turn help stabilize meganets. Like-minded groups will find one another, and meganets will enable them to create their own accounts of the world and ignore other accounts. With these groups increasingly isolated from one another, and with each group having its own interpretation of large-scale events, flash points between groups will become less common. It could well be that the cultural wars we see around us now will subside not through any societal advancement or resolution but simply from the sides becoming increasingly unaware of one another, then fracturing into smaller factions, lacking the unifying specter of a common enemy. Discourse will be so hermetic and regularized within each faction that members will lose their frame of reference the moment they find themselves out of their home territory. Workplaces and other spaces that bring members of different factions together will handle the difference with their own domain-specific argots, focused on the task at hand. At work, you will talk about work and only work with your coworkers because you will increasingly have little else in common with most of them.

All of this standardization and fracture will create a greater unity within each meganet. Each individual will increasingly play her part in the overall direction of a meganet, much in the way a neuron does in the brain or an air current does in the atmosphere: with great complexity on the whole but with regularity and predictability in isolation. Individuals will still make decisions in their lives to inhabit one or another part of each meganet, but once such decisions are made, their roles will be tightly constrained through a combination of social conformity and algorithmic coercion. Hard as it is to imagine, that constraint won't be enforced by any central entity; it will arise purely through the natural self-organizing properties of the meganet. Humans and computer networks, joined together, create something greater than either of them, and that creation, on its own, will bring a new kind of order to its components.

In 1907, Henry Adams famously wrote of a near-religious experience on seeing a hall of small and large dynamos (motors) that were to power automobiles and airships.

> Satisfied that the sequence of men led to nothing and that the sequence of their society could lead no further, while the mere sequence of time was artificial, and the sequence of thought was chaos, he turned at last to the sequence of force; and thus it happened that, after ten years' pursuit, he found himself lying in the Gallery of Machines at the Great Exposition of 1900, his historical neck broken by the sudden irruption of forces totally new. . . . To Adams the dynamo became a symbol of infinity. As he grew accustomed to the great gallery of machines, he began to feel the forty-foot dynamos as a moral force, much as the early Christians felt the Cross. The planet itself seemed less impressive, in its old-fashioned, deliberate, annual or daily revolution, than this huge wheel, revolving within arm's-length at some vertiginous speed, and barely murmuring,—scarcely humming an audible warning to stand a hair's-breadth further for respect of power,—while it would not wake the baby lying close against its frame. Before the end, one began to pray to it; inherited instinct taught the natural expression of man before silent and infinite force. Among the thousand symbols of ultimate energy the dynamo was not so human as some, but it was the most expressive.

Such motors restructured the world, laying down new pathways of transport and communication. Adams's flood of awe stemmed from a force that worked of its own accord, with indifference to human will or human history. So it is with the meganet. The irony, however, is that humans constitute an integral part of the meganet. The force removing human self-determination is paradoxically a force in which we are a necessary part.

The meganet works from a basis of computable data, and so what the meganet shows us is a skewed, selective ensemble of very partial slices of human existence, selected and transformed by algorithms. The sheer immensity, overpowering speed, and incessant spread of the meganet's workings—their volume, velocity, and virality—condition our view of the world at every level, from the personal scale to the global scale, and the flood of what the meganet brings to us through our devices is so great as to give us little room to resist its restructuring of life. Time and again in this book, we have seen how meganets have unanticipated, unintended, and frequently negative effects. Sometimes the genie was put back in the bottle, but the inertia is in the other direction, toward systems like Aadhaar and cryptocurrency whose loss of control will prove uncontainable once deployed.

Each generation takes for granted whatever it was that disturbed the previous generation as new, anomalous, and unthinkable. Whether it was the deployment of the automobile and airplane, the arrival of television and mass media, or the spread of the internet, those who grow up with the new technologies adjust to them naturally in a way that their parents cannot. What will it look like when meganets and the loss of control they bring with them will feel as normal to us as cars or television? What will happen when a generation stops worrying about the invasiveness, the chaos, the errors, and most of all the sheer lack of human knowledge brought to us by the incomprehensible scale of meganets? It may just leave the older generation nostalgic for a time of greater individuality and greater understanding of the world's workings, but there's also reason to believe that the meganet will not integrate itself as peacefully as these past revolutions. We may never stabilize.

The technological changes since the Industrial Revolution have turned the world upside down many times, but they nonetheless left power at the human level. When a plane crashes, for example, it is possible (and necessary) to understand exactly what went wrong and ensure it does not happen again. But the exponential growth of meganets augurs an age in which catastrophic phenomena, akin to the financial crisis of 2008 but far less controllable, become regular events:

Warcraft's Corrupted Blood on a global scale. Cryptocurrency is currently ground zero here, its May 2022 crash sending shockwaves far beyond its own market into the entire economy, with the promise of future such shocks. But any meganet of sufficient size and importance, whether governmental, military, or private, runs the risk of suddenly and catastrophically spiraling out of control in unpredictable ways thanks to the lightning-fast runaway interactions of people and algorithms. What we see on social media will look quite orderly and tame compared to what meganets will bring in the future.

I've argued that this uncontrollable complexity is something that simply can't be eliminated from meganets. The very qualities that cause them to grow and take increasingly prominent (and often useful) places in our lives are the same qualities that remove human agency and deindividualize people. These systems can be tempered, however, even if they can't be fixed. I have provided wide-scale, nontargeted prescriptions in the hopes of influencing meganets in more beneficial and less dangerous directions. All of them are geared toward dampening the aggressive feedback loops that meganets generate, preventing spontaneous, explosive anomalies from gaining quite as much traction. These approaches are meant to work for most meganets, at the cost of removing some of their power and benefits (for meganets do have many benefits). Making meganets less useful is the price we must pay for making them less dangerous.

And here there is something of a paradox: If, as I've said, meganets remove the ability of leaders to take decisive action, then how can my recommendations be implemented? The answer is that we must do so with what agency we do have left. The agency must come independently from multiple sources, both from top-down elite organizations like governments and tech companies, as well as from the emergent desires of humans to be rid of the more noxious effects that meganets are having on their lives. In that sense, we are waging war against the force of new, semiautonomous entities that have already begun to direct large parts of human existence; we are struggling to exert human force to tame that which is greater than the human. It is an uphill battle.

As meganets grow, the degree to which they will resemble natural forces will grow as well, and it will be increasingly obvious that we cannot debug them any more than we can debug the weather. We can only cope with them. Meganets self-organize remarkably well, but they do not stabilize in ways that necessarily benefit humans. The overall meganet endures its catastrophes far better than its human participants do. We may come to accept meganets' capricious ways, however much damage they do in the process. We may come to see that we are less individuals and more peculiar cogs of these giant entities that algorithmically merge human wills into an unreasoning leviathan. Having built them, we may have no choice but to pass the torch of leadership to them, accepting our essential but subordinate role.

That ceding of human agency is what we have already done in global economic matters, relying on the self-organizing processes and partial human intervention that ensure that supply chains and markets remain stable (most of the time) despite a dearth of central planning. There is no guarantee that meganets will behave as well, however. Their tendency to amplify rather than stabilize could lead us to enter a world of accelerated crises of all sorts, whether economic, social, or political. We will only discover how destabilizing they can be as we go forward—but we will indeed discover it.

If we must continue to cede power to meganets, we can at minimum remember how we got here. There is so much information flooding us through meganets' channels that we hardly have any time or space to understand how we arrived at our present state of affairs. We are too tied up with the increasingly out-of-control present. This book is an attempt to strengthen the thin connecting thread so we don't forget entirely. The pre-internet world of 1985 is forgotten. The pre-Google world of 1995 is distant. The pre-Facebook world of 2005 is fading. But without the ability to contrast today with yesterday, we won't understand where we are, and we will miss out on insights that might help us temper the meganet's excesses.

Despite my critical eye, the meganet is hardly all bad. The level of information and connection it brings to people has countless beneficial effects. Meganets are now an essential and ubiquitous component of society, and we have no choice to take the bad with the good, and so the bad requires intense attention in the hopes of mitigating it as best we can. Perhaps, as Franz Kafka is claimed to have said, there is "infinite hope, just not for us" because our own meganet dynamos have usurped our hope alongside our control. But the transfer of control is not total. Perhaps we can be content with finite hope.

Acknowledgments

> Now with a voice grown unfamiliar,
> I speak to silences of altered rooms,
> Shaken by knowledge of recurrence and return.
>
> WELDON KEES, "Covering Two Years"

THIS BOOK WAS forged in the tumultuous crucible of the last half decade, and it stands as one mere person's attempt of making sense of how that chaos arose out of what had come before. Countless people have helped me in this effort. I am grateful for their insight and support and apologize to any I may have omitted.

Immense thanks to John Mahaney and Andrew Stuart for their incalculable work in shepherding the creation of this book.

Equally great gratitude is due to the following for their discussion and support: Scott Aaronson, Jon Abbey, Hannes Bajohr, Scott Brown, Vikram Chandra, Stephen Cogle, John Crowley, Vladislav Davidzon, Simon DeDeo, Brian Dorman, Noémie Elhadad, Adam Elkus, Jordan Ellenberg, John Emerson, Jessie Ferguson, Jessica Flack, William Flesch, Martin Ford, Sam Frank, Brett Fujioka, Lauren Gabriele, Genese Grill, Chris Hardgrove, Josh

Harrison, Joel Hernandez, Maggie Jackson, Claudia Jou, Annie Kim, Park MacDougald, Daniel Mattila, Mary McMullen, Melanie Mitchell, Simona Moldovan, Eireene Nealand, Reza Negarestani, Frank Pasquale, Meredith Patterson, Nicole Perrin, Blakely Phillips, Marco Roth, Mohammad Salemy, Lisa Samuels, Evan Selinger, Anastasia Senenko, Sara Shacket, Kate Shanks, Harry Siegel, Jacob Siegel, Laura Skorina, Mali Sridharan, Rebecca Starks, Jannon Stein, Galen Strawson, Elizabeth Tinsley, London Tsai, Kate Tsurkan, Carisa Véliz, Bina Venkatamaran, Brian Vickers, Ron Winchel, Pete Wolfendale, and Josephine Wolff.

This book was built atop a collective edifice of thought and knowledge too immense to describe or quantify, but some of the most luminous guiding spirits include W. Ross Ashby, James Beniger, Ann E. Berthoff, Hans Blumenberg, Margaret Boden, John Tyler Bonner, Jacob Bronowski, Jacob Burckhardt, Kenneth Burke, Myles Burnyeat, Ernst Cassirer, Rosalie Littell Colie, Denis Diderot, Thomas M. Disch, Georges Dreyfus, Ralph Ellison, William Empson, Jeanne Fahnestock, Erving Goffman, Johan Huizinga, Laura (Riding) Jackson, Hugh Kenner, Stanisław Lem, G. E. R. Lloyd, George Herbert Mead, Robert Musil, Joseph Needham, Isidore Okpewho, Heinz Pagels, Jaak Panksepp, Charles Sanders Peirce, Henri Poincaré, I. A. Richards, Gian-Carlo Rota, Johanna Seibt, Wilfrid Sellars, Mark Siderits, Georg Simmel, Brian Skyrms, Barbara Maria Stafford, Lev Vygotsky, Norbert Wiener, and Ludwig Wittgenstein.

Part of Chapter 7 previously appeared in *MIT Technology Review* in a significantly different form.

My parents and family have always been there as a source of encouragement. Above all, my two children, Eleanor and Iris, have served as constant inspiration, and this book is for them.

Notes

INTRODUCTION: THE NEW MINDS OF THE WORLD

1. Eric Ravenscraft, "What Is the Metaverse, Exactly?," *Wired*, April 25, 2022, https://www.wired.com/story/what-is-the-metaverse/.

2. Hunt Allcott, Luca Braghieri, Sarah Eichmeyer, and Matthew Gentzkow, "The Welfare Effects of Social Media," Stanford University, November 8, 2019, http://web.stanford.edu/~gentzkow/research/facebook.pdf; and Lydia Emmanouilidou and Brandi Fullwood, "We Asked Listeners Why They Can't Quit Facebook. Here's What You Said," *The World*, February 4, 2019, https://www.pri.org/stories/2019-02-04/we-asked-listeners-why-they-cant-quit-facebook-heres-what-you-said.

3. Mike Murphy, "Zuckerberg Said to Say of Facebook Ad Boycott: 'All These Advertisers Will Be Back' Soon Enough," MarketWatch, July 4, 2020, https://www.marketwatch.com/story/zuckerberg-on-facebook-ad-boycott-all-these-advertisers-will-be-back-soon-enough-2020-07-01.

4. Monika Bickert, "Combatting Vaccine Misinformation," Meta, March 7, 2019, https://about.fb.com/news/2019/03/combatting-vaccine-misinformation/; and Robert McMillan and Brianna Abbott, "Facebook Cracks Down on Vaccine Misinformation," *Wall Street Journal*, March 7, 2019, https://www.wsj.com/articles/facebook-cracks-down-on-vaccine-misinformation-11551989347.

5. Jeff Horwitz, "Facebook Pledged Crackdown on Vaccine Misinformation. Then Not Much Happened," *Wall Street Journal*, May 30, 2019,

https://www.wsj.com/articles/facebook-pledged-crackdown-on-vaccine-misinformation-then-not-much-happened-11559243847.

6. Mark Zuckerberg, Facebook, March 3, 2020, https://www.facebook.com/4/posts/10111615249124441.

7. Sam Schechner, Jeff Horwitz, and Emily Glazer, "How Facebook Hobbled Mark Zuckerberg's Bid to Get America Vaccinated," *Wall Street Journal*, September 17, 2021, https://www.wsj.com/articles/facebook-mark-zuckerberg-vaccinated-11631880296.

8. Jennifer Kasten, "What Judy Mikovits Gets Wrong—Pretty Much Everything, Pathologist Argues," MedPage Today, May 12, 2020, https://www.medpagetoday.com/infectiousdisease/generalinfectiousdisease/86461.

9. Matthew Kearney, Shawn Chiang, and Philip Massey, "The Twitter Origins and Evolution of the COVID-19 'Plandemic' Conspiracy Theory," *Harvard Kennedy School Misinformation Review* 1, no. 3 (2020), https://misinforeview.hks.harvard.edu/article/the-twitter-origins-and-evolution-of-the-covid-19-plandemic-conspiracy-theory/.

10. David Klepper and Amanda Seitz, "Facebook Froze as Anti-Vaccine Comments Swarmed Users," Associated Press, October 26, 2021, https://apnews.com/article/the-facebook-papers-covid-vaccine-misinformation-c8bbc569be7cc2ca583dadb4236a0613.

11. Schechner, Horwitz, and Glazer, "How Facebook Hobbled Mark Zuckerberg's Bid to Get America Vaccinated."

12. Mark Zuckerberg, Facebook, September 3, 2020, https://www.facebook.com/zuck/posts/10112270823363411.

13. Andrew Marantz, "Why Facebook Can't Fix Itself," *New Yorker*, October 12, 2020, https://www.newyorker.com/magazine/2020/10/19/why-facebook-cant-fix-itself.

14. Julia Carrie Wong, "How Facebook Let Fake Engagement Distort Global Politics: A Whistleblower's Account," *Guardian* (Manchester, UK), April 12, 2021, https://www.theguardian.com/technology/2021/apr/12/facebook-fake-engagement-whistleblower-sophie-zhang.

15. Kenneth Burke, *Permanence and Change: An Anatomy of Purpose* (New York: New Republic, 1935), 351.

16. Kevin Helms, "Goldman Sachs Sees the Metaverse as $8 Trillion Opportunity," Bitcoin.com, January 24, 2022, https://news.bitcoin.com/goldman-sachs-metaverse-8-trillion-opportunity/.

17. Natasha Dailey, "JPMorgan Opens a Decentralized Lounge Featuring a Tiger as the Bank Seeks to Capitalize on $1 Trillion Revenue Opportunity from the Metaverse," Insider, February 15, 2022, https://markets.businessinsider.com/news/currencies/jpmorgan-decentraland-onyx-lounge-metaverse-virtual-real-estate-crypto-dao-2022-2.

18. Chris Flood, "Crypto Risks 'Destabilizing' Emerging Markets, Says Senior IMF Official," *Financial Times*, January 31, 2022, https://www.ft.com/content/45ca2229-485e-4043-b709-deda943e9ddb.

19. Robert McMillan, "The Inside Story of Mt. Gox, Bitcoin's $460 Million Disaster," *Wired*, March 3, 2014, https://www.wired.com/2014/03/bitcoin-exchange/.

20. Hannah Murphy, Richard Waters, Alex Barker, and Jamie Smyth, "Media Blackout: Why Facebook Pulled the Plug on News in Australia," *Financial Times*, February 27, 2021, https://www.ft.com/content/f4e09ffb-4ca9-4004-9f8e-33bf13080ce9.

21. Elaine Moore, "If Big Tech Has Our Data, Why Are Targeted Ads So Terrible?," *Financial Times*, March 11, 2021, https://www.ft.com/content/b013d9a2-c69d-4c17-aaeb-020eb2e33403.

22. "Ultimate Guide to EU Cookie Laws," PrivacyPolicies, November 15, 2021, https://www.privacypolicies.com/blog/eu-cookie-law/.

23. Mark Hertsgaard, "A Second Trump Term Would Be 'Game Over' for the Climate, Says Top Scientist," *Guardian* (Manchester, UK), October 2, 2020, https://www.theguardian.com/us-news/2020/oct/02/donald-trump-climate-change-michael-mann-interview.

CHAPTER 1: A WORLD TOO BIG TO KNOW

1. Future City, "'Crypto-Park' Project Review," 2019, https://web.archive.org/web/20200216044949/https://futurecity.ir/en/cryptopark/.

2. Emilio Janus, "Iran Unveils a Crypto-Mining, Water-Sliding, Sanction-Busting Skyscraper," Bitcoinist, 2019, https://bitcoinist.com/iran-crypto-mining-water-skyscraper/.

3. Cambridge Bitcoin Electricity Consumption Index, 2021, https://cbeci.org/cbeci/index/comparisons.

4. Stefania Palma, "Singapore's Seniors Turn to Wearable Tech to Fight Covid," *Financial Times*, November 16, 2020, https://www.ft.com/content/588984ac-0396-4db2-b39d-4f78b6ebe622.

5. David Sun, "TraceTogether Data Was Accessed in May 2020 for Punggol Fields Murder Investigation," *Straits Times* (Singapore), February 2, 2021, https://www.straitstimes.com/singapore/politics/tracetogether-data-was-accessed-in-may-2020-for-punggol-fields-murder.

6. Kenny Chee, "Bill Introduced to Make Clear TraceTogether, SafeEntry Data Can Be Used to Look into Only 7 Types of Serious Crimes," *Straits Times* (Singapore), February 1, 2021, https://www.straitstimes.com/singapore/proposed-restrictions-to-safeguard-personal-contact-tracing-data-will-override-all-other.

7. Kersti Kaljulaid, "Estonia Is Running Its Country Like a Tech Company," *Quartz*, February 19, 2019, https://qz.com/1535549/living-on-the-blockchain-is-a-game-changer-for-estonian-citizens/.

8. Petteri Kivimäki, "There Is No Blockchain Technology in X-Road," Nordic Institute for Interoperability Solutions, April 26, 2018, https://www.niis.org/blog/2018/4/26/there-is-no-blockchain-technology-in-the-x-road.

9. Arvind Narayanan, "'Private Blockchain' Is Just a Confusing Name for a Shared Database," Freedom to Tinker, September 18, 2015, https://freedom-to-tinker.com/2015/09/18/private-blockchain-is-just-a-confusing-name-for-a-shared-database/.

10. Narayanan, "'Private Blockchain' Is Just a Confusing Name."

11. Justin Elliott, "Does the NSA Tap That? What We Still Don't Know About the Agency's Internet Surveillance," ProPublica, July 22, 2013, https://www.propublica.org/article/what-we-still-dont-know-about-the-nsa-secret-internet-tapping.

12. Paul Mozur, Raymond Zhong, and Aaron Krolik, "In Coronavirus Fight, China Gives Citizens a Color Code, with Red Flags," *New York Times*, March 1, 2020, https://www.nytimes.com/2020/03/01/business/china-coronavirus-surveillance.html.

13. Wenxin Fan, "China Fires Official for Abusing Covid Tracking Codes to Thwart Protesters," *Wall Street Journal*, June 23, 2022, https://www.wsj.com/articles/china-fires-official-for-abusing-covid-tracking-codes-to-thwart-protesters-11655986238.

14. SINTEF, "Big Data, for Better or Worse: 90% of World's Data Generated over Last Two Years," ScienceDaily, May 22, 2013, https://www.sciencedaily.com/releases/2013/05/130522085217.htm.

15. Thomas Pynchon, "Is It O.K. to Be a Luddite?" *New York Times*, October 28, 1984, https://archive.nytimes.com/www.nytimes.com/books/97/05/18/reviews/pynchon-luddite.html.

16. David Rotman, "We're Not Prepared for the End of Moore's Law," *MIT Technology Review*, February 24, 2020, https://www.technologyreview.com/2020/02/24/905789/were-not-prepared-for-the-end-of-moores-law/.

17. Diego Doval, "Cray 2 v iPhone XS: Fight!," Medium, December 16, 2018, https://medium.com/@diego./cray-2-v-iphone-xs-fight-6f05b494efe1.

18. Shoshana Zuboff, *The Age of Surveillance Capitalism: The Fight for a Human Future at the New Frontier of Power* (New York: PublicAffairs, 2019), 53.

19. Tim Bradshaw, "Cloud Glitch Brings Down Thousands of Websites," *Financial Times*, June 8, 2021, https://www.ft.com/content/0d5b9430-750b-44b7-b238-6e2160c3c591.

20. "Greek Word Study Tool," Perseus Hopper, accessed June 24, 2022, http://www.perseus.tufts.edu/hopper/morph?l=me%2Fgas&la=greek&can=me%2Fgas0#lexicon.

21. Russ Rowlett, "Metric and SI Unit Prefixes," ibiblio, April 26, 2018, https://www.ibiblio.org/units/prefixes.html.

22. Rowlett, "Metric and SI Unit Prefixes."

23. Lexico, METAVERSE English Definition and Meaning, accessed June 24, 2022, https://www.lexico.com/en/definition/metaverse.

24. Merriam-Webster, "What Is the 'Metaverse'? A Real Word for a Virtual World," October 30, 2021, https://www.merriam-webster.com/words-at-play/meaning-of-metaverse.

25. Associated Press, "Explainer: What Is the Metaverse and How Will It Work?," ABC News, October 28, 2021, https://abcnews.go.com/Business/wireStory/explainer-metaverse-work-80842516.

26. Matthew Ball, "Payments, Payment Rails, and Blockchains, and the Metaverse," MatthewBall.vc, June 29, 2021, https://www.matthewball.vc/all/metaversepayments.

27. Sara Fischer, "Metaverse Bull Market," Axios, November 16, 2021, https://www.axios.com/2021/11/16/metaverse-wall-streets-favorite-buzzword.

28. Meta Quest, "Horizon Worlds," accessed June 24, 2022, https://www.oculus.com/horizon-worlds/.

29. "Metaverse," Wikipedia, last modified May 9, 2022, https://en.wikipedia.org/wiki/Metaverse.

30. Associated Press, "Facebook Wants to Lean into the Metaverse. Here's What It Is and How It Will Work," NPR, October 28, 2021, https://www.npr.org/2021/10/28/1050280500/what-metaverse-is-and-how-it-will-work.

31. Sarah Austin, "The New Wave of Web 3.0 Metaverse Innovations," *Entrepreneur*, September 8, 2021, https://www.entrepreneur.com/article/380250.

32. Shoshana Zuboff, interview by Lance Farrell, "Shoshana Zuboff: Rendering Reality and Cash Cows," Science Node, October 17, 2017, https://sciencenode.org/feature/shoshana-zuboff,-part-two-rendering-reality.php.

CHAPTER 2: NO CENTER TO HOLD

1. Robin Wigglesworth, "The 'Tesla-Financial Complex': How Carmaker Gained Influence over the Markets," *Financial Times*, November 22, 2021, https://www.ft.com/content/17f0cd1f-e751-4ddb-b13c-ea4e685b55c0.

2. Carmen Ang, "A Decade of Elon Musk's Tweets, Visualized," Visual Capitalist, March 9, 2022, https://www.visualcapitalist.com/a-decade-of-elon-musks-tweets-visualized/.

3. Victor Tangermann, "Elon Musk Explains Why He Is 'Pro Doge,' Not Bitcoin," Futurism, December 23, 2021, https://futurism.com/elon-musk-pro-doge-bitcoin.

4. Elon Musk, "Staying Public," Tesla, August 24, 2018, https://www.tesla.com/blog/staying-public.

5. Tina Nguyen, "Trump and Musk Unite over Twitter, the Moon and Sticking It to the Establishment," Politico, May 27, 2020, https://www.politico.com/news/2020/05/27/trump-musk-moon-space-283608.

6. "Tesla Starts Accepting Once-Joke Cryptocurrency Dogecoin," BBC, January 15, 2022, https://www.bbc.com/news/business-60001144.

7. Lucy Kellaway, "Beyond Order, by Jordan Peterson—More Orders from Chaos," *Financial Times*, March 10, 2021, https://www.ft.com/content/a060f834-428d-49e2-83b1-99a2e016a93d.

8. Merriam-Webster, "The Story Behind 'Stonks,'" accesssed June 24, 2022, https://www.merriam-webster.com/words-at-play/stonks-stocks-meme-words-were-watching.

9. Julia-Ambra Verlaine and Gunjan Banerji, "Keith Gill Drove the GameStop Reddit Mania. He Talked to the Journal," *Wall Street Journal*, January 29, 2021, https://www.wsj.com/articles/keith-gill-drove-the-gamestop-reddit-mania-he-talked-to-the-journal-11611931696.

10. Ortenca Aliaj, Michael Mackenzie, and Laurence Fletcher, "Melvin Capital, GameStop and the Road to Disaster," *Financial Times*, February 6, 2021, https://www.ft.com/content/3f6b47f9-70c7-4839-8bb4-6a62f1bd39e0; and Laurence Fletcher, "Hedge Fund That Bet Against GameStop Shuts Down," *Financial Times*, June 21, 2021, https://www.ft.com/content/397bdbe9-f257-4ca6-b600-1756804517b6.

11. CNBC Television, "Keith Gill Delivers His Testimony at GameStop Hearing: 'I Like the Stock,'" YouTube video, 5:23, February 18, 2021, https://www.youtube.com/watch?v=ukXQGBpXaVM.

12. US Securities and Exchange Commission, *Staff Report on Equity and Options Market Structure Conditions in Early 2021* (Washington, DC: U.S. Securities and Exchange Commission, 2021), https://www.sec.gov/files/staff-report-equity-options-market-struction-conditions-early-2021.pdf.

13. Yishan Wong, comment on "The accuracy of Voat regarding Reddit: SRS admins?," Reddit, October 24, 2016, https://www.reddit.com/r/TheoryOfReddit/comments/58zaho/the_accuracy_of_voat_regarding_reddit_srs_admins/d95a7q2/.

14. Maddy King, "Reddit Tried to Stop the Spread of Hateful Material. New Research Shows It May Have Made Things Worse," Triple J, Hack (podcast), November 11, 2020, https://www.abc.net.au/triplej/programs/hack/reddit-stop-spread-hateful-material-did-not-work/12874066.

15. Lee Hae-rin, "Deaths of Athlete, Streamer Ignite Calls for Harsher Punishments for Internet Trolling," *Korea Times*, February 7, 2022, https://www.koreatimes.co.kr/www/nation/2022/02/251_323370.html.

16. Lee Jian, "Jo Jang-Mi, Internet Personality, Is Dead at 27," *Korea JoongAng Daily*, February 6, 2022, https://koreajoongangdaily.joins.com/2022/02/06/entertainment/television/bj-jammi-suicide-korea/20220206190428388.html.

17. Yim Hyun-su, "After Being Called Feminists, These Women Faced Online Harassment," *Korea Herald*, February 11, 2022, http://www.koreaherald.com/view.php?ud=20220210000628.

18. S. Nathan Park, "Why So Many Young Men in South Korea Hate Feminism," *Foreign Policy*, June 23, 2021, https://foreignpolicy.com/2021/06/23/young-south-korean-men-hate-liberals-feminists/.

19. So Yun Alysha Park, "A Move Forward for the Korean Women's Movement," Verso (blog), October 4, 2018, https://www.versobooks.com/blogs/4064-a-move-forward-for-the-korean-women-s-movement.

20. Emily Singh, "Megalia: South Korean Feminism Marshals the Power of the Internet," *Korea Exposé*, July 30, 2016, https://www.koreaexpose.com/megalia-south-korean-feminism-marshals-the-power-of-the-internet/.

21. Yeji Jesse Lee, "Megalia: South Korea's Radical Feminist Community," *10 Magazine*, August 2, 2016, https://10mag.com/megalia-south-koreas-radical-feminism-community/.

22. Wonyun Lee, "Responding to Misogyny, Reciprocating Hate Speech—South Korea's Online Feminism Movement: Megalia," DASH, 2019, https://nrs.harvard.edu/URN-3:HUL.INSTREPOS:37366046.

23. Yoo Seong-woon, "A Social Dispute Causes Justice Party Members to Defect," *Korea JoongAng Daily*, August 3, 2016, https://koreajoongangdaily.joins.com/news/article/Article.aspx?aid=3022158.

24. "South Korea," Freedom House, June 1, 2020–May 31, 2021, https://freedomhouse.org/country/south-korea/freedom-net/2021.

25. Kim Arin, "Lee Jun-seok and the Rise of Anti-feminism," *Korea Herald*, September 6, 2021, http://www.koreaherald.com/view.php?ud=20210906000932.

26. Jake Kwon, "Why a Hand Gesture Has South Korean Companies on Edge," CNN Business, October 7, 2021, https://www.cnn.com/2021/10/02/business/south-korea-business-gender-war-intl-hnk-dst/index.html.

27. Jihae Koo and Minchul Kim, "Feminism Without Morality, Neoliberalism as Feminist Praxis: A Computational Textual Analysis of Womad, a South Korean Online 'Feminist' Community," *International Journal of Communications* 15, no. 21 (2021): 1900, https://ijoc.org/index.php/ijoc/article/view/14736/3421.

28. Heewon Kim, "Korean Radical Feminist Allegedly Committed Child Sexual Assault in Australia," *Korea Daily*, November 20, 2017, https://www.koreadailyus.com/korean-radical-feminist-allegedly-committed-child-sexual-assault-australia/.

29. "Korean Woman Shares How She Sexually Assaulted Australian Boy, Gets Arrested Immediately," Koreaboo, November 23, 2017, https://us-central.koreaboo.com/news/korean-woman-shares-sexually-assaulted-australian-boy-gets-arrested-immediately/; and Thomas Duff, "South Korean Woman, 29, Accused of Horrific Child Porn Offences Is Allowed to Leave Australia

After a Bureaucratic Bungle," *Daily Mail* (London), March 10, 2019, https://www.dailymail.co.uk/news/article-6793243/Notorious-female-child-pornographer-29-flees-Australia-bureaucratic-bungle.html.

30. Claire Lee, "'Isu Station' Assault Case Triggers Online Gender War in South Korea," *Korea Herald*, November 18, 2018, http://www.koreaherald.com/view.php?ud=20181118000177.

31. Lee Suh-yoon, "Isu Station Assault Sparks Gender-Charged Debate Online," *Korea Times*, November 15, 2018, https://www.koreatimes.co.kr/www/nation/2018/11/251_258756.html.

32. Yoo Young-gyu, "Fines for Both Men and Women in 'Isu Station Assault Case' That Caused Gender Conflict," SBS News, June 4, 2020, https://news.sbs.co.kr/news/endPage.do?news_id=N1005819802.

33. "Facebook Scandal 'Hit 87 Million Users,'" BBC, April 4, 2018, https://www.bbc.com/news/technology-43649018.

34. David Ingram and Peter Henderson, "Trump Consultants Harvested Data from 50 Million Facebook Users: Reports," Reuters, March 16, 2018, https://www.reuters.com/article/us-facebook-cambridge-analytica/trump-consultants-harvested-data-from-50-million-facebook-users-reports-idUSKCN1GT02Y.

35. Izabella Kaminska, "Cambridge Analytica Probe Finds No Evidence It Misused Data to Influence Brexit," *Financial Times*, October 7, 2020, https://www.ft.com/content/aa235c45-76fb-46fd-83da-0bdf0946de2d.

36. Kaminska, "Cambridge Analytica Probe Finds No Evidence It Misused Data to Influence Brexit."

37. Mike Isaac, "How Misinformation Can Affect Facebook Employees' Morale," *New York Times*, November 25, 2020, https://www.nytimes.com/2020/11/25/technology/how-misinformation-can-affect-facebook-employees-morale.html.

38. Mark Zuckerberg, "A Privacy-Focused Vision for Social Networking," Facebook, March 12, 2021, https://www.facebook.com/notes/mark-zuckerberg/a-privacy-focused-vision-for-social-networking/10156700570096634/.

39. Katie Paul, "Thousands of Facebook Groups Buzzed with Calls for Violence Ahead of U.S. Election," Reuters, November 6, 2020, https://www.reuters.com/article/us-usa-election-facebook-focus/thousands-of-facebook-groups-buzzed-with-calls-for-violence-ahead-of-u-s-election-idUSKBN27M2UN.

40. Mark Zuckerberg, "The US elections are just two months away . . . ," Facebook, September 3, 2020, https://www.facebook.com/zuck/posts/10112270823363411.

41. Hannah Murphy, "Facebook and Google Quietly Extend Bans on Political Advertising," *Financial Times*, November 11, 2020, https://www.ft.com/content/a88fe3fc-c75b-4814-95e5-612f085b124c.

42. Zuckerberg, "The US elections are just two months away."

43. Jay Sullivan, "Introducing a Forwarding Limit on Messenger," Meta, September 3, 2020, https://about.fb.com/news/2020/09/introducing-a-forwarding-limit-on-messenger/.

44. Felix Richter, "Facebook Keeps On Growing," Statista, February 4, 2021, https://www.statista.com/chart/10047/facebooks-monthly-active-users/.

45. "Number of Monthly Active Facebook Users Worldwide as of 1st Quarter 2022," Statista, April 28, 2022, https://www.statista.com/statistics/264810/number-of-monthly-active-facebook-users-worldwide/.

46. Maximilian Schrems, "Facebook's Data Pool," Europe Versus Facebook, accessed June 24, 2022, http://www.europe-v-facebook.org/EN/Data_Pool/data_pool.html.

47. Bobby Goodlatte, "I'm really disappointed by what's going on tonight . . . ," Facebook, November 9, 2016, https://www.facebook.com/g/posts/10101648538367704.

48. Matthew Ingram, "The Facebook Armageddon," *Columbia Journalism Review*, Winter 2018, https://www.cjr.org/special_report/facebook-media-buzzfeed.php.

49. US Securities and Exchange Commission, Form S-1 Registration Statement, Facebook, Inc., 7370, February 1, 2012, https://www.sec.gov/Archives/edgar/data/1326801/000119312512034517/d287954ds1.htm.

50. Nick Dourian, "ZYNGA Employee Spills the Beans on America's Most Hated Gaming Company," Unleash the Fanboy, June 5, 2013, http://www.unleashthefanboy.com/video-games/zynga-employee-spills-the-beans-on-americas-most-hated-gaming-company/57673.

51. Simon Parkin, "Catching Up with Jonathan Blow," Game Developer, December 6, 2010, https://www.gamasutra.com/view/feature/134595/catching_up_with_jonathan_blow.php.

52. Cyrus Farivar, "How Zynga Went from Social Gaming Powerhouse to Has-Been," Ars Technica, September 12, 2013, https://arstechnica.com/information-technology/2013/09/how-zynga-went-from-social-gaming-powerhouse-to-has-been.

53. David Auerbach, interview by Jeff Wise, "Slate's David Auerbach on What's Wrong (and Right) with the Media," *Intelligencer* (Doylestown, PA), July 24, 2016, https://nymag.com/intelligencer/2016/07/david-auerbach-problem-with-media.html.

54. For a deeper examination of what sort of human-generated data computers encourage, see my book *Bitwise: A Life in Code* (New York: Pantheon, 2018).

55. Jason Murdock, "Facebook Racial Ad Targeting Options Quietly Dropped After Years of Criticism," *Newsweek*, September 1, 2020, https://www.newsweek.com/facebook-racial-ad-targeting-multicultural-affinity-updates-criticism-1528877.

56. Alex Schultz, "What Do People Actually See on Facebook in the US?" Meta, November 10, 2020, https://about.fb.com/news/2020/11/what-do-people-actually-see-on-facebook-in-the-us/.

57. See Eli Pariser, *The Filter Bubble* (New York: Penguin, 2011).

58. George W. S. Trow, *Within the Context of No Context* (New York: Atlantic Monthly Press, 1997), 117–118.

59. James Traub, "It's Time for the Elites to Rise Up Against the Ignorant Masses," *Foreign Policy*, June 28, 2016, https://foreignpolicy.com/2016/06/28/its-time-for-the-elites-to-rise-up-against-ignorant-masses-trump-2016-brexit/.

60. Michael Gold and Sharon Otterman, "N.Y. Pushes Vaccines with Mandates and $100, but Stops Short of More Masking," *New York Times*, July 28, 2021, https://www.nytimes.com/2021/07/28/nyregion/new-york-vaccine-mandate-one-hundred-dollars.html.

CHAPTER 3: DISCOVERING THE MEGANET

1. Victor Luckerson, "'Crush Them': An Oral History of the Lawsuit That Upended Silicon Valley," The Ringer, May 18, 2018, https://www.theringer.com/tech/2018/5/18/17362452/microsoft-antitrust-lawsuit-netscape-internet-explorer-20-years.

2. I discuss my own journey through this period in *Bitwise: A Life in Code* (New York: Pantheon, 2018), chapter 2.

3. Christopher D. Manning, Prabhakar Raghavan, and Hinrich Schütze, *Introduction to Information Retrieval* (New York: Cambridge University Press, 2008), 1–2.

4. IBM, "What Is a Digital Twin?," https://www.ibm.com/topics/what-is-a-digital-twin.

5. Jim Leichenko, "The Top 10 Most Expensive Keywords on Google," Kantar, September 4, 2018, https://www.kantar.com/inspiration/advertising-media/most-expensive-keywords-on-google.

6. See David Auerbach, "You Are What You Click: On Microtargeting," *Nation*, February 13, 2013, https://www.thenation.com/article/archive/you-are-what-you-click-microtargeting/.

7. Lawrence Page, Sergey Brin, Rajeev Motwani, and Terry Winograd, "The PageRank Citation Ranking: Bringing Order to the Web," Stanford InfoLab, 1999, http://ilpubs.stanford.edu:8090/422/1/1999-66.pdf.

8. Loren Baker, "20+ Years of SEO: A Brief History of Search Engine Optimization," *Search Engine Journal*, February 27, 2021, https://www.searchenginejournal.com/seo-101/seo-history.

9. Frederik Stjernfelt and Anne Mette Lauritzen, *Your Post Has Been Removed: Tech Giants and Freedom of Speech* (Cham, Switzerland: Springer, 2019), 139–172, https://link.springer.com/chapter/10.1007/978-3-030-25968-6_12.

10. Julie Jargon, "Teen Girls' Sexy TikTok Videos Take a Mental-Health Toll," *Wall Street Journal*, February 5, 2022, https://www.wsj.com/articles/teen-girls-sexy-tiktok-videos-take-a-mental-health-toll-11644016839.

11. David Streitfeld, "What Happened to Amazon's Bookstore?," *New York Times*, December 3, 2021, https://www.nytimes.com/2021/12/03/technology/amazon-bookstore.html.

12. "How Many Products Does Amazon Actually Carry? And in What Categories?," Business Wire, June 14, 2016, https://www.businesswire.com/news/home/20160614006063/en/How-Many-Products-Does-Amazon-Actually-Carry-And-in-What-Categories.

13. Ray Davis, "Community Service for the Public Domain," Pseudopodium (blog), December 24, 2004, https://www.pseudopodium.org/ht-20041224.html.

14. Steve Landsburg, "On the Amazon," The Big Questions, November 10, 2009, http://www.thebigquestions.com/2009/11/10/on-the-amazon/.

15. Amazon, "Coriolanus: Notes," accessed June 24, 2022, https://www.amazon.com/dp/0602210526.

16. Amazon, "The Snake's Skin," accessed June 24, 2022, https://www.amazon.com/dp/1628971266; see also Amazon, "Mysteria," accessed June 24, 2022, https://www.amazon.com/dp/1556438818/, for David Ulansey's similarly unpublished *Mysteria*.

17. Shira Ovide, "How Fake Amazon Reviews Hurt Us and Amazon," *New York Times*, November 19, 2020, https://www.nytimes.com/2020/11/19/technology/fake-reviews-amazon.html.

18. Ganda Suthivarakom, "Welcome to the Era of Fake Products," Wirecutter (blog), February 11, 2020, https://www.nytimes.com/wirecutter/blog/amazon-counterfeit-fake-products/.

CHAPTER 4: THE MEGANET AS GAME AND COMMERCE

1. Paresh Dave, "Zuckerberg Says Facebook's Future Is Going Big on Private Chats," Reuters, March 6, 2019, https://www.reuters.com/article/us-facebook-zuckerberg/zuckerberg-says-facebooks-future-is-going-big-on-private-chats-idUSKCN1QN2JR.

2. Ryan Vlastelica, "Meta's Stock-Market Wipeout Is Unmatched in the Megacap Era," Bloomberg, February 18, 2022, https://www.bloomberg.com/news/articles/2022-02-18/meta-s-collapse-is-unmatched-in-the-era-of-big-tech-tech-watch.

3. Caitlin Ostroff and Caitlin McCabe, "Facebook Parent Meta's Stock Plunges, Loses More Than $200 Billion in Value," *Wall Street Journal*, February 3, 2022, https://www.wsj.com/articles/facebook-owner-metas-stock-price-plunges-premarket-jolting-tech-investors-11643887542.

4. Kevin Helms, "Goldman Sachs Sees the Metaverse as $8 Trillion Opportunity," Bitcoin, January 24, 2022, https://news.bitcoin.com/goldman-sachs-metaverse-8-trillion-opportunity/.

5. Addison Blu, "The Most Expensive Ships in Star Citizen," GameSkinny, October 22, 2015, https://www.gameskinny.com/7pxq0/the-most-expensive-ships-in-star-citizen.

6. FT Collections, "Tech Exchange," *Financial Times*, https://www.ft.com/content/7d2a185c-7ab1-4fb2-80ca-aaa1fa7267ba.

7. Cabanatuan City, "NFT Gaming in the Philippines," Play-to-Earn, YouTube video, 18:09, May 13, 2021, https://youtu.be/Yo-BrASMHU4?t=345.

8. Jet Encila, "Axie Infinity's SLP Currency Value Now Almost Zero," Bitcoinist, April 14, 2022, https://bitcoinist.com/axie-infinitys-slp-currency-now-zero/.

9. See Georg Simmel, *The Philosophy of Money*, edited by David Frisby (London: Routledge, 2004).

10. See David Auerbach, *Bitwise: A Life in Code* (New York: Pantheon, 2018), chapter 4.

11. Tom Fish, "25 Most Popular Mobile Games of the Decade," *Newsweek*, September 4, 2021, https://www.newsweek.com/most-popular-mobile-games-decade-1625270.

12. Jeffrey Rousseau, "Newzoo: Mobile Game Revenue Generated $93.2Bn in 2021," Game Industry, January 20, 2022, https://www.gamesindustry.biz/articles/2022-01-20-newzoo-mobile-game-revenue-generated-usd93bn-in-2021.

13. Statista, "Number of Mobile Gaming Users Worldwide in 2021, by Region," September 7, 2021, https://www.statista.com/statistics/512112/number-mobile-gamers-world-by-region/.

14. Megan Graham, "Apple's Seismic Change to the Mobile Ad Industry Is Drawing Near, and It's Rocking the Ecosystem," CNBC, December 15, 2020, https://www.cnbc.com/2020/12/15/apples-seismic-change-to-the-mobile-ad-industry-draws-near.html; Ryan Whitman, "Google Prepares to Let Everyone Delete Their Android Advertising IDs," Android Police, February 16, 2022, https://www.androidpolice.com/google-delete-android-advertising-ids/.

15. Matthew Ingram, "The Facebook Armageddon," *Columbia Journalism Review*, Winter 2018, https://www.cjr.org/special_report/facebook-media-buzzfeed.php.

16. Power Word: Gold, "World of Warcraft Subscribers 2005–2013 (and Beyond)" (blog), July 26, 2013, http://powerwordgold.blogspot.com/2013/07/world-of-warcraft-subscribers-2005-2013.html.

17. Richard Waters, "Satya Nadella: 'Being Great at Game Building Gives Us Permission to Build the Next Internet,'" *Financial Times*, February 3, 2022, https://www.ft.com/content/7d2a185c-7ab1-4fb2-80ca-aaa1fa7267ba.

18. Ge Jin, "Gold Farmers Part1.mov," YouTube video, 6:10, September 20, 2010, https://www.youtube.com/watch?v=q3cmCKjPLR8.

19. Richard Heeks, "Understanding 'Gold Farming' and Real-Money Trading as the Intersection of Real and Virtual Economies," *Journal for Virtual Worlds Research* 2, no. 4 (2010), https://jvwr-ojs-utexas.tdl.org/jvwr/article/view/868.

20. Ge Jin, "Gold Farmers Part2.mov," YouTube video, 12 mins., September 20, 2010, https://www.youtube.com/watch?v=3rezLLMhwSM.

21. Dibbell, "The Decline and Fall of an Ultra Rich Online Gaming Empire."

22. Joshua Green, *Devil's Bargain: Steve Bannon, Donald Trump, and the Storming of the Presidency* (New York: Penguin, 2017), chapter 4.

23. Dibbell, "The Decline and Fall of an Ultra Rich Online Gaming Empire."

24. Andrew Rosati, "Desperate Venezuelans Turn to Video Games to Survive," Bloomberg, December 6, 2017, https://www.bloomberg.com/news/articles/2017-12-05/desperate-venezuelans-turn-to-video-games-to-survive.

25. M. Mitchell, "How Would You Soft Reset World of Warcraft's In-Game Economy?," Blizzard Watch, September 16, 2019, https://blizzardwatch.com/2019/09/16/soft-reset-world-warcrafts-game-economy/.

26. Döt, World of Warcraft Forums, 2021, https://us.forums.blizzard.com/en/wow/t/gold-reset-question-nobody-is-asking/872166/6.

27. Wowpedia, "Corrupted Blood (debuff)," accessed June 24, 2002, https://wowpedia.fandom.com/wiki/Corrupted_Blood_(debuff).

28. Wowpedia, "Corrupted Blood (debuff)."

29. Eric T. Lofgren and Nina Fefferman, "The Untapped Potential of Virtual Game Worlds to Shed Light on Real World Epidemics," *Lancet* 7, no. 9 (September 2007): 625–629, https://www.thelancet.com/journals/laninf/article/PIIS1473-3099(07)70212-8/fulltext.

30. Accenture, "BugTraq," accessed June 24, 2022, https://www.securityfocus.com/news/11330.

31. Mark Ward, "Deadly Plague Hits Warcraft World," BBC, September 22, 2005, http://news.bbc.co.uk/2/hi/technology/4272418.stm.

32. Wowpedia, "Corrupted Blood (debuff)."

33. The original case for it modeling real-world pandemics was made by Lofgren and Fefferman, "The Untapped Potential of Virtual Game Worlds"; Peter Earle makes the case against: Peter C. Earle, "World of Warcraft's Corrupted Blood Outbreak Is Not a Model for COVID-19," AIER, May 28, 2020, https://www.aier.org/article/world-of-warcrafts-corrupted-blood-outbreak-is-not-a-model-for-covid-19/.

34. Earle, "World of Warcraft's Corrupted Blood Outbreak."

35. Mansoor Iqbal, "Pokémon Go Revenue and Usage Statistics (2022)," Business of Apps, May 10, 2022, https://www.businessofapps.com/data/pokemon-go-statistics/. Pokémon GO's first year (2016) attracted a boom of 250 million

users before a significant fall-off in 2017, but Niantic has steadily regained users and revenue in subsequent years, their 2020 revenue beating 2016.

36. Boon Hun, "Have $20,000? You Can Buy a High-Level Pokémon GO Account," Goody Feed, August 16, 2016, https://goodyfeed.com/20000-can-buy-high-level-pokemon-go-account/.

37. Reddit, PokemonGoSpoofing, accessed June 24, 2022, https://www.reddit.com/r/PokemonGoSpoofing/.

38. Axie Infinity, "Axie Infinity," November 2021, https://whitepaper.axieinfinity.com/.

39. Level Dash, "How Much It Costs to Start Playing Axie Infinity," LevelDash.com, July 12, 2021, https://leveldash.com/how-much-to-start-playing-axie-infinity/.

40. Isabella James, "10 Most Expensive 'Axie Infinity' Tokens So Far," *Tech Times*, July 29, 2021, https://www.techtimes.com/articles/263499/20210729/10-most-expensive-axie-infinity-tokens-so-far.htm.

41. Google Docs, "Axie Growth Data," accessed June 24, 2022, https://docs.google.com/spreadsheets/d/1g4d2lzBytC-Wo4_rKGHjR3vGeJHb8hd1jb55qRf_S2g/edit#gid=0, and @YggAlerts, https://mobile.twitter.com/officialAAPH/status/1422100979680366592; and CoinMarketCap, "Smooth Love Potion," accessed June 24, 2022, https://coinmarketcap.com/currencies/smooth-love-potion/.

42. Derek Lim, "Explaining Axie Infinity and Its Mercurial Rise," Tech in Asia, July 28, 2021, https://www.techinasia.com/explaining-axie-infinity-mercurial-rise.

43. Luis Buenaventura, "Investigating the Axie Phenomenon," Cryptoday, July 8, 2021, https://cryptoday.substack.com/p/investigating-the-axie-phenomenon.

44. Kristine Servando and Philip Lagerkranser, "Axie Infinity Owner 'Fully Committed' to Reimbursing Players After Hack," Bloomberg, March 30, 2022, https://www.bloomberg.com/news/articles/2022-03-30/axie-owner-fully-committed-to-reimbursing-players-after-hack.

45. Ravie Lakshmanan, "Lazarus Group Behind $540 Million Axie Infinity Crypto Hack and Attacks on Chemical Sector," Hacker News, April 16, 2022, https://thehackernews.com/2022/04/lazarus-hackers-behind-540-million-axie.html.

46. Joshua Oliver, Nikou Asgari, and Kadhim Shubber, "FTX: Inside the Crypto Exchange that 'Accidentally' Lost $8bn," *Financial Times*, November 18, 2022, https://www.ft.com/content/913ff750-d1f4-486a-9801-e05be20041c1.

47. Packy McCormick, "The Great Online Game," Not Boring, May 10, 2021, https://www.notboring.co/p/the-great-online-game.

48. Aella, "Maximizing Your Slut Impact: An Overly Analytical Guide to Camgirling," Knowingless, November 19, 2018, https://knowingless.com/2018/11/19/maximizing-your-slut-impact-an-overly-analytical-guide-to-camgirling/.

49. Jasmine Ramer, "How Much Do Cam Girls Make? (2022 Cam Girl Salary Report)," Ready Set Cam, May 2, 2022, https://readysetcam.com/blogs/camming-101/how-much-do-cam-girls-make.

50. McCormick, "The Great Online Game."

CHAPTER 5: MAJORITY RULES

1. "Tech Bubbles Are Bursting All over the Place," *Economist*, May 14, 2022, https://www.economist.com/business/2022/05/14/tech-bubbles-are-bursting-all-over-the-place.

2. Dan Conway, "How I Got Sucked into the Cryptocurrency Craze and Walked Away with $13 Million," Hustle, November 9, 2019, https://thehustle.co/how-i-made-13-million-cryptocurrency-ethereum/.

3. Conway, "How I Got Sucked into the Cryptocurrency Craze."

4. Vitalik Buterin, "Bitcoin and the Goldbugs," Bitcoin Weekly, June 12, 2011, https://web.archive.org/web/20110617050611/http://bitcoinweekly.com/articles/bitcoin-and-the-goldbugs.

5. Olga Kharif, "Crypto Market Cap Surpasses $2 Trillion After Doubling This Year," Bloomberg, April 5, 2021, https://www.bloomberg.com/news/articles/2021-04-05/crypto-market-cap-doubles-past-2-trillion-after-two-month-surge; and CoinMarketCap, "Cryptocurrency Prices, Charts and Market Capitalizations," accessed July 12, 2022, https://coinmarketcap.com/currencies/smooth-love-potion/.

6. Eva Szalay, "Wall Street Banks Diverge in Views on Bitcoin Boom," *Financial Times*, March 22, 2021, https://www.ft.com/content/c3cb412e-e2b1-4837-a092-bcbc3eda81a1.

7. Andrew Galbraith and Samuel Shen, "Explainer: What Beijing's New Crackdown Means for Crypto in China," Reuters, May 19, 2021, https://www.reuters.com/world/china/what-beijings-new-crackdown-means-crypto-china-2021-05-19/.

8. Bitcoin Forum, "Strange block 74638," 2010, https://bitcointalk.org/index.php?topic=822.0

9. Robert Stevens, "The Day Someone Created 184 Billion Bitcoin," Decrypt, August 26, 2020, https://decrypt.co/39750/184-billion-bitcoin-anonymous-creator.

10. George Friedman, "Opinion: Why It Matters If Bitcoin Is a Currency or a Commodity," MarketWatch, December 13, 2017, https://www.marketwatch.com/story/why-it-matters-if-bitcoin-is-a-currency-or-a-commodity-2017-12-13.

11. On the relation of currency and function, see Georg Simmel's *The Philosophy of Money* (London: Routledge, 2004), and its application to cryptocurrency at David Auerbach, "Understanding the Ethics of Bitcoin Through the Ideas of 19th-Century Thinker Georg Simmel," Tablet, November 30, 2018,

https://www.tabletmag.com/sections/news/articles/understanding-the-ethics-of-bitcoin-through-the-ideas-of-19th-century-thinker-georg-simmel.

12. Bitcoin Wiki, "Value Overflow Incident," accessed June 24, 2022, https://en.bitcoin.it/wiki/Value_overflow_incident.

13. Stevens, "The Day Someone Created 184 Billion."

14. Ethereum creator Vitalik Buterin chronicled the accidental fork immediately after in "Bitcoin Network Shaken by Blockchain Fork," *Bitcoin Magazine*, March 13, 2013, https://bitcoinmagazine.com/technical/bitcoin-network-shaken-by-blockchain-fork-1363144448. The underlying cause was that Ethereum version 0.8 switched to a more efficient underlying database, which was able to handle more transactions per block than 0.7 could. When a block with a sufficiently large number of transactions was then created (block 225430, with over ten thousand transactions), 0.7 rejected it while 0.8 accepted it, causing the fork and the existence of two independent blockchains from that block onward.

15. Buterin, "Bitcoin Network Shaken by Blockchain Fork."

16. This transcript is the version clarified by Arvind Narayanan, replacing handles with real names, at Arvind Narayanan, "Analyzing the 2013 Bitcoin Fork: Centralized Decision-Making Saved the Day," Freedom to Tinker, July 28, 2015, https://freedom-to-tinker.com/2015/07/28/analyzing-the-2013-bitcoin-fork-centralized-decision-making-saved-the-day/.

17. Narayanan, "Analyzing the 2013 Bitcoin Fork."

18. Jamie Redman, "Bitcoin's Software Has Been Rolled Back Before," Bitcoin.com, May 9, 2019, https://news.bitcoin.com/bitcoins-software-has-been-rolled-back-before/.

19. Werner Vermaak, "Bitcoin vs Bitcoin Cash vs Bitcoin SV," Alexandria, updated May 2022, https://coinmarketcap.com/alexandria/article/bitcoin-vs-bitcoin-cash-vs-bitcoin-sv.

20. Laura Shin chronicles the labyrinthine infighting around the Segregated Witness (SegWit) transaction scaling proposal in Shin, "Will This Battle for the Soul of Bitcoin Destroy It?," *Forbes*, October 23, 2017, https://www.forbes.com/sites/laurashin/2017/10/23/will-this-battle-for-the-soul-of-bitcoin-destroy-it/?sh=7563a14c3d3c.

21. Wolfie Zhao, "Binance Considered Pushing for Bitcoin 'Rollback' Following $40 Million Hack," CoinDesk, May 7, 2019, https://www.coindesk.com/binance-may-consider-bitcoin-rollback-following-40-million-hack.

22. Eric Olszewski, "No, You Can't Just 'Rollback Bitcoin,'" Medium, May 9, 2019, https://medium.com/@eolszewski/no-you-cant-just-rollback-bitcoin-f2e7217bfb5a.

23. One short introduction to smart contracts in Ethereum is CoreLedger, "What Are Smart Contracts? A Breakdown for Beginners," Medium, October 9, 2019, https://medium.com/coreledger/what-are-smart-contracts-a-breakdown-for-beginners-92ac68ebdbeb.

24. The Attacker, "An Open Letter," PasteBin, June 18, 2016, https://pastebin.com/CcGUBgDG.

25. As chronicled at Osman Gazi Güçlütürk, "The DAO Hack Explained: Unfortunate Take-Off of Smart Contracts," Medium, August 1, 2018, https://ogucluturk.medium.com/the-dao-hack-explained-unfortunate-take-off-of-smart-contracts-2bd8c8db3562. A third option of a "soft fork" was considered but rejected because of a bug in Ethereum itself that would have opened up all of Ethereum to attack, as described here: Tjaden Hess, River Keefer, and Emin Gün Sirer, "Ethereum's DAO Wars Soft Fork is a Potential DoS Vector," Hacking, Distributed, June 28, 2016, https://hackingdistributed.com/2016/06/28/ethereum-soft-fork-dos-vector/.

26. Jeffrey Wilcke, "To Fork or Not to Fork," Ethereum Foundation Blog, July 15, 2016, https://blog.ethereum.org/2016/07/15/to-fork-or-not-to-fork/.

27. Antonio Madeira, "The Dao, the Hack, the Soft Fork and the Hard Fork," CryptoCompare, March 12, 2019, https://www.cryptocompare.com/coins/guides/the-dao-the-hack-the-soft-fork-and-the-hard-fork/.

28. Samuel Falkon, "The Story of the DAO—Its History and Consequences," The Startup, December 24, 2017, https://medium.com/swlh/the-story-of-the-dao-its-history-and-consequences-71e6a8a551ee.

29. Yogita Khatri, "Ethereum Classic Suffers Another 51% Attack in Five Days," The Block, August 6, 2020, https://www.theblockcrypto.com/linked/74130/ethereum-classic-another-51-attack.

30. CoinDesk, Ethereum Classic price, retrieved July 12, 2022, https://www.coindesk.com/price/ethereum-classic.

31. Hugh Son, "Morgan Stanley Becomes the First Big U.S. Bank to Offer Its Wealthy Clients Access to Bitcoin Funds," CNBC, March 17, 2021, https://www.cnbc.com/2021/03/17/bitcoin-morgan-stanley-is-the-first-big-us-bank-to-offer-wealthy-clients-access-to-bitcoin-funds.html.

32. Sandy Kaul, Richard Webley, Jonathan Klein, Shobhit Maini, Omid Malekan, and Ioana Niculcea, "Bitcoin at the Tipping Point," Citi GPS, March 2021, https://www.citivelocity.com/citigps/bitcoin/.

33. Kaul et al., "Bitcoin at the Tipping Point."

34. Slickcharts, "Cryptocurrency Market Data," accessed July 27, 2022, https://www.slickcharts.com/currency.

35. Kaul et al., "Bitcoin at the Tipping Point."

36. James Fontanella-Khan, Hannah Murphy, and Miles Kruppa, "Facebook Gives Up on Crypto Ambitions with Diem Asset Sale," *Financial Times*, January 26, 2022, https://www.ft.com/content/e237df96-7cc1-44e5-a92f-96170d34a9bb.

37. Siddharth Venkataramakrishnan and Joe Rennison, "Tether's Commercial Paper Disclosure Places It Among Global Giants," *Financial Times*, June 9, 2021, https://www.ft.com/content/342966af-98dc-4b48-b997-38c00804270a.

38. Nikhilesh De and Marc Hochstein, "Tether's First Reserve Breakdown Shows Token 49% Backed by Unspecified Commercial Paper," CoinDesk, May 13, 2021, https://www.coindesk.com/markets/2021/05/13/tethers-first-reserve-breakdown-shows-token-49-backed-by-unspecified-commercial-paper/.

39. Frances Coppola, "Tether's Smoke and Mirrors," Coppola Comment (blog), May 17, 2021, https://www.coppolacomment.com/2021/05/tethers-smoke-and-mirrors.html.

40. Patrick McKenzie, "Tether: The Story So Far," Kalzumeus, October 29, 2019, https://www.kalzumeus.com/2019/10/28/tether-and-bitfinex/. His conclusions are drawn from the affidavit of Bitfinex and Tether's general counsel Stuart Hoegner at Kalzumeus: Supreme Court of New York, County of New York, *Letitia James, Attorney General of the State of New York v. iFinex Inc., BFXNA Inc., BFSWW Inc., Tether Holdings Limited, Tether Operations Limited, BFXWW / Tether Limited, Tether International Limited*, April 30, 2019, http://media.kalzumeus.com/tether-docs/bitfinex-response-to-nyag.pdf.

41. Letitia James, "Attorney General James Ends Virtual Currency Trading Platform Bitfinex's Illegal Activities in New York," press release, February 23, 2021, https://ag.ny.gov/press-release/2021/attorney-general-james-ends-virtual-currency-trading-platform-bitfinexs-illegal.

42. John M. Griffin and Amin Shams, "Is Bitcoin Really Un-Tethered?," SSRN, November 5, 2019, https://dx.doi.org/10.2139/ssrn.3195066.

43. Eva Szalay, "Stablecoins Could Trigger Credit Market Contagion, Warns Fitch," *Financial Times*, July 1, 2021, https://www.ft.com/content/b734b2e8-db37-46fe-93b1-d47a59f74068.

44. Lyle Daly, "5 Things to Know Before You Buy Tether," The Ascent, July 3, 2021, https://www.fool.com/the-ascent/cryptocurrency/articles/5-things-to-know-before-you-buy-tether/.

45. Emily Nicolle, "'Everything Broke': Terra Goes from DeFi Darling to Death Spiral," Bloomberg, May 11, 2022, https://www.bloomberg.com/news/articles/2022-05-11/-everything-broke-terra-goes-from-defi-darling-to-death-spiral.

46. James, "Attorney General James Ends Virtual Currency Trading Platform."

47. Kaul et al., "Bitcoin at the Tipping Point."

CHAPTER 6: THE LIMITS OF CONTROL

1. Warren S. McCulloch, "What Is a Number, That a Man May Know It, and a Man, That He May Know a Number?," *General Semantics Bulletin*, no. 26/27 (1960): 7–18.

2. Steven Melendez and Alex Pasternack, "Here Are the Data Brokers Quietly Buying and Selling Your Personal Information," *Fast Company*, March 2, 2019, https://www.fastcompany.com/90310803/here-are-the-data-brokers

-quietly-buying-and-selling-your-personal-information, lists the hundred-plus data brokers in Vermont thanks to a law requiring registration. See also, Natasha Singer, "A Data Broker Offers a Peek Behind the Curtain," *New York Times*, August 31, 2013, https://www.nytimes.com/2013/09/01/business/a-data-broker-offers-a-peek-behind-the-curtain.html; David Auerbach, "You Are What You Click: On Microtargeting," *Nation*, February 13, 2013, https://www.thenation.com/article/archive/you-are-what-you-click-microtargeting/; and Brad Adgate, "Increasingly Agencies Are Using 'Big Data' as Part of Their Advertising Strategy," *Forbes*, September 10, 2021, https://www.forbes.com/sites/bradadgate/2021/09/10/increasingly-agencies-are-using-big-data-as-part-of-their-advertising-deliverables/.

3. James Risen and Laura Poitras, "N.S.A. Gathers Data on Social Connections of U.S. Citizens," *New York Times*, September 28, 2013, https://www.nytimes.com/2013/09/29/us/nsa-examines-social-networks-of-us-citizens.html.

4. Shiv Sahay Singh, "Whiff of Starvation in Jharkhand Deaths," *Hindu* (Chennai, India), October 28, 2017, https://www.thehindu.com/news/national/whiff-of-starvation-in-jharkhand-deaths/article19940690.ece.

5. "Of 42 'Hunger-Related' Deaths Since 2017, 25 'Linked to Aadhaar Issues,'" The Wire, September 21, 2018, https://thewire.in/rights/of-42-hunger-related-deaths-since-2017-25-linked-to-aadhaar-issues.

6. Reetika Khera, "These Digital IDs Have Cost People Their Privacy—and Their Lives," *Washington Post*, August 9, 2018, https://www.washingtonpost.com/news/theworldpost/wp/2018/08/09/aadhaar/.

7. Menaka Rao, "Why Aadhaar Is Prompting HIV Positive People to Drop Out of Treatment Programmes Across India," Scroll.in, November 17, 2017, https://scroll.in/pulse/857656/across-india-hiv-positive-people-drop-out-of-treatment-programmes-as-centres-insist-on-aadhaar.

8. Prashant Reddy Thikkavarapu, "Scaremongering over HIV and Aadhaar," The Hoot, November 19, 2017, http://asu.thehoot.org/media-watch/media-practice/scaremongering-over-hiv-and-aadhaar-10395.

9. Shankkar Aiyar, *Aadhaar: A Biometric History of India's Twelve-Digit Revolution*, (New Delhi: Westland, 2017).

10. "Learning with the Times: What Is Aadhaar?," *Times of India*, October 4, 2010, https://timesofindia.indiatimes.com/india/Learning-with-the-Times-What-is-Aadhaar/articleshow/6680601.cms.

11. Prithwis Mukerjee, "Aadhaar Is Not Fault-Free, but Criticism Against It Is Misguided," *Swarajya*, February 9, 2018, https://swarajyamag.com/magazine/aadhaar-is-not-fault-free-but-criticism-against-it-is-misguided.

12. Yoginder K. Alagh, "Aadhaar and Inefficiency," *Indian Express*, December 19, 2017, https://indianexpress.com/article/opinion/columns/aadhaar-and-inefficiency-4988795/.

13. See, for example, Shekhar Gupta, "God, Please Save India from Our 'Wine 'n Cheese' Aadhaarophobics," ThePrint, September 25, 2018, https://theprint.in/opinion/save-india-wine-n-cheese-aadhaarophobics/27456/.

14. See, for example, Reetika Khera, "The Real Beneficiary," *Indian Express*, June 2, 2017, https://indianexpress.com/article/opinion/columns/uidai-aadhaar-card-the-real-beneficiary-4684994/; and Jean Drèze and Reetika Khera, "Aadhaar's $11-bn Question: The Numbers Being Touted by Govt Have No Solid Basis," *Economic Times*, February 8, 2018, https://economictimes.indiatimes.com/news/economy/policy/aadhaars-11-bn-question-the-numbers-being-touted-by-govt-have-no-solid-basis/articleshow/62830705.cms.

15. Aiyar, *Aadhaar*.

16. Héctor José García Santiago, "Transition to the Digital ID Card: Closing the Digital Divide in Colombia," *Digital Future*, January 20, 2021, https://www.digitalfuturemagazine.com/2021/01/20/transition-to-the-digital-id-card-closing-the-digital-divide-in-colombia/.

17. Kristine Schachinger, "Real Names: Google+, Government & the Identity Ecosystem," Search Engine Watch, September 1, 2011, https://www.searchenginewatch.com/2011/09/01/real-names-google-government-the-identity-ecosystem/.

18. Schachinger, "Real Names: Google+, Government & the Identity Ecosystem."

19. Kashmir Hill, "Google's Eric Schmidt Says Plus Is an 'Identity Service' Not a Social Network," *Forbes*, August 29, 2011, https://www.forbes.com/sites/kashmirhill/2011/08/29/googles-eric-schmidt-says-plus-is-an-identity-service-not-a-social-network/.

20. Schachinger, "Real Names: Google+, Government & the Identity Ecosystem."

21. Yitz Jordan, "Facebook's 'Real Name' Policy Isn't Just Discriminatory, It's Dangerous," *Quartz*, September 17, 2014, https://qz.com/267375/facebooks-real-name-policy-isnt-just-discriminatory-its-dangerous/.

22. Nadia Drake, "Help, I'm Trapped in Facebook's Absurd Pseudonym Purgatory," *Wired*, June 19, 2015, https://www.wired.com/2015/06/facebook-real-name-policy-problems/.

23. "What Types of ID Does Facebook Accept?," Facebook, accessed May 14, 2022, https://www.facebook.com/help/159096464162185.

24. Ram Sewak Sharma, *The Making of Aadhaar: World's Largest Identity Platform* (New Delhi: Rupa Publications, 2020).

25. Sharma, *The Making of Aadhaar*.

26. Aria Thaker, "Aadhaar Security Failure: Government Webpages Provide Unsecured Access to Demographic Authentication," *Caravan*, June 21, 2018, https://caravanmagazine.in/science-technology/aadhaar-security-failure-government-webpages-provide-unsecured-access-to-demographic-authentication.

27. Sharma, *The Making of Aadhaar*.

28. See Prashant Reddy Thikkavarapu's arguments. Thikkavarapu, "Scaremongering over HIV and Aadhaar."

29. Aiyar, *Aadhaar*.

30. Divya Trivedi, "'Aadhaar Is Useless for Identification,'" *Frontline*, October 26, 2018, https://frontline.thehindu.com/cover-story/article25164776.ece.

31. Alexandra Bruell, "Amazon Surpasses 10% of U.S. Digital Ad Market Share," *Wall Street Journal*, April 6, 2021, https://www.wsj.com/articles/amazon-surpasses-10-of-u-s-digital-ad-market-share-11617703200.

32. Aiyar, *Aadhaar*.

33. Karan Saini, "Aadhaar Remains an Unending Security Nightmare for a Billion Indians," The Wire, May 11, 2018, https://thewire.in/government/aadhaar-remains-an-unending-security-nightmare-for-a-billion-indians.

34. Khera, "The Real Beneficiary."

35. "Aadhaar Is Mass Surveillance System, Will Lead to Civil Death for Indians: Edward Snowden," *India Today*, August 20, 2018, https://www.indiatoday.in/technology/news/story/aadhaar-is-mass-surveillance-system-will-lead-to-civil-death-for-indians-edward-snowden-1319121-2018-08-20.

36. "Sec 57 of Aadhaar Act Struck Down. Here's What It Means for You," The Quint, September 26, 2018, https://www.thequint.com/news/india/supreme-court-strikes-down-section-57-of-aadhaar-act-what-it-means-for-you.

37. Nehaa Chaudhari, "Supreme Court Has Banned Private Companies from Using Aadhaar. What Does It Actually Mean?," Scroll.in, October 4, 2018, https://scroll.in/article/896771/supreme-court-has-banned-private-companies-from-using-aadhaar-what-does-it-actually-mean.

38. "Aadhaar Judgement: Supreme Court Upholds Validity but Says Don't Need to Link to Bank Accounts, Mobile Phones," The Wire, September 26, 2018, https://thewire.in/law/supreme-court-upholds-validity-of-aadhaar-but-cant-link-to-bank-accounts-and-mobile-phones.

39. Billy Perrigo, "India Has Been Collecting Eye Scans and Fingerprint Records from Every Citizen. Here's What to Know," *Time*, September 28, 2018, https://time.com/5409604/india-aadhaar-supreme-court/.

40. "Government Tables Bill to Allow Voluntary Use of Aadhaar for SIMs, Bank Account," *Economic Times*, January 2, 2019, https://economictimes.indiatimes.com/news/politics-and-nation/government-introduces-aadhaar-amendment-bill-in-lok-sabha/articleshow/67347885.cms?from=mdr.

41. Sruthisagar Yamunan, "Aadhaar Act Amendments Let Private Firms Resume Use of Biometric ID, Sustain Arbitrary Surveillance," Scroll.in, January 4, 2019, https://scroll.in/article/908067/aadhaar-act-amendments-let-private-firms-resume-use-of-biometric-id-sustain-arbitrary-surveillance.

42. This argument is made several times in Sharma, *The Making of Aadhaar*.

43. Amy Hawkins, "Chinese Citizens Want the Government to Rank Them," *Foreign Policy*, May 24, 2017, https://foreignpolicy.com/2017/05/24/chinese-citizens-want-the-government-to-rank-them/.

44. Liu Xuanzun, "Social Credit System Must Bankrupt Discredited People: Former Official," *Global Times*, May 20, 2018, https://web.archive.org/web/20180522052535/https://www.globaltimes.cn/content/1103262.shtml.

45. Liu, "Social Credit System Must Bankrupt Discredited People."

46. Matthew Carney, "Leave No Dark Corner," ABC, September 18, 2018, https://www.abc.net.au/news/2018-09-18/china-social-credit-a-model-citizen-in-a-digital-dictatorship/10200278.

47. Nathan Vanderklippe, "Chinese Blacklist an Early Glimpse of Sweeping New Social-Credit Control," *Globe and Mail*, January 3, 2018, https://www.theglobeandmail.com/news/world/chinese-blacklist-an-early-glimpse-of-sweeping-new-social-credit-control/article37493300/.

48. Kevin McSpadden, "Fewer Babies, Altered Expectations and a Desire for Connection: How Modern Society Is Forcing Chinese Filial Piety to Adapt to New Times," *South China Morning Post*, June 14, 2021, https://www.scmp.com/news/people-culture/china-personalities/article/3136992/fewer-babies-altered-expectations-and.

49. Vanderklippe, "Chinese Blacklist an Early Glimpse."

50. Rogier Creemers, "China's Social Credit System: An Evolving Practice of Control," SSRN, May 9, 2018, https://dx.doi.org/10.2139/ssrn.3175792.

51. Rogier Creemers, "Planning Outline for the Construction of a Social Credit System (2014–2020)," China Copyright and Media (blog), June 14, 2014, https://chinacopyrightandmedia.wordpress.com/2014/06/14/planning-outline-for-the-construction-of-a-social-credit-system-2014-2020/.

52. Creemers, "Planning Outline for the Construction of a Social Credit System."

53. Frank Pasquale, "Data Nationalization in the Shadow of Social Credit Systems," Balkinization (blog), June 21, 2018, https://balkin.blogspot.com/2018/06/data-nationalization-in-shadow-of.html; Jay Stanley, "China's Nightmarish Citizen Scores Are a Warning for Americans," ACLU, October 5, 2015, https://www.aclu.org/blog/privacy-technology/consumer-privacy/chinas-nightmarish-citizen-scores-are-warning-americans; and Vanderklippe, "Chinese Blacklist an Early Glimpse."

54. Carney, "Leave No Dark Corner."

55. Ryan McMorrow and Cheng Leng, "'Digital Handcuffs': China's Covid Health Apps Govern Life but Are Ripe for Abuse," *Financial Times*, June 27, 2022, https://www.ft.com/content/dee6bcc6-3fc5-4edc-814d-46dc73e67c7e.

56. Joy Dong, "A Chinese City May Have Used a Covid App to Block Protesters, Drawing an Outcry," *New York Times*, June 16, 2022, https://www.nytimes.com/2022/06/16/business/china-code-protesters.html.

57. Huizhong Wu, "Residents Say China Used Health Tracker for Crowd Control," Associated Press, June 17, 2022, https://apnews.com/article/covid-technology-health-government-and-politics-7b1ea828f10f76e8190410457a05286f.

58. John Liu, Paul Mozur, and Kalley Huang, "In a Big Potential Breach, a Hacker Offers to Sell a Chinese Police Database," *New York Times*, July 5, 2022, https://www.nytimes.com/2022/07/05/business/china-police-data-breach.html.

59. Creemers, "China's Social Credit System."

60. Liu Lipeng, interview by Protocol, "Censored Word Lists Are 'Proprietary Assets' for Chinese Big Tech," *Protocol*, June 4, 2021, https://www.protocol.com/china/china-censorship-interview.

61. Creemers, "China's Social Credit System."

62. "Report from Beijing, China: Are Thermal Cameras the Next Wave of Digital Authoritarianism?," The Doe, November 2020, https://www.thedoe.com/narratives/china-thermal-cameras-digital-authoritarianism; and Eric Feigl-Ding (@DrEricDing), "14) meanwhile, Police in Shanghai . . . ," Twitter, April 10, 2022, https://twitter.com/DrEricDing/status/1513062922280484876.

CHAPTER 7: INSIDE THE MEGANET'S BRAIN

1. Micah Lanier, "TayTweets with Trolls: Microsoft Research's Painful Lesson in Conversation Crowdsourcing," Digital Innovation and Transformation, March 17, 2017, https://digital.hbs.edu/platform-digit/submission/taytweets-with-trolls-microsoft-researchs-painful-lesson-in-conversation-crowdsourcing/.

2. Anonymous, "Tay-New AI from Microsoft," /pol/-Politically Incorrect, March 23, 2016, http://archive.4plebs.org/pol/thread/68537741.

3. Chloe Rose Stuart-Ulin, "Microsoft's Politically Correct Chatbot Is Even Worse Than Its Racist One," *Quartz*, July 31, 2018, https://qz.com/1340990/microsofts-politically-correct-chat-bot-is-even-worse-than-its-racist-one/.

4. Vaughn Highfield, "Microsoft's Chatbot, Zo, Has Gone Rogue and Is Slating Windows," Alphr, July 24, 2017, https://www.alphr.com/technology/1006395/microsoft-s-chatbot-zo-has-gone-rogue-and-is-slating-windows/.

5. Peter Lee, "Learning from Tay's introduction," Official Microsoft Blog, March 25, 2016, https://blogs.microsoft.com/blog/2016/03/25/learning-tays-introduction/.

6. Marc Daalder (@marcdaalder), "Having received my first #antisemitic tweets, I'd like to apply to join the cabal now . . . ," Twitter, September 18, 2016, https://twitter.com/marcdaalder/status/777566366933057536.

7. This example taken from my article: David Auerbach, "If Only AI Could Save Us from Ourselves," *MIT Technology Review*, December 13, 2016, https://www.technologyreview.com/2016/12/13/6076/if-only-ai-could-save-us-from-ourselves/.

8. These two paragraphs adapted from my article: David Auerbach, "It's Easy to Slip Toxic Language Past Alphabet's Toxic-Comment Detector," *MIT Technology Review*, February 24, 2017, https://www.technologyreview.com/2017/02/24/153573/its-easy-to-slip-toxic-language-past-alphabets-toxic-comment-detector/.

9. Pablo Delgado, "How El País Used AI to Make Their Comments Section Less Toxic," The Keyword (blog), March 21, 2019, https://blog.google/outreach-initiatives/google-news-initiative/how-el-pais-used-ai-make-their-comments-section-less-toxic/.

10. See, for example, Nicolas Kayser-Bril, "Automated Moderation Tool from Google Rates People of Color and Gays as 'Toxic,'" Algorithm Watch, May 19, 2020, https://algorithmwatch.org/en/story/automated-moderation-perspective-bias/.

11. Ewen Callaway, "'It Will Change Everything': DeepMind's AI Makes Gigantic Leap in Solving Protein Structures," *Nature*, November 30, 2020, https://www.nature.com/articles/d41586-020-03348-4.

12. Grace Lindsay, *Models of the Mind: How Physics, Engineering and Mathematics Have Shaped Our Understanding of the Brain* (London: Bloomsbury 2021), chapter 6.

13. Ian Goodfellow, Yoshua Bengio, and Aaron Courville, *Deep Learning* (Cambridge, MA: MIT Press, 2016), 20.

14. Melanie Mitchell's *Artificial Intelligence* (New York: Farrar, Straus and Giroux, 2019) is a superb introduction to these mechanisms.

15. Yann LeCun, Corinna Cortes, and Christopher J. C. Burges, "The MNIST Database of Handwritten Digits," accessed June 24, 2022, http://yann.lecun.com/exdb/mnist/.

16. Nils J. Nilsson, *The Quest for Artificial Intelligence: A Guide for Thinking Humans* (Cambridge: Cambridge University Press, 2009), 105.

17. Jeffrey Dastin, "Amazon Scraps Secret AI Recruiting Tool That Showed Bias Against Women," Reuters, October 10, 2018, https://www.reuters.com/article/us-amazon-com-jobs-automation-insight/amazon-scraps-secret-ai-recruiting-tool-that-showed-bias-against-women-idUSKCN1MK08G.

18. Jeff Larson, Surya Mattu, Lauren Kirchner, and Julia Angwin, "How We Analyzed the COMPAS Recidivism Algorithm," ProPublica, May 23, 2016, https://www.propublica.org/article/how-we-analyzed-the-compas-recidivism-algorithm.

19. David Auerbach, "'A Cannon's Burst Discharged Against a Ruinated Wall': A Critique of Quantitative Methods in Shakespearean Authorial Attribution," *Authorship* 7, no. 2 (2018), https://doi.org/10.21825/aj.v7i2.9737.

20. Rana el Kaliouby, *Girl Decoded: A Scientist's Quest to Reclaim Our Humanity by Bringing Emotional Intelligence to Technology* (New York: Currency, 2020).

21. Kaliouby, *Girl Decoded.*

22. Yann LeCun, Yoshua Bengio, and Geoffrey Hinton, "Deep Learning," *Nature* 521, no. 7553 (2015): 438, https://www.nature.com/articles/nature14539.

23. Goodfellow, Bengio, and Courville, *Deep Learning*.

24. Jasper, "Meet Jasper, the Future of Writing," 2022, https://www.jasper.ai/.

25. Sam Heggie-Collins, "Cogito Announces the AI Coaching System for the Enterprise," *Directors Club News*, December 14, 2020, https://directorsclub.news/2020/12/14/cogito-announces-the-ai-coaching-system-for-the-enterprise/.

26. "Cogito Announces the AI Coaching System for the Enterprise," Business Wire, December 9, 2020, https://www.businesswire.com/news/home/20201209005554/en/Cogito-Announces-The-AI-Coaching-System-for-the-Enterprise.

27. For a representative overview of current views of algorithmic bias, see Nicol Turner Lee, Paul Resnick, and Genie Barton, "Algorithmic Bias Detection and Mitigation: Best Practices and Policies to Reduce Consumer Harms," Brookings, May 22, 2019, https://www.brookings.edu/research/algorithmic-bias-detection-and-mitigation-best-practices-and-policies-to-reduce-consumer-harms/.

28. Juan G. Roederer, *Information and Its Role in Nature* (Heidelberg, Germany: Springer, 2005), 206.

29. Martin Ford, *Rule of the Robots: How Artificial Intelligence Will Transform Everything* (New York: Basic Books, 2021), 120.

30. Nicholas Furl, P. Jonathan Phillips, and Alice J. O'Toole, "Face Recognition Algorithms and the Other-Race Effect: Computational Mechanisms for a Developmental Contact Hypothesis," *Cognitive Science* 26, no. 6, (2002): 797–815, https://www.sciencedirect.com/science/article/abs/pii/S0364021302000848.

CHAPTER 8: TAMING THE MEGANET

1. Philip Kitcher, *The Main Enterprise of the World: Rethinking Education* (New York: Oxford University Press, 2021).

2. For an overview of the more severe actions taken by China, see "World Report 2022: China," Human Rights Watch, https://www.hrw.org/world-report/2022/country-chapters/china-and-tibet.

3. Robby Soave, "Facebook Said My Article Was 'False Information.' Now the Fact-Checkers Admit They Were Wrong," *Reason*, December 29, 2021, https://reason.com/2021/12/29/facebook-masks-false-information-science-feedback-wrong-covid/.

4. Simon Oxenham, "'I Was a Macedonian Fake News Writer,'" BBC, May 28, 2019, https://www.bbc.com/future/article/20190528-i-was-a-macedonian-fake-news-writer.

5. Priyanjana Bengani, "Hundreds of 'Pink Slime' Local News Outlets Are Distributing Algorithmic Stories and Conservative Talking Points," Tow Center Reports, December 18, 2019, https://www.cjr.org/tow_center_reports/hundreds-of-pink-slime-local-news-outlets-are-distributing-algorithmic-stories-conservative-talking-points.php.

6. Judd Legum, Tesnim Zekeria, and Rebecca Crosby, "Right-Wing Operatives Deploy Massive Network of Fake Local News Sites to Weaponize CRT," Popular Information, November 8, 2021, https://popular.info/p/right-wing-operatives-deploy-massive.

7. Julian Kauk, Helene Kreysa, and Stefan R. Schweinberger, "Understanding and Countering the Spread of Conspiracy Theories in Social Networks: Evidence from Epidemiological Models of Twitter Data," *PloS One* 16, no. 8 (August 12, 2021): e0256179, https://doi.org/10.1371/journal.pone.0256179.

8. Madhumita Murgia, "Ways to Make Social Media Less 'Viral,'" *Financial Times*, November 22, 2021, https://www.ft.com/content/b9ed8ce4-4fb0-4ef3-ae0b-95ea37368d16.

9. Murgia, "Ways to Make Social Media Less 'Viral.'"

10. Robin Wigglesworth, "The 'Tesla-Financial Complex': How Carmaker Gained Influence over the Markets," *Financial Times*, November 22, 2021, https://www.ft.com/content/17f0cd1f-e751-4ddb-b13c-ea4e685b55c0.

11. David Freedlander, "Nobody Knows How NYC's New Voting System Will Affect the Mayoral Race," *Intelligencer* (Doylestown, PA), February 12, 2021, https://nymag.com/intelligencer/2021/02/how-will-ranked-choice-voting-affect-nycs-mayoral-race.html.

12. Samar Khurshid, "Poll Shows Adams Ahead, Garcia Jump, and 'Undecided' Leading the Field in Mayoral Primary," *Gotham Gazette*, May 26, 2021, https://www.gothamgazette.com/city/10508-adams-garcia-yang-undecided-lead-new-poll-nyc-mayor; and Pat Kiernan (@patkiernan), "One note of explanation on this: It's a 'today' simulation that started by removing the undecided voters. Mainly to give insight into how the ranked-choice counting would play out . . . ," Twitter, April 19, 2021, https://twitter.com/patkiernan/status/1384114814021111817.

13. Liza Lin, "TikTok to Adjust Its Algorithm to Avoid Negative Reinforcement," *Wall Street Journal*, December 16, 2021, https://www.wsj.com/articles/tiktok-to-adjust-its-algorithm-to-avoid-negative-reinforcement-11639661801.

14. See for example Elisabeth Rosenthal, "How to Prevent Coronavirus? Wash Your Hands," *New York Times*, January 28, 2020, https://www.nytimes.com/2020/01/28/opinion/coronavirus-prevention-tips.html; Donald G. McNeil Jr., "Mask Hoarders May Raise Risk of a Coronavirus Outbreak in the U.S.," *New York Times*, January 29, 2020, https://www.nytimes.com/2020/01/29/health/coronavirus-masks-hoarding.html; and Terry Nguyen, "Coro-

navirus Has Americans Rushing to Buy Face Masks, but Health Officials Warn to Not Hoard Them," Vox, February 25, 2020, https://www.vox.com/the-goods/2020/2/6/21124979/wuhan-coronavirus-face-masks-hoarding.

15. Emmarie Huetteman, "COVID Vaccine Hesitancy Drops Among All Americans, New Survey Shows," KHN, March 30, 2021, https://khn.org/news/article/covid-vaccine-hesitancy-drops-among-americans-new-kff-survey-shows/.

16. "Facebook Apology as AI Labels Black Men 'Primates,'" BBC, September 6, 2021, https://www.bbc.com/news/technology-58462511.

17. Stuart Fieldhouse, "Is Monero in Danger of Being Used by Organised Crime as an Alternative to Bitcoin?," Armchair Trader, June 17, 2021, https://www.thearmchairtrader.com/monero-organised-crime-bitcoin/.

CONCLUSION: GRACEFULLY PASSING THE TORCH

1. "National Wastewater Surveillance System," CDC, March 21, 2022, https://www.cdc.gov/healthywater/surveillance/wastewater-surveillance/wastewater-surveillance.html.

2. "Ingestible, Expanding Pill Monitors the Stomach for Up to a Month," Nanowerk News, January 30, 2019, https://www.nanowerk.com/nanotechnology-news2/newsid=52012.php.

Index

© VICTOR JEFFREYS

DAVID B. AUERBACH is a writer, technologist, and software engineer who worked at Google and Microsoft after graduating from Yale University. His writing has appeared in the *Times Literary Supplement*, *MIT Technology Review*, the *Nation*, *UnHerd*, *n+1*, Tablet, The Daily Beast, and *Bookforum*, among many other publications. He was Slate's technology columnist from 2013 to 2016, and he was nominated for a National Magazine Award for his coverage of the HealthCare.gov hearings. He teaches on the history of computation at the New Centre for Research and Practice and is a frequent guest at the institute's events. He has lectured around the world on technology, literature, and philosophy and, in addition, has done scholarly research on James Joyce, William Shakespeare, and artificial intelligence. His first book, *Bitwise: A Life in Code*, was published by Pantheon in 2018.

PublicAffairs is a publishing house founded in 1997. It is a tribute to the standards, values, and flair of three persons who have served as mentors to countless reporters, writers, editors, and book people of all kinds, including me.

I. F. Stone, proprietor of *I. F. Stone's Weekly*, combined a commitment to the First Amendment with entrepreneurial zeal and reporting skill and became one of the great independent journalists in American history. At the age of eighty, Izzy published *The Trial of Socrates*, which was a national bestseller. He wrote the book after he taught himself ancient Greek.

Benjamin C. Bradlee was for nearly thirty years the charismatic editorial leader of *The Washington Post*. It was Ben who gave the *Post* the range and courage to pursue such historic issues as Watergate. He supported his reporters with a tenacity that made them fearless and it is no accident that so many became authors of influential, best-selling books.

Robert L. Bernstein, the chief executive of Random House for more than a quarter century, guided one of the nation's premier publishing houses. Bob was personally responsible for many books of political dissent and argument that challenged tyranny around the globe. He is also the founder and longtime chair of Human Rights Watch, one of the most respected human rights organizations in the world.

• • •

For fifty years, the banner of Public Affairs Press was carried by its owner Morris B. Schnapper, who published Gandhi, Nasser, Toynbee, Truman, and about 1,500 other authors. In 1983, Schnapper was described by *The Washington Post* as "a redoubtable gadfly." His legacy will endure in the books to come.

Peter Osnos, *Founder*